AN INTRODUCTION TO POST-COMMUNIST BULGARIA

MANCHESTER
UNIVERSITY PRESS

SERIES EDITORS THOMAS CHRISTIANSEN AND EMIL KIRCHNER

already published

Committee governance in the European Union
THOMAS CHRISTIANSEN AND EMIL KIRCHNER (EDS)

Theory and reform in the European Union
DIMITRIS N. CHRYSSOCHOOU, MICHAEL J. TSINISIZELIS, KOSTAS IFANTIS, STELIOS STAVRIDIS

The European Union and the Cyprus conflict
Modern conflict, postmodern union
THOMAS DIEZ

The time of European governance
MAGNUS EKENGREN

Greece in a changing Europe
Between European integration and Balkan disintegration?
KEVIN FEATHERSTONE AND KOSTAS IFANTIS (EDS)

The new Germany and migration in Europe
BARBARA MARSHALL

Turkey's relations with a changing Europe
MELTEM MÜFTÜLER-BAC

Righting wrongs in Eastern Europe
ISTVAN POGANY

Two tiers or two speeds?
The European security order and the enlargement of the European Union and Nato
JAMES SPERLING (ED.)

Recasting the European order
Security architectures and economic cooperation
JAMES SPERLING AND EMIL KIRCHNER

The Emerging Euro-Mediterranean system
DIMITRIS K. XENAKIS AND DIMITRIS N. CHRYSSOCHOOU

Emil Giatzidis

AN INTRODUCTION TO POST-COMMUNIST BULGARIA

POLITICAL, ECONOMIC AND SOCIAL TRANSFORMATIONS

MANCHESTER UNIVERSITY PRESS
Manchester and New York

distributed exclusively in the USA by Palgrave

Published by Manchester University Press
Oxford Road, Manchester M13 9NR, UK
and Room 400, 175 Fifth Avenue, New York, NY 10010, USA
www.manchesteruniversitypress.co.uk

Distributed exclusively in the USA by
Palgrave, 175 Fifth Avenue, New York,
NY 10010, USA

Distributed exclusively in Canada by
UBC Press, University of British Columbia, 2029 West Mall,
Vancouver, BC, Canada V6T 1Z2

British Library Cataloguing-in-Publication Data
A catalogue record for this book is available from the British Library

Library of Congress Cataloging-in-Publication Data applied for

ISBN 0 7190 6094 X *hardback*
0 7190 6095 8 *paperback*

First published 2002

10 09 08 07 06 05 04 03 02 10 9 8 7 6 5 4 3 2 1

Typeset in Minion with Lithos
by Northern Phototypesetting Co Ltd, Bolton
Printed in Great Britain
by Bell & Bain Ltd, Glasgow

Contents

	List of tables	*page* vi
	Preface	vii
	List of abbreviations	viii
	Chronology of events	ix
1	Introduction	1
2	The historical background	10
3	The political landscape	44
4	Economic transformation	79
5	The ‘rebirth’ of civil society	110
6	International relations in the post-Communist era	133
7	Conclusion	160
	References	168
	Select bibliography	175
	Index	177

Tables

2.1 Annual average growth, 1953–60 to 1986–89 *page* 26

2.2 Direction of foreign trade, 1960–80 33

2.3 Exports and imports, 1985 34

3.1 Main parties in the National Assembly, 1990–97 53

4.1 Annual growth of GDP, 1989–94 85

4.2 Key economic indicators, 1994–99 91

4.3 Average monthly wage through 1996 108

Preface

The collapse of Communism in the late 1980s represented fundamental and far-reaching changes in European history, ideology and geography. The divisions that separated the continent for almost half a century no longer exist and Bulgaria is searching for a place in the new configuration. For the first time in its history Bulgaria is seeking to establish liberal democratic politics and to become an equal partner in the construction of an integrated Europe. At the same time Bulgaria is striving to close the historical circle that opened with the country's independence in 1878 and to fulfil the dreams of past generations. This book attempts to provide, in an accessible way, an overview of the development and direction of Bulgarian policies since 1989, placing them in cultural and historical context and within the frame of the new European reality.

The book was begun in 1996, while I was still a postgraduate student at the University of Sheffield, when television images of thousands of protesting Bulgarians stirred my interest in the reasons for the different course of Bulgarian post-Communist development. More than ten years after the remarkable events of 1989 the post-Communist situation has still not been resolved, so keeping pace with developments in a topic that is still a moving target has been the main limitation of the book. Precisely because of the immensity of the events that happened so quickly and the diversity and complexity of the subject, extensive use has been made of a range of both primary and secondary sources. More than thirty interviews were conducted by the author, a short list of which is given in the references, that were extremely helpful, as they provided a clearer understanding of what happened in Bulgaria over the 1990s and offered interpretations of events and developments.

Finally, I wish to express my deep appreciation to all the people who contributed to the completion of the book. I would particularly like to thank Ian Kerns, who stimulated my interest in the region and the emerging post-Communist democracy. I also want to thank Venetta, Ivan and Sunny for their hospitality and assistance during the time I spent in Bulgaria as well as my parents and Nicky for their valuable support.

Abbreviations

AIC	agro-industrial complexes
BANU	Bulgarian Agrarian National Union
BCP	Bulgarian Communist Party
BGL	Bulgarian lev
BIBA	Bulgarian International Business Association
BSECZ	Black Sea Economic Co-operation Zone
BSP	Bulgarian Socialist Party
CEECs	Central and East European Countries
CEFTA	Central European Free Trade Area
CMEA	Council for Mutual Economic Assistance
EAPC	Euro-Atlantic Partnership Council
EU	European Union
FDI	foreign direct investment
FIA	Foreign Investment Act
FRY	Federal Republic of Yugoslavia
FYROM	Former Yugoslav Republic of Macedonia
GDP	gross domestic product
GNP	gross national product
IMF	International Monetary Fund
LC	Liquidation Council
LOUAL	Law on the Ownership and Use of Agricultural Land
MRF	Movement for Rights and Freedom
NACC	North Atlantic Co-operation Council
NATO	North Atlantic Treaty Organisation
NEM	New Economic Mechanism
NGO	non-governmental organisation
OECD	Organisation for Economic Co-operation and Development
PA	Privatisation Agency
PfP	Partnership for Peace
SOE	State-owned enterprise
UDF	Union of Democratic Forces
UNDP	United Nations Development Programme
USAID	United States Agency for International Development

Chronology of events

3 March 1878	The San Stefano Treaty is signed between the Ottoman and Russian empires. It designates Bulgaria as an independent principality under the Ottoman Empire's suzerainty. After 1989 it is celebrated as a national holiday
1908	Bulgaria declares its formal independence and becomes a kingdom
October 1912	Beginning of the First Balkan War
16 June 1913	Bulgaria attacks Serbia and Greece and the Second Balkan War breaks out
6 October 1919	The BANU, under Alexander Stamboliski's leadership, wins the elections
9 June 1923	The BANU government is violently overthrown and six days later Alexander Stamboliski is beheaded
1 March 1941	Bulgaria joins the Axis
5 September 1944	Soviet Union declares war on Bulgaria and three days later the Red Army invades the territory of Bulgaria
9 September 1944	The Fatherland Front, under BCP guidance, comes to power
10 September 1944	Bulgaria and the Fatherland Front government declare war on Germany and its allies
November 1945	Georgi Dimitrov returns to Bulgaria
27 October 1946	Elections are held and Fatherland Front candidates win over 70 per cent of the votes
23 September 1947	The main opposition leader, Nicola Petkov, is executed by the Communists
4 December 1947	Bulgaria is proclaimed a People's Republic
June 1949	Georgi Dimitrov dies in a sanatorium near Moscow
February 1954	Todor Zhivkov is appointed General Secretary of the BCP
9 August 1988	Diplomatic relations established between Bulgaria and the European Community
May 1989	The first sign of public dissidence when the Muslim minority demonstrate against their oppression
3 November 1989	A demonstration by some 5,000 Ecoglasnost supporters in Sofia is broken up by the police

10 November 1989	Todor Zhivkov resigns and Petar Mladenov is appointed head of state and Andrey Lukanov Prime Minister
7 December 1989	UDF is formed, with Dr Zhelyu Zhelev as its leader
16 January 1990	Launch of the round-table talks with the participation of the BCP and the UDF
8 May 1990	Signing of Trade and Co-operation Agreement between Bulgaria and European Union
10–17 June 1990	First post-Communist elections won by the BSP, followed by the UDF, BANU and MRF
6 July 1990	Petar Mladenov resigns under public pressure
1 August 1990	Zhelyu Zhelev is elected President of the Bulgarian Republic
29 August 1990	Bulgaria establishes diplomatic relations with NATO
17 September 1990	Bulgaria joins the Phare programme
19 December 1990	Andrey Lukanov resigns. Dimitar Popov becomes Prime Minister and forms a coalition government
22 December 1990	Bulgarian parliament adopts a resolution expressing Bulgaria's wish to join the European Union
9 July 1991	A new constitution is ratified
13 October 1991	Parliamentary elections won by the UDF with relative majority and the first non-Communist government is formed under Filip Dimitrov, supported by the MRF
17 December 1991	Zhan Videnov is elected chairman of the BSP
19 February 1992	First presidential elections under the new constitution, won by UDF candidate Zhelyu Zhelev
7 May 1992	Bulgaria becomes member of the Council of Europe
28 October 1992	Following the withdrawal of the MRF's parliamentary support, the UDF government resigns
28 December 1992	Professor Lyuben Berov forms a coalition government, supported by the MRF and the BSP
8 March 1993	Bulgaria signs the Association Agreement with the European Union which enters into force on 2 January 1995
14 February 1994	Bulgaria joins the NATO initiative Partnership for Peace
18 December 1994	Early parliamentary elections won by the BSP and Zhan Videnov becomes Prime Minister
29 December 1994	Ivan Kostov succeeds Filip Dimitrov as UDF chairman
6 March 1995	Bulgaria becomes an associate member of the Western European Union

1 December 1995	Parliament ratifies Bulgaria's official EU membership application
2 October 1996	Bulgaria becomes member of the World Trade Organisation
3 October 1996	Former Prime Minister Andrey Lukanov is assassinated
3 November 1996	Presidential elections won by the UDF candidate, Petar Stoyanov
23 December 1996	Georgi Parvanov replaces Zhan Videnov as leader of the BCP. Five days later Videnov also resigns from the post of Prime Minister
10 January 1997	Demonstrations around the parliament begin. A month later political parties agree to hold early parliamentary elections
19 April 1997	Parliamentary elections won by the UDF. Ivan Kostov becomes Prime Minister
1 January 1999	Bulgaria joins CEFTA
10 December 1999	EU Council invites Bulgaria to open accession negotiations

1

Introduction

> What a fantastic year this has been for freedom! 1989 will be remembered for decades to come as the year when the people of half our continent began to throw off their chains. (Margaret Thatcher)

At the close of the twentieth century democracy became one of the most fashionable terms in political science, as during the last century democratisation has been a major global phenomenon and probably the most important political trend, with democratic politics emerging in various parts of the world previously suffering authoritarian domination. But it was the breakdown of the Communist regimes in the former Soviet Union and Central and Eastern Europe, which resulted in the unprecedented event of almost thirty countries moving simultaneously in a democratic direction and seeking to establish democratic political systems, that triggered the recent surge in the literature on democracy. The revolutions of 1989, that differed widely from place to place, marked the end of an era for the Communist states from the Baltic to the Balkans and signalled the revival of democratic ideas and principles on the European continent. The unprecedented nature of the democratic transition in Central and Eastern Europe resides also in the fact that the process of political change from an authoritarian and single-party political system to liberal democracy is taking place simultaneously with the replacement of a centrally planned system of economic production and distribution with a market-oriented economy. In this respect, democratic transitions in Central and Eastern Europe presented a very different form from those, for instance, in Southern Europe, where domestic economic systems had been harmonised with the international economic environment before regime changes occurred. This fact alone makes a research study carried out on these transitions, at least, fascinating.

The countries of Central and Eastern Europe followed diverging paths in the process of political and economic transformation over the 1990s and the euphoria that accompanied the revolutions of 1989 lasted longer in some countries than in others. The disintegration of the state socialist system and the momentous political changes that ensued, which no one could have predicted, created a totally new order in these countries. It is the analysis of this new order that poses a challenge to political scientists. What caused the demise of the past regime, what was its legacy, how and under what conditions a new democratic system has been established in these countries, why has the advance of democracy been more successful in some of those countries and less in others and, especially, whether and how democracy will consolidate and become sustainable are just a few of the questions political science should answer. These questions set the general context of this book.

This study is about a complex political development: whether a country that went through almost half a century of totalitarianism can establish a stable and enduring democratic political system. The object is not to explain in depth how the totalitarian regime collapsed or how the new democratic system came into existence. It is more an effort to analyse how this democratic system can become viable and strengthened in a way that can be considered, not simply in terms of liberal electoral politics, as consolidated. While Bulgaria is on the road to political, economic and social transformation, the consolidation of its newly established democratic political system and the issue of joining the Euro-Atlantic organisations are the main challenges for the country.

Among the former Communist Bloc countries, Bulgaria is one of the most interesting cases for study, as it presents with a set of characteristics different from those observed elsewhere in Central and Eastern Europe. Bulgaria had almost no experience of democratic politics prior to the Communist period, in contrast to some other Eastern European countries, which means that Bulgaria is lacking in the necessary democratic tradition and culture. Unlike almost all other Central and Eastern European countries, where Communist ideology was foreign, in Bulgaria there was a strong indigenous Communist movement in the inter-war period which implies that Bulgarians were more inclined to accept the Communist system. Bulgarian people, in addition, even before the Communist experience, had developed traditional friendly sentiments towards Russia while during the Communist era Bulgaria was the country most closely attached to the Soviet Union, which perhaps indicates that Bulgarians may find it more difficult to overcome the Communist past in both political and economic terms. Like all post-Communist countries, Bulgaria has had to implement simultaneous political and economic reforms, yet, unlike the countries of Central Europe, Bulgaria has been characterised by political instability and lacklustre economic reform. Being also a Balkan country, Bulgaria is strongly affected by the regional environment, which is not promoting democracy, as the political scene of the region is still dominated by nationalistic fundamentalism, a paternalistic mentality and endemic corruption. Finally, Bulgaria, having earned in the past the reputation of troublemaker, and owing to lack of knowledge, is often confronted with misunderstanding and prejudice among Western scholars and political figures.

Before going any further a brief clarification of certain terms should be offered and a distinction should be made between the process of democratic transition and democratic consolidation. Transition is understood as a process in time rather than in terms of what it actually designates, which is rather vague. The dismantling of the previous authoritarian regime marks the initiation of the transition process which lasts until the new democratic structures become operative. As Linz and Stepan put it,

> a democratic transition is complete when sufficient agreement has been reached about political procedures to produce an elected government, when a government comes to power that is the direct result of a free and popular vote, when this government *de facto* has the authority to generate new policies, and when the executive, legislative and judicial power generated by the new democracy does not have to share power with other bodies *de jure*. (Linz and Stepan, 1996: 3)

Democratic transition can be initiated either from the authoritarian political elite in power (transition from above) or by opposition groups (transition from below) or even in some cases transition may occur as a result of the actions of both government and opposition groups. Yet it is important to assert that there is no transition whose beginning is not the consequence – direct or indirect – of important shifts within the authoritarian regime itself. In Bulgaria, it was the reformist sector within the Communist nomenclature which, calculating its own interests and desires, initiated and guided the transition and the whole process of political change took a form of negotiated reform. It was an elite-centred process that made possible the peaceful transition to a plural political system without the elimination of the previous ruling elite but instead allowed the participation of elements of the previous regime in the shaping of the new democratic system and gave the opportunity to former Communists to participate in the new democratic procedures and institutions. In this process, the elements of the previous elite and the opponents of the Communist regime who formed the new political elite settled the terms of the transition, forged agreement upon fundamental changes and laid the foundations for the creation of democratic political institutions and a market economy. 'A most interesting and important facet of the transition to democracy in Bulgaria is the awareness exhibited by political leaders of all stripes about the importance of learning and instilling the democratic rules of the game' (Melone, 1998: 4). Based on this arrangement, Bulgaria immediately relinquished one-party rule, held multi-party elections based upon electoral competition, established representative institutions, adopted a democratic constitution and since then has had regular elections, but are these elements alone sufficient for democracy to be consolidated?

Transitions may begin but may never be completed, since the overthrow of the old regime and the recovery of freedom are necessary but not sufficient conditions for the birth of democracy, and in this context the collapse of the Communist system was not automatically leading to democratisation. The contemporary tendency is to perceive democracy as a political system which supplies regular constitutional opportunities for changing the governing officials and which is based on the principles of social tolerance, civil rights and liberties, determining also the mode of the relationship between society and state. Secret balloting, universal suffrage, civic freedoms, periodic elections and party competition are the basic elements in conceptualising modern democracy. In this respect, Samuel Huntington's view about a consolidated democracy is that a country has established a democratic system when power has been passed between parties on two occasions by peaceful, electoral competition – the 'two turnover test'.[1] O'Donnell and Przeworski offer another aspect on this issue, arguing that an elite consensus on the democratic procedures and a strategic conception of actors are necessary. Thus a country can be considered as a consolidated democracy when at a minimum it entails:

> the compliance of most political actors with constitutional rules of political conduct and the emergence of a procedural consensus about the rules of the game; the subordination of those who exercise the monopoly of coercion, the military and security apparatus, under democratic control; and the vanishing of popular beliefs that there are feasible and attractive alternatives to democracy. (Kitschelt *et al.*, 1995: 143)

This approach basically places emphasis on the political actors agreeing to abide by democratic rules and to reject all alternatives to democracy.

According to both these arguments Bulgaria has not only managed to consolidate its democracy but existed as one for most of the 1990s. Bulgaria certainly meets Huntington's 'two turnover test', has a government that operates in a democratic fashion, and is a country where human rights are safeguarded, the military and security forces are under the direct control of the executive, and society and all political actors have become aware of the fact that there is no alternative to democracy. Yet, as most political and state institutions have become estranged from the people and have consequently lost public trust and support, as society is characterised by disenchantment and seems to be in a chronic state of social disintegration, the contention that Bulgaria has come through the initial period of learning about the working of democracy and has become truly democratic is disputable. Democratic consolidation involves both the elimination of residues of the old system that are incompatible with the workings of a democratic regime and, most of all, and most urgently, involves the building of democratic institutions that reinforce the democratic rules of the game. Democratic institutions promote but at the same time are promoted by a democratic political culture. Thus democratic consolidation is connected with both behavioral and institutional changes that normalise democratic politics and narrow its uncertainty. That is because democracy must not be seen just as a competitive political market, and therefore one has to look beyond the forms and the procedures to observe the actual operation of democracy. No matter how realistic this argument is, democracy should be defined not only in terms of procedures but also (and more important) in terms of substantive policy. Philippe C. Schmitter conceived democracy as

> a principle, embodied in a set of rules, expressed through a complex of institutions, which is aimed at establishing or sustaining a certain quality of relationship between those who rule and those who are ruled. Its guiding principle is that of citizenship, that is, the right to be treated by fellow human beings as equal and the obligation to respect the legitimacy of choices made by collective deliberation among equals. (Schmitter, 1983: 887)

In this approach, the term 'citizenship' itself entails much more than merely the act of voting but asserts the right of all citizens to take part themselves in decision making, to share in making the decisions that will affect their lives, and certainly in the deliberations and group activities of all kinds that lead to these decisions, thus facilitating the integration of the citizen into society. It is essential for this that the people, instead of acting as political consumers, see themselves as active participants and must exert and develop their own capacities in order to 'exercise the maximum amount of control over their own lives and environment' (Pateman, 1970: 43). In this way – and this is perhaps the most important aspect – democracy can be self-sustaining, since the very qualities that are required of individual citizens in order for the system to work successfully in the long term are those that the process of political participation itself develops and fosters. The more the individual citizen participates in public affairs, the more he takes control of his life at a variety of levels, and the more stable, profound and efficient democracy is.

Democracy requires the political participation of the people and this presupposes recognition by the state that individuals, informal groups and formal institutions should be free to pursue their interests and ideals independent of the state in most spheres of life. Without such intermediate organisations and groups, democracy is restricted to the relatively small circle of professional politics, leaving the population few opportunities for political participation. In other words, modern democratic regimes should be characterised by the existence, legality and legitimacy of various organisations and associations that are relatively independent in relation to the state, the government and one another, thus not permitting the individual to be wholly absorbed into the state. Their importance lies in the fact that such organisations provide people with the opportunities to be active participants in society, to become citizens, to engage actively in public life, to encourage citizen activism and to facilitate civil co-operation. This is the notion of civil society which Larry Diamond defined as:

> a network of formal and informal groups, voluntary, self-generating, (largely) self-supporting, autonomous from the state, representing different social, political, professional and economic groups. It is distinct from 'society' in general in that it involves citizens acting collectively in a public sphere to express their interests, passions, and ideas, exchange information, achieve mutual goals, make demands on the state, and hold state officials accountable. (Diamond, 1994: 59)

Civil society occupies the space between government and the private sector, in which by free association individuals can reinforce their social webs and articulate their relationships, implying a general sense of community. Civil society is an intermediary entity, standing between the private sphere and the state, not only restricting state power but also legitimising state authority when it is based on the rule of law. An active and healthy civil society lies short of the state and can mitigate conflicts, protecting the citizen from arbitrary decisions (coming from political authorities, the police, the military, etc.) and hence improving the quality of citizenship. In contrast, Communist regimes had no civil society, since Communist society was totally patronised and controlled by a party that was equivalent to the state. Societies that lack such autonomous intermediate groups are much more likely to be dominated by a centralised power apparatus – an absolute monarchy, an oriental despotism, an authoritarian or totalitarian dictatorship. The consolidation of democracy requires the expansion of citizen access, the development of democratic citizenship and culture, the broadening of leadership recruitment and training, the presence of strong and independent social groups and other functions that civil society performs. In this realm, the more active, plural, resourceful, institutionalised and active civil society is, and the more effectively it balances the tensions in its relations with the state, the more likely it is that democracy will endure. Consequently, civil society can play a significant role, perhaps on occasion even a decisive one, in building and consolidating democracy. Alternatively, of course, this also means that an absence of a vibrant civil society can prevent democracy from becoming established and consolidated. Especially in cases where civil society has been suppressed by the previous regime, as in Bulgaria in the Communist era, its reconstitution is an absolute necessity for a successful democratisation. Nevertheless, it usually takes decades or even generations for a previously atomised society to overcome the legacy of mistrust and to develop the basic norms associated with civil society and a civic culture. The organisation of the party system, as well, has a profound effect on the consolidation of democratic rule. Unstable and fragmented party systems tend to impede the negotiation of sustainable understandings between interest groups and undermine co-ordination within the state apparatus itself. Other factors that could accelerate or impede the evolution of civil society and consequently the consolidation of democracy are the prior democratic experience, a more industrialised and modern economy, which entails a more complex society and educated population, an external environment supportive of democracy, the way political elites and public respond to the problems that the new democracy confronts.

In the case of the former Communist countries, special attention should be paid to the issue of economic consolidation, since the adoption and the implementation of programmes to stabilise and more fundamentally to reform economies have posed formidable political challenges that have implications that go well beyond their immediate economic effects. The ultimate success or failure of those programmes is widely viewed as having a significant influence on the fate of democratic political systems because, to a large extent, the success of the economic transition is crucial in maintaining the popularity and credibility of the new democratic governments. Economic deregulation and the heavy cost of economic reform, in terms of growing unemployment, inflation and inequality, may lead to the dominance of the already wealthy (both at the political and at the economic level) and thereby to the alienation of the middle class, may undermine the stability and erode the legitimacy of the evolving democratic system and may turn crucial social actors against democratisation and result in oligarchy. In retrospect, democratic transition looks like a fairly easy process which requires various structural changes in a very limited period of time, while the consolidation of a democratic regime requires deep changes in the psychology and attitudes of people, which inevitably are slow. The central object of this book, therefore, is to assess the post-Communist period in Bulgaria, to examine how the democratisation process has developed thus far, to see whether civil society has developed sufficiently to assist democratic consolidation, to look at Bulgaria's prospects of developing as a stable and democratic entity and hence to follow the road that eventually leads to full EU and NATO membership.

For such a study to be carried out, in terms of the structure of the book, the first necessity is a brief historical overview of the period which preceded the imposition of Communism, along with the performance of the Communist regime and its legacy. The second chapter, thus, examines the historical development of the Bulgarian state, the political tradition and economic development prior to Communist rule. The second section concentrates on Bulgaria under Communism and in particular discusses the elimination of political opposition and the ability of the regime to limit dissent, the policies of collectivisation and industrialisation that were able to drastically change the whole country and radically improved living standards, and attempts to describe the main problems Bulgarian society was facing at the end of the 1980s which form a crucial part of the context in which the subsequent attempt to build democracy develops.

Chapter 3 reviews the transition period, studies the role of the public and the political elite in the overthrow of the totalitarian regime, and the formation of the new democratic political institutions, and looks at how the former Communists retained the political initiative and managed to maintain a relatively strong influence over the transition process. The second half chronicles political events and explores the way the post-Communist political situation has developed, the role, positions and performance of political parties, how the state and its institutions have coped with the problems of the post-Communist period and the effects on society, and studies the political culture in the years since 1989. Only by addressing these issues will it be revealed whether the political framework favours the development of civil society, and whether the political conditions for democratic consolidation exist.

Another critical issue for the consolidation of democracy in Bulgaria, which is the subject of Chapter 4, is the way the economic transition has progressed. Chapter 4 analyses economic conditions at the beginning of the 1990s, the strategies and the programmes implemented and attempts to explain why, despite the pledges and the intentions, successive governments proved incapable of handling the economic transition, causing a deepening economic crisis. Chapter 4 also discusses economic development during the 1990s, the main trends in areas such as privatisation and foreign investment and the prospects of economic recovery. The chapter therefore explores these issues and the implications of the economic transformation in Bulgaria as a further important aspect of the context in which democratic change is being attempted.

Chapter 5 discusses the role of emerging civil society in the process of democratic consolidation. The chapter assesses the way civil society and its organisations have developed during the post-Communist period, how the economic crisis and political instability affected the development of civil society and what has been achieved ten years after the democratic transition. In order to address these issues in a satisfactory way, the book focuses on the main ingredient of a civil society, voluntary civic associations or non-governmental organisations (NGOs). After defining the actual role and meaning of the NGOs, Chapter 5 looks at the relevant Bulgarian tradition and provides an account of the number of NGOs in Bulgaria, their character, their features and their problems, and examines the reasons why the state and the NGOs have not yet managed to co-operate with each other, and ultimately, whether the position of the third sector in Bulgaria has improved.

Chapter 6 examines the profound changes in the conduct of foreign policy after 1989 as for the first time in its history Bulgaria attempts to move from Europe's periphery and become member of the core European institutions. The chapter first reviews political and economic relations between Bulgaria and the European Union, looking at the problems and the impediments to consider whether and how Bulgaria will meet key conditions of the *acquis communautaire*. Chapter 6 also looks at progress in Bulgaria's campaign to join NATO and discusses the related but controversial issue of relations with Russia in the post-Communist period. Another important foreign policy question is the country's relations with its Balkan neighbours. Bulgaria's relations with Turkey, Greece, Macedonia, Serbia and Romania are treated, as well as the country's position and role in the Balkan region. Only by examining all the above issues does it become possible to answer the main questions raised in the book.

Finally, the conclusion, summarising the findings of the previous chapters, focuses on the obstacles Bulgaria may encounter in the creation of a vigorous civil society, the dangers for its democratic politics and the prospects of participation in European integration.

From the discussion of the meaning of democracy it can safely be concluded that there is no absolute definition of democracy and that it is not an all-or-nothing affair, which is either realised completely or not at all; it is a matter of quality and degree, of the extent to which the principles of popular control and political equality are realised in practice. In this respect, democracy in Bulgaria already exists, as the country has made considerable democratic gains in the post-Communist period. Whether these are irreversible and whether there are more to be achieved is another matter.

Note

1 'By this test, a democracy may be viewed as consolidated if the party or group that takes power in the initial election at the time of transition loses a subsequent election and turns over power to those election winners, and if those election winners then peacefully turn over power to the winners of a late election. Selecting rulers through elections is the heart of democracy, and democracy is real only if rulers are willing to give up power as a result of elections' (Huntington, 1991: 267).

2

The historical background

The modern history of Bulgaria, according to R. McIntyre, may be divided into three periods:

> 1396–1878 under Ottoman rule and largely cut off from commercial or cultural contact with the rest of Europe; 1878–1944, a period of four wars and dramatically changing national borders as the drive for long-delayed modernisation and national self-actualisation led to an aggressive and expansionist foreign policy. Internal developments in this period moved first in the direction of parliamentary democracy and social change through essentially social democratic policies, followed by a fascist coup and quasi-totalitarian rule from 1923 to 1944. (McIntyre, 1988: 16)

The third period began with the gradual seizure of power by the Bulgarian Communist Party just after the Second World War. In 1989 a new post-Communist era began.

Bulgaria prior to Communist rule

1396–1878

Although contemporary Bulgaria is a young nation state, the history of an autonomous Bulgarian state traces its roots back to the seventh century, when the Byzantine Empire signed a peace treaty recognising the existence and military success of a combined Slav–Bulgarian state. Bulgaria is the result of a merger of Bulgarian tribes, who had migrated to the Balkans and had gradually been assimilated by the indigenous Slav population. The Bulgarians were in a minority and, though they gave their name and political framework to the nation, the language and the way of life remained Slavic, particularly since the country had taken on an agricultural character typical of the Slav. Due to the geographical proximity to the Byzantine Empire, Bulgarians were the first Slavic people to be Christianised

y Christianised more than a century later). Thus, with its
Christian Orthodox scholarship, Bulgaria became the first
vic culture, characterised not only by the establishment of
ligious institutions and territorial vastness but also by high
accomplishments, while the Cyrillic alphabet, formulated at
ually adopted by the majority of eastern Slavs, including the
ans. It was at that point, as Crampton notes, that Bulgarians established 'a form of national cultural consciousness'. And he goes on to argue that despite the fact that it was far from the idea of modern nationalism, this 'sense of identity was strong enough to preserve the concept of Bulgaria as a distinct religious, cultural, and, perhaps, political entity' (Crampton, 1987: 5).

The early Bulgarian empire peaked in the tenth century and subsequently declined when the Byzantine forces dominated again. However, as the Byzantine influence began to decay the Bulgarians re-established their independence, which lasted from the late twelfth century to the late fourteenth, when the Ottoman Empire conquered the Balkans and resulted in almost five centuries of Turkish domination over Bulgaria. During that period Bulgarians were deprived of social and political organisations of their own and were forced to live under a state and political system that was substantially different from and distinctly alien to the European political, economic and cultural model, separated from the progressive trends of European development. Under Ottoman rule Bulgaria went through a lengthy period of political dependence and cultural limitation, from Turks as well as Greeks. (The latter, feeling culturally superior, encouraged Bulgarians to abandon their native ways and become Hellenised.) The spiritual and cultural achievements of the past, along with long national traditions, provided the basis for the unity of the Bulgarian people during the centuries of foreign rule. During that time, although the national identity and culture were preserved in the rural areas, they did not drive a national self-determination movement until the late eighteenth century, when the Ottoman Empire was clearly in decline. The eighteenth century brought the development of the modern Bulgarian vernacular and a rise of cultural nationalism in the region.

The decline of the Ottoman state was one of the strongest incentives for the considerable economic growth of the Bulgarian people during the second half of the nineteenth century. The reorganisation of craft manufacture along with the incorporation of the Ottoman Empire into the European economic system gave further impetus to manufacture and trade.

> Trade activity was extended beyond the Turkish Empire's borders. Bulgarian goods were exported increasingly to Western Europe and modern manufacturing equipment, mainly textile machinery, was imported. Trade brought the idea of achieving modernisation in Bulgarian life and culture, as more Bulgarians traveled to the West for business or for education. (Dobrin, 1973: 4)

Over time, Bulgarians' ethnic awareness evolved into a national consciousness that came to be expressed in national institutions and ultimately in the suppressed revolt of 1876 (the 'April uprising'). However, it was not so much the realisation of the vision of the national revolutionaries that led to freedom as the Russian victory in the Russo-Turkish War of 1877–78. Russia's interests in the region coincided with the existence of an independent Bulgarian state and hence in 1878 Bulgaria was again established as an independent country.[1] The task of building up a nation state began under the direct guidance of the temporary Russian administration, which mapped out the state institutions and called a Constituent National Assembly in Turnovo (the ancient capital) which was to draft the Bulgarian Constitution. This was the first broad political forum of the liberated Bulgarians (Todorov, 1977: 68). The Turnovo Constitution, which was adopted in 1879, represented one of the most advanced and democratic of Basic Laws laws in the world at that time and remained the foundation of the Bulgarian state for sixty-five years.[2] As a result, soon after its adoption, the country's political, judicial and administrative system took shape. Nevertheless,

> in practice the Turnovo Constitution failed to live up to its promise. Despite the provisions that limited the role of the monarch and provided for parliamentary supremacy, actual power steadily gravitated to the royal head-of-state. As in all Balkan countries during that era, the monarch exerted a substantial influence on political life by manipulating the parties and cabinets. (Tanchev, 1998: 66)

Besides, the Constitution was frequently amended and often violated, owing to impulsive actions and personal ambitions that can be attributed to lack of experience and the general absence of self-government.

As it was primarily the Russian Empire that led to Bulgarian liberation, Russia's role in Bulgarian history prior the Second World War can hardly be overestimated. This fact increased the prestige of Russia among a broad stratum of the Bulgarian society in the following years – though the affiliation between Russians and Bulgarians should not be exaggerated, as it usually is among Westerners (i.e. the 'Russian big brother'). The building of the independent Bulgarian state and the whole subsequent history of Bulgaria are marked by the competition between various preferences and orientations in foreign policy. The pro-Russian orientation was soon counteracted by a pro-European one. Decisive for the prevalence of one orientation or another at a most general level were such factors and considerations as the move towards industrialism and modernisation (in this respect the European states had much more to offer than Russia), the strategies for the solution of the 'national question', etc. The nascent Bulgarian political society was very receptive to European political models and political ideas, as Europe was synonymous with progress, advancement, liberalisation and enlightenment. The pro-European orientation of Bulgaria reached its peak when power passed into the hands of Stefan Stambolov (Prime Minister from 1887 to 1893), who catalysed the modernisation process.

The influence of European political models was also reflected in the formation of the political parties, which borrowed the names, ideologies and programmes of those in European countries. Not only were the political parties modelled on European analogues but there were preferences among them for one or other of the 'great powers' as a potential patron of the country, and this was essential part of a party's identity. 'There has not been a single political party or political project which did not declare its sympathy for some foreign state or other ... The foreign state is emblematic of the proposed political model, and the declared sympathy with it did not constitute 'national treason' (Todorov, 1999: 7). On the other hand, in order to gain the favour of the Bulgarian political elite, the 'great powers' pursued such strategies as offering them educational opportunities abroad, promoting their respective 'cultures' in Bulgaria; they also exerted an economic influence or direct political pressure at certain moments (e.g. on the eve of the World Wars).

As Germany tended to prevail over the others, this dichotomy produced the ironic result of Bulgaria being 'on the wrong side' in both World Wars. Taking the side of Germany, Bulgaria suffered the harsh consequences of the post-1918 peace, and would have had a similar fate in 1945 had not the Soviet Union ensured that Bulgaria was not punished.

1878–1944

Liberation brought fundamental political, social and economic changes. In the political sphere, though the country adopted a democratic form of government,

> power was always in the hands of a politically active elite composed of the country's few large landowners, merchants, political bosses on the small town and village level, lawyers, clergy, officers, teachers, and those educated in Bulgarian communities abroad. After the Liberation these men took up the reins of government, staffing the civil service and officer corps of the new state. (Bell, 1977: 5)

The declared domestic policy hardly differed from one party to another, and this period is filled with political tension, conflicts and conspiracies, an intensified struggle for the spoils of office, a proliferation of bureaucracy, pervasive corruption, and the exclusion of the bulk of the population from the political arena. Political life was debased by polarisation, splits in the political parties, frequent Cabinet changes, pro-monarchy and anti-monarchy *coups*, intimidation, violence and counterfeiting. In addition the country had to bear the heritage of centuries of paternalist rule that was marked by the Ottoman Empire's hostility to the autonomous political consolidation of intermediary groups. The operation of the Bulgarian political system, therefore, was based on restricted popular participation and on a strongly centralised state controlled by a few notable families and professional politicians. It was characteristic that, on election days in any village, the police were more influential than the most idealistic opposition speeches.

> The peasantry, four-fifths of the population, lacked the education, organisation, and experience to act as a brake on political degeneration. Its role in government was reduced to casting ballots in what were more and more frequently rigged or meaningless elections. By the close of the nineteenth century most educated

> Bulgarians were aware that two societies had arisen: the urban 'political intelligentsia' and the common people. (Bell, 1977: 7)

Nevertheless, during the Stambolov (nicknamed the 'Bulgarian Bismarck') years political life showed signs of a gradual change. As he was known for his revolutionary past, Stambolov enjoyed wider popular recognition than his predecessors. Establishing a virtual dictatorship by acquiring total control over the state apparatus (the military, the police, the civil authorities), Stambolov managed to smother political opposition and to suppress military uprisings and conspiracies with an iron hand. Thus when he was deposed in 1894 political life lost some of the features which had characterised it before. Abysmal political standards, furthermore, were matched by the absence of any significant economic progress.

After the break-up of the great estates formerly held by Ottoman proprietors, Bulgaria emerged from Ottoman rule a poor agricultural country of small landowning peasants with exceedingly traditional and primitive agricultural methods, so that agrarian capitalist development rested on a base of smallholdings. In a population of 3,774,000 in 1900, over 80 per cent were peasants, most families owning their land. With one of the least developed economies in Europe, gradual industrialisation in a smallholder economy and rapid modernisation through state efficiency were the main policies pursued until 1944. The encouragement of certain branches of industry, the large-scale construction of railways and roads, along with the development of the mining industry, were mainly the result of government investment and policy.

In contrast to previous governments, Stambolov paid greater attention to Bulgaria's many internal problems. Thus the stimulation of industry began under his rule, as he succeeded in laying the foundations of economic growth with a package of laws sanctioning the construction of roads and railways, legal and commercial contacts with other countries and the establishment of national institutions in education, culture and health services.

> Stambolov introduced measures which greatly accelerated the process of modernisation of Bulgarian society. Not only did the rebuilding of the capital and its transformation into a modern European city begin, with the establishment of a new university, but infant industry also was encouraged by mild protectionism and new railways and new highways. His policies in that respect were continued by the next cabinets, and Bulgaria witnessed quite a steady tendency to economic growth.[3] (Pantev, 1996: 11)

Despite this tendency, Bulgaria was still far from achieving the necessary industrial transformation, as large-scale industry did not gain much ground and the economic structure preserved its traditional agricultural character. An index was the fact that the number of industrial enterprises in 1887 increased from thirty-six to 345 in 1911, with 16,000 workers, and almost 90 per cent of the goods manufactured being food or other products closely related to agriculture. Industry remained too reliant upon imported raw materials and semi-manufactured goods, mainly because local products were not of a high enough quality for use in manufacturing. Heavy industry (the production of machinery and other advanced manufacturing techniques) was almost completely absent, and the machinery imported was not the type characteristic of industrialisation.[4] Thus, by 1920, still only about 13 per cent of the population were engaged in industry, handicrafts, and transport, while 75 per cent were still in agriculture; the rest, 12 per cent, were in government service and the professions (Dobrin, 1973: 8; Berend and Ranki, 1974: 143).

Despite the fact that there was almost no change in its social structure, from the turn of the century and up to the Balkan Wars (1912–13) Bulgaria experienced a time of progress. 'But the living conditions of the broad masses did not improve since much of the material progress was financed by borrowing heavily abroad, requiring periodical tax increases and the establishment of special state monopolies over goods of general use to service the loans' (Berend and Ranki, 1974: 109). The peasantry, thus, had to bear not only the costs of a heavily centralised administrative machine and of maintaining a large and well equipped army (preparing for the forthcoming wars) but also the payments on the loans contracted abroad.[5] On the other hand, the political elite was interested in rural welfare only as far as it was a steady source of revenue and was largely responsible for turning national strategy away from social and economic problems and into nationalist, irredentist, non-productive and ruinous projects. Smallholdings, at the same time, were repeatedly subdivided through inheritance, and farming methods were not improving, as peasants who gained ownership of the land possessed no capital and were unable to acquire adequate loans to carry out modernisation. Subsequently

> peasant discontent mounted steadily. This group had certain definite demands; it wanted, for example, loans to be available at reasonable rates, guaranteed markets for crops, and the assurance of low prices for staples, such as matches, soap, and sugar. The peasants particularly disliked the rising costs of consumer goods when their own incomes were declining. (Jelavich and Jelavich, 1977: 194)

In 1899 these conditions, coupled with the fact that peasants realised that governmental policies and national politics affected them, gave rise to the Bulgarian Agrarian National Union (BANU). BANU became a major political force when the already impoverished condition of the masses deteriorated and the slow pace of development was even more retarded as Bulgaria was drawn into two regional wars and the First World War.[6]

Having supported the central powers during the war, Bulgaria found itself on the losing side and had to submit to the harshest terms. For years the Bulgarians remained bitter about the results of the Second Balkan War and the First World War, what they called the 'national catastrophe', and they would welcome any opportunity in international affairs for revision. The destruction caused by these wars and the losses through reparations in peacetime drained the already limited national resources. (For instance, Bulgaria was required to pay an indemnity of

$450 million over thirty-eight years.) The poorest nation in the Balkans, aside from Albania, Bulgaria was placed under an impossible burden.

The war defeats, the intolerable scarcities and the corruption among the ruling circles discredited the traditional political institutions – the monarchy, the bourgeois parties and the parliament – and created a revolutionary wave nourished by popular suffering and crushing national disappointment. In this situation, two radical parties came to the forefront of the political stage: the BANU and the Bulgarian Social Democratic Party, which subsequently changed its name to the Bulgarian Communist Party (BCP). The BANU won the elections in 1919 (the BCP came second) and under the leadership of Alexander Stamboliski, who had formulated an indigenous ideology of 'Agrarianism' as a third way between capitalism and Marxism, found a chance to step in and undertook to reshape Bulgaria.

Once in power, and during the three years of his governance, 'Stamboliski implemented an Agrarian programme which placed Bulgaria well on the road to recovery after the disasters of the First World War. But his programme aroused resentments among the urban political formations, including the military, which Stamboliski had reduced drastically'[7] (Moser, 1994: 17).

In 1923 the Agrarian regime was violently overthrown by a fascist military-political coalition and an authoritarian order was restored. Acts of violence and clashes between right-wing and left-wing paramilitary groups now characterised the country's unstable politics. This pattern lasted until 1935, when a *coup d'état*, mounted by Tsar Boris, with the support of the military, established what no one doubted was a royal dictatorship though the outward forms of parliamentary democracy were maintained.

In sum, since the liberation, every attempt to create a viable democratic system was unsuccessful, as workable democratic parliamentary governments were the exception rather than the rule. In the twentieth century, moreover, democratic principles hardly stood a chance in Bulgaria, where the unresolved national problem, the absence of genuine reform, the heavily centralised political system, the weak middle class, political fragmentation and clientism, civil strife and political violence, along with an inefficient, dictatorial and corrupt administration that continued to follow the traditions and methods of the Ottoman Empire as well as the model established by other fascist regimes of the time (mainly the Italian one), proved too much for Bulgarian democracy. In addition, the Great Depression – albeit the crisis in Bulgaria was not as profound as in most Western countries, owing to the high share of agriculture in the formation of incomes – made the situation even worse for the already poor population, leaving people with almost no interest in liberal democracy and democratic structures. Consequently political participation remained the privilege of the elite. This is what Nicos Mouzelis calls 'oligarchic parliamentary rule', a system dominated by only a few people who managed to maintain a liberal system of representation (with the usual civil liberties) while at the same time excluding the bulk of the lower classes from the political arena (Mouzelis, 1986: 3).

In this way the peasantry, still constituting the majority of the population, continued to view the state and politics as alien, feeling a growing sense of deference and helplessness, and faced the world outside its village with greater suspicion. Especially as the outside world was mainly responsible for the impoverishment of the agrarian sector and the low living standards.[8]

Agriculture was burdened with serious problems stemming from

> the uneconomic system of scattered strip distribution, which was once a venerable form of insurance against hail but by this period obsolete and irrational; the primitive level of agronomic technology; ... the high level of rural overpopulation and underemployment. Low productivity, low consumption, and low capital formation in agriculture fed each other in a tight circle. (Rothschild, 1974: 331)

The inter-war period brought very few changes in the social and economic structure. On the eve of the Second World War, Bulgaria was still a primarily agricultural country, and the size of industrial units, like that of farms, remained small. So, for instance, from 1929 to 1939 industrial production grew by about 52 per cent, a relatively high figure, but still agriculture's share of GNP was 60 per cent in 1924 and 52 per cent in 1939, when the share of industrial production was no more than 5.6 per cent in 1938 (the lowest proportion in Southeastern Europe, Albania excepted), not much different from the 5.1 per cent of 1926 (Crampton, 1987: 141).

In the economic realm, moreover, the major characteristics were overdependence on exports of agricultural products (particularly tobacco), and the fact that Bulgaria was drawn into the German economic orbit. The links that had been forged in the First World War were maintained in the 1920s, when Germany took a quarter of all Bulgaria's exports. The economic crisis of 1929, the Great Depression and later the monarchic regime of Boris further aligned Bulgaria with Nazi Germany in economic as well as in diplomatic terms. Besides being unable to react flexibly and adequately to changing economic conditions, Bulgaria found itself internationally isolated, confined and unbalanced, as trade with the West and the Balkan countries atrophied and thus, in many respects, was forced into close co-operation with Germany. The Bulgarian and German economies were naturally complementary, and Bulgaria benefited a great deal from the relationship with Germany. (In 1939 exports to Germany reached 71.1 per cent of the total figure and imports 69.5 per cent.)

> Know-how, industrial installations, and credit flowed in from Germany in return for agricultural products. Many new roads were built. The mining industry grew. Thousands of Bulgarian workers found jobs in Germany and gained experience, and capital returned to the country. The construction, chemical, machine building industries, and metallurgy made significant advances, though the main advance was in food processing. (Dobrin, 1973: 9)

But whatever economic progress Bulgaria was making was once again interrupted, by the Second World War. Bulgaria repeated the mistake of 1914 and became an ally of Germany for the purpose of obtaining the territories envisaged at San Stefano, declaring war on Great Britain, France, the United States but not on the Soviet Union.[9] Bulgaria's involvement in the war was minimal – indeed, the country was largely untouched by it – and when defeat appeared inevitable Bulgaria sought to break away from the Axis pact. Its plea for an armistice with the Allies was disregarded by the Soviet Union, which in September 1944 proceeded to declare war and occupy the country. (Under the terms of the armistice Bulgaria was once again forced to evacuate the territories it had occupied in Greece and Yugoslavia.)

Bulgaria under Communist rule

Early stages of Communism and the seizure of power

Bulgaria has a history of an indigenous Communist movement, and the BCP was considerably stronger than some others Communist parties in Eastern Europe, perhaps because of the country's tradition of peasant radicalism. Certainly the BCP, throughout its history, benefited from popular admiration of Russia, which was stronger in Bulgaria than in any other country in Europe. The historical roots of Bulgarian Communism can be traced back to the 1890s, when Dimitar Blagoev, a Russian-educated intellectual considered the 'father' of Bulgarian Communism, introduced the Communist ideology. The movement that received its inspiration at that time failed to grow during its early years, firstly owing to the split (1903) into 'narrow' and 'broad' factions (the Bolshevik–Menshevik split) and secondly because of the absence of a substantial urban proletariat, since smallholder peasants were not susceptible to easy organisation. The 'broad' group, realising that an almost wholly agrarian economy like Bulgaria's would be unable to support the classical Marxist approach, evolved into the Bulgarian Social Democratic Party. The 'narrow' faction, under Blagoev, advocating policies based on an industrialised economy, formed the nucleus of the Communist Party. Politically intransigent, the 'narrow' Communists had, at first, less popular following than the 'broad' socialists but this trend was reversed at the end of the First World War, when, having assumed the name of the BCP, the Communists became the second strongest political force in the country.

Nevertheless the Communists faced difficulties such as constant interference in their affairs by the Comintern in Moscow, ineptitude and misjudgement on the part of their leaders at home, and fitful periods of rigorous persecution by the Bulgarian authorities. Especially after 1923, when the Communists, led by Georgi Dimitrov, attempted a *coup*, the BCP was declared illegal and faded for several years almost into insignificance. About 3,000 Communists fled to Russia to avoid capture. It revived again considerably in popularity and organisational strength in 1931–32 as the Bulgarian Workers' Party, a Communist front organisation, saw thirty-one of its candidates win seats as deputies in the general elections, an outstanding achievement. Later, although persecuted again by successive regimes, the Communists retained their relative strength and would have done even better but for the internal upheavals they experienced. In fact during that period the BCP acquired most of the characteristics typical of a Communist party.

> Illegality encouraged the Communists to develop the conspiratorial principle of rigid organisation, a central hierarchy, military discipline and cell structures; to distrust autonomous action; to favour 'entryism', the infiltration of other, potentially friendly organisations like trade unions, and the creation of front organisations; to promote the cultivation of the disciplined cadre party, the group of battle-hardened activists, professional revolutionaries ready to accept whatever instructions they received and to scorn recruitment on a large scale. (Schöpflin, 1993: 47)

During the Second World War there was a certain amount of small-scale partisan activity in Bulgaria, directed against government troops because there were no Germans to fight. The Communist underground had been harried by the police, and by 1942 the party and its organisational superstructure had been weakened considerably (though relatively strong, with a claimed total membership of about 30,000). Throughout the war the Soviet leadership encouraged the formation of partisan organisations and Communist collaboration with certain other parties in front organisations. It was the general tactic pursued by the Communist parties in several countries (Greece, for instance) since the 1935 Comintern decision. In Bulgaria the BCP stood behind the Fatherland Front, a weak combination of political organisations and parties that had often been rivals in the past. The main components of the Fatherland Front, apart from the core constituted by the Communists, were left-wing Agrarians and left-wing Social Democrats. The only well organised political force in it was the BCP, which had its own local cells throughout the country, an underground press, and a guerrilla movement towards which the remaining member parties of the Front showed an unwilling attitude. Finally, in September 1943, the Front took organisational shape through the formation of its first National Committee. 'From then on the Communists had an instrument with which to work, and this proved increasingly viable as the war drew to its close and the victorious Soviet troops approached ever nearer' (Brown, 1970: 8).

According to Crampton, in Bulgaria, as in other parts of Europe, the general atmosphere of the initial post-war period was, for a number of reasons, in favour of left-wing groups:

> the Communists' record of resistance was a fact which to many legitimised their participation in the government; the Soviet Union and the Red Army were widely respected, and a government with Communist participation would be favorably regarded by Moscow making Soviet patronage more secure and effective; the notion of a planned economy was generally attractive to a generation that had only experienced the dismal failure of capitalism in the 1930s and still faced considerable problems. (Crampton, 1987: 146)

Therefore, as soon as Soviet troops entered the country, with the absence of opposition, and the full co-operation of the police and the army, the Fatherland

Front simply took over the government on 9 September 1944 – a day that became the most celebrated in the Bulgarian Communist calendar.[10]

However, as Nissan Oren noted, to the Communists victory came suddenly and almost unexpectedly. Despite the fact that Communism had been strong in Bulgaria and the Communist Party did not have to be reinvented, the Communists in 1944, in almost all respects, were substantially weaker than they had been in the early and mid-1920s. This was a striking deviation from the general direction of European Communism. Yet their relative position on the domestic scene was favourable, since they had been able to maintain most of their political organisation during the preceding decades, while their potential rivals had not (Oren, 1973: 82).

After September 1944 the political scene underwent radical transformation as only those political parties represented in the Front were permitted the right to organise formally, and purges and trials ranged far and wide. In 1947, when the opposition Agrarian Union was in effect dissolved and its leader, Nikola Petkov, executed, the last obstacle to the Communists had been removed. Stalinisation took hold in Bulgaria with great aggressiveness, and a large number of persons (nearly 3,000) who were considered a threat to the regime were tried and summarily executed. In the meantime the Communists completely reorganised local government to their own advantage, and once they had eliminated all the enemies of the new regime they set about removing all vestiges of independence from the Fatherland Front. The pattern followed by the BCP in order to seize power was common throughout Eastern Europe. The BCP initially formed a genuine coalition behaving as a true political actor in the political system, then gradually assumed total control of the coalition and finally centralised the entire political system under Communist power. By September 1946 the Communist regime consolidated its grip. and this was the moment at which the party leader, Georgi Dimitrov, proclaimed the Bulgarian People's Republic.[11]

The political transformation

Once political opposition had been eliminated and all political organisations outside the BCP had been destroyed, the Communists faced no difficulty in ratifying a new Constitution under which the party's 'leading role within society' was formalised. From that moment, Bulgaria became another state of the Communist Bloc and as such the country's political course displayed all the characteristics of a Communist regime.

The Communist system (as it was transformed by Stalin) has been widely identified not only as authoritarian but as presented with all the features of totalitarianism:

> one ruling party, one single ideology, the predominance of the leader in all matters, extensive police repression often directed randomly against the whole population and not just against 'enemies of the state', all the economy under state control, direct and overt control of the mass media and practice of government censorship, consistent deception of the masses outside the Party, frequent party purges to demonstrate

> the guiding principle, 'those who are not with us, are against us', great emphasis placed on the role of rituals and symbols such as marches, stage-managed expressions of goodwill for party leaders and so on. (Crawford, 1996: 46)

But the single most important feature of totalitarianism, its central characteristic, was the complete suppression and destruction of civil society and its institutions.[12] Civil society, by its own nature, could potentially threaten the monopoly of power and thus the Communist regime had to ensure its fragmentation and dissolution. The regime achieved this objective first by abolishing or by putting under the control of the state all the autonomous, voluntary, non-governmental organisations. Political organisations, trade unions, religious and academic organisations, publishing houses, even sports clubs – in short, all forms of communal activity – were annihilated. Either these organisations were replaced by new ones created by the state and the party (a separation between them was virtually impossible) or they had to change their organisational structures in order to become an integral part of the system with the responsibility to promote Marxism-Leninism. The values and principles represented by civil institutions were eliminated and replaced by the values and the ideology of the omnipotent state while the nomenclature of the new regime was formed by social categories hitherto excluded from political society (mainly the peasants). In that way the Communist state extended and imposed the principles of its bureaucratic hierarchy on to civil society, which ceased to exist as an arena defined by its autonomy from the state.

> The imposition of a totalizing system, legitimated in terms of perfection, managed by convinced utopians and backed up by terror, resulted in the elimination of much of what makes a society a society, as distinct from an agglomeration of individuals. Autonomies and solidarities, terms of trust, codes of interpersonal behaviour, the rules governing micro-level transactions were shattered. (Schöpflin, 1993: 78)

The totalitarian system thus led to the total degradation of civil organisations into state-controlled entities and from that point the system, by producing atomisation, did not have citizens but subjects. That was because the regime managed to destroy 'the values indispensable to democratic life: honesty, trust and responsibility. Bulgarians lived in a milieu whose daily conflicts between their public and private selves eroded the "inner integrity" and "moral identity" of the individual and produced the "total abdication of personal responsibility"' (Meininger and Radoeva, 1996: 55). The state did not want citizens, as, in contrast to a democratic regime, the supreme political value was not the individual but the collective interest, which only the party could determine. Although the regime encouraged participation by involving people in the political process through voting (about 99 per cent was the usual electoral turnout) and through membership of mass organisations such as youth clubs, women's associations and trade unions, this participation was hollow and even coerced, since it was totally controlled and regulated by the party. These fictitious autonomous organisations were used for political propaganda while every activity had to be strictly scheduled – from the number of new members to that of obligatory gatherings. The promotion of such a form of participation was an attempt by the party to foster the dissemination of the new ideology and to achieve the better implementation of control of the civil society structures and through them to control both society and citizens. In addition, because of the strictly hierarchical, disciplined, regimented, bureaucratic centralised political structure of the party, and by virtue of its monopoly status, the centre of all power was the leader. (It was especially true during the Stalinist period.[13]) The leader could control the party, while the party could control the state and the state provided the necessary institutions (police, army, judiciary) to enforce this control over civil society. As Z. Zhelev argued, in his famous account of fascism and totalitarianism,

> in reality, the leaders of the totalitarian system were also the sole representatives of the civil society. They alone were entitled to speak on behalf of the civil society or, which is much the same, to be the 'citizens' who represented society before the state. The tyranny of politics over all other public domains allowed these people to claim total superiority: they were the smartest, worthiest, most principled, most honest, etc. (Zhelev, 1997: 156)

Besides this there was no room in the system for intermediary organisations since there were no interests to be expressed other than those reflecting the will of the party. The purpose of the existing organisations was solely the execution of party policies and the best fulfilment of party goals. This meant that the individuals and the institutions were supposed to represent only the party's interests instead of their own. The members of trade unions, for instance, were expected to fight for the fulfilment of the plans even if it meant the deterioration of their standard of living. Especially since the unions' senior officials were coming under the nomenclature of the party it was impossible to articulate the interests of the work force. Under such conditions 'the mass associations adequately performed interest articulation functions only where the relevant issues were non-controversial, where there was no conflict between official and group definitions of an interest' (Lovenduski and Woodall, 1987: 302).

But this was hardly the case during the Communist era because, in an attempt to manage all dimensions of the society, the state left no area beyond its responsibility and beyond its reach. With the end of the 1950s even the Bulgarian Church lost its autonomy and thus was unable to play a role similar to that of the Catholic Church in Poland.[14] As Z. Rau asserted, the state's final goal was not just the destruction of civil society but its irreversible elimination. 'In order to make the disappearance of civil society irreversible, the state found it necessary to deprive individuals of their will to rebuild the structures of that society and that could be achieved only by changing the very consciousness of the population' (Rau, 1991: 11). As the political system was driven by ideology, everything was political and capable of being understood only through politics (the 'tyranny of politics'). But there was only one set of values, thus not permitting the possibility of argument over different propositions and policies. The ideology of Marxism-Leninism was able to provide unmistakable answers to every question, in any domain, in any branch of human knowledge. As Zhelev noted,

> the totalitarian state imposed authoritarian rule on the intellectual sphere, because its fiercely centralised bureaucratic hierarchy promoted authority and faith in the undoubted correctness of its decisions into the supreme judge of truth, so in effect, rather than authority depending on truth, it was the reverse: truth depended on authority. (Zhelev, 1997: 154)

Disagreement, doubt and debate were considered antagonistic, hostile, antisocial and irrational, deserving punitive action. The 'luxury of having been sceptical' could result in time in a concentration camp, while compliance could lead to political power, wealth and social prestige. In this attempt to merge the public and private spheres, no aspect of life, no activity, however apolitical it might appear, remained outside the ideological purview of the regime. Even family values were expected to give way to serving the party goals. This is what Zhelev described as the 'uniformity' of the entire life of society.

> Uniformity is the question by which the totalitarian party imposed its control over the state and, through the state, over the civil society. It was a political uniformity through which the totalitarian party extended its monopoly onto those areas of civil society which in traditional bourgeois democracies are free of state or political party control: the arts, literature, tastes, entertainment etc., right down to private family affairs. (Zhelev, 1997: 95)

From this argument it is apparent that when a separation of the party from the state was taking place, the disintegration of the totalitarian system and the re-emergence of civil society became inevitable. This was proved in 1989.

In political terms, Bulgaria followed the pattern similar to all the Eastern European countries. After the brutal consolidation of Communist rule, the bloody struggle between 'native' and 'Moscow' Communists ended in victory for the latter. One-man dictatorship was established, under Vulko Chervenkov – as Dimitrov died in 1949 – sanctioned by Moscow. Stalin's death was followed by relaxations and the denunciation of the previous leadership. A 'native' Communist, Todor Zhivkov, a man of no especial reputation at that point, became First Secretary of the party in 1954 and – after a period of asserting his control – the unchallenged leader of the country until 1989. Under his rule Bulgaria was unquestionably loyal to Moscow, and was unaffected politically or ideologically by the upheavals in Hungary in 1956, in Czechoslovakia in 1968 or the anti-Communist movement in Poland in 1980. By a combination of ruthlessness and accommodation, Zhivkov managed to keep Bulgarian society well under control, even during such troubled times.

The economic transformation

After a new constitution had been enacted, stating that the national economy would be planned, the major preoccupations of the newly installed regime were to integrate Bulgaria into the Soviet camp and to construct a socialist society based on modernisation, social welfare and class equality. With this regard, by spring 1948 Bulgaria had signed treaties of friendship and co-operation with all the other states of Eastern Europe, and in 1949 was a founder member of the Council of Mutual Economic Assistance (CMEA), and of the Warsaw Pact in 1955. On the domestic scene, the economic policies adopted after the war closely followed the Soviet pattern and were modelled and introduced with the assistance of Soviet experts and managers.[15] The basic features of the model were the virtually complete nationalisation of industrial assets and land, and the replacement of the market by an all-encompassing system of central planning.

The market system of the capitalist world was rejected as unscientific, wasteful and geared to the gratification of private interest at public expense. In its place was substituted a planned, scientific approach to all aspects of economic life. The state sought to design an integrated plan to meet the goals specified by the political authorities. Government stipulated the objectives, or 'targets', and the way in which they were to be achieved was the task of the planners – the preparation of these plans, usually made on a five-year basis, absorbed a great deal of the attention of the government and party officials. There was thus produced a command economy, designed to respond to instructions from the top and to obey the orders of those in political control. Power and authority were removed from the individual production unit, known as the 'enterprise' (Morris, 1984: 77).

In this way the centrally planned economy provided an opportunity for resolving simultaneously the formidable problems of capital accumulation, effective demand and income distribution. The system, in order to achieve a given objective, was able to mobilise and direct resources and manpower, could use hitherto unexploited labour reserves, such as the excess agricultural population and women, and introduce more easily from above advanced technologies (Jelavich, 1983: 347). There were certain weaknesses in the central planning system, as, for example, it was completely dependent on the ability of the planners, who were faced with an unmanageable problem of data collection and plan co-ordination, it was quite rigid, which meant that adjustments could not be easily made, and, most crucial of all, the state was committed to support production units whether or not they were profitable. This was very common in the Communist economies, since the lack of incentives and competition within the system often led enterprises to operate at a low level of efficiency and to produce shoddy goods at a high cost. Enterprises were no longer autonomous economic actors relying on market signals (such as supply and demand), but instead they were transformed into the lowest level of a vast bureaucratic apparatus geared not to profit, but to meeting the political priorities of the regime. Besides, 'the main quality fostered in managers was not entrepreneurial flair but political conformity with the dictates of their bureaucratic superiors, and unquestioning fulfilment of commands, no matter how economically irrational they might be from the point of view of the enterprise or the economy in general' (Batt, 1993: 208).

The Soviet development strategy, moreover, could be briefly defined as 'rapid growth of heavy industry to be achieved through concentrated investment from the state budget and a labor force augmented by peasant influx. A smaller rural labor force would be left on the mechanized collective farms to produce the surplus needed to feed a growing urban population' (Lampe, 1986: 139). Despite the development of a number of distinctly idiosyncratic features Bulgaria maintained this Soviet strategy and model of state ownership, central planning of industry and central direction of agriculture with considerable fidelity and more closely than did any of the other Communist regimes in Eastern Europe for four decades.

Accordingly, the main task of the new economic system was to secure government ownership of all the means of production, either through nationalisation or, in the case of land, through collectivisation. Initial nationalisation of industry took place in 1946, but it was fully accomplished only at the end of 1947, together with nationalisation of the financial apparatus.[16] The year 1948 saw the nationalisation of wholesale trade and the establishment of a foreign-trade monopoly. The production and distribution of most goods and services came under the control of the state. Thus the central administration had to determine matters such as what products should be produced, where they should be manufactured, their exact specifications and prices, questions that had previously been determined by the rules of the free market.

Irrespective of the fact that economic policy in all Eastern European countries gave priority to heavy industry, this policy was possibly most widespread in Bulgaria. Following the Soviet pattern, and under the need to break the economy out of the cycle of self-perpetuating underdevelopment, Bulgaria embarked on the road of rapid (or forced) industrialisation with collectivisation, placing emphasis almost completely on heavy industry, in particular on metallurgy and engineering. Impressive enterprises, such as giant iron, steel and fertiliser complexes, power plants and hydro-electric projects were to be built, and further development of secondary sectors such as building materials, basic chemical production, electric power and transport took place in order to support industrialisation. The goal for Bulgaria was to acquire a strong industrial base for the future and the driving motto was that the present should be sacrificed to the future. But for the creation of a strong industrial sector state planners subordinated every aspect of the national economy: investment, money supply, wages, employment policies, the provision of consumer goods, welfare expenditure.

All these projects involved very high investment outlays and Bulgaria lacked the necessary capital. Since Soviet credits, although available, were small, this rapid advance in one part of the economy had to be paid for by the peasantry and consumers. The peasant producer carried much of the burden of the economic revolution while there was a steady flow of labour displaced from the land to service the industrial sector. Similarly, the average citizen was forced to accept a reduced standard of living, because consumer industries and services were regularly sacrificed to the alternative goal, a high level of industrial growth[17] (Jelavich, 1983: 346).

Still, the policy of rapid industrialisation produced results and wrought changes in the economic structure. Agriculture soon lost its dominance among contributions to the national income, and the country was well on its way to becoming agricultural-industrial. Whereas in 1948 more than half the national income was produced by agriculture and only a quarter by industry, already by 1960 this trend had been reversed. The balance between industry and agriculture in 1939 had been 75 : 25 in favour of agriculture; in 1949 it stood at 70 : 30, and by 1956 it had swung to 67 : 32 to the advantage of industry. This structural change in the economy is also reflected in employment by economic sector: in 1948 agricultural workers still made up 82 per cent of the total work force; by 1970 the figure was 36 per cent and by 1988 19 per cent. Industrial employment in 1948 amounted only to about 8 per cent of the labour force but by 1967 the industrial proportion had already grown 28 per cent (Dobrin, 1973: 152; Brown, 1970: 47).

Table 2.1 Annual average growth, 1953–60 to 1986–89 (%)

Period	*Official data (NMP)*	*Western calculation (GNP)*
1953–60	9.40	n.a.
1961–65	6.70	6.6
1966–70	8.75	4.7
1971–75	7.80	4.5
1976–80	6.10	1.2
1981–85	3.70	0.9
1986–89	3.10	–1.8

Source: Wyzan (1996: 80).

Apart from the structural transformation, these early economic policies generated impressive economic growth even by international standards (see table 2.1). Yet by the mid-1960s this performance had started to lose momentum and the official approach was to experiment with various innovative models of economic reform. First, in an obvious attempt to correct some of the serious deficiencies in the economy, a reorganisation of both government and the economy away from the previous centralised lines was begun (the so-called 'New Economic System'). The general features were the decentralisation of the decision-making process, greater use of market forces to which enterprises were expected to respond, the introduction of the concept of profit and loss, and the tying of wages to production. Nonetheless, by 1969 the market-oriented reforms had been abandoned as the expected results had not materialised, for many of the reform's features were neither worked out nor implemented.[18] New plans involved borrowing, better management and growing pressure from above for the dissemination of technical progress on a large scale, but, without sufficiently powerful and motivating incentives at the lower levels, again this technical progress initiative proved unrealistic and did not work.

By the mid-1970s it was clear that, although industrialisation had brought about some improvements in living standards, the evidence of deteriorating performance was mounting. Plan targets remained largely unfulfilled, and shortages, irregularities in supply and eccentricities of quality had not been eliminated. Economic performance was disappointing not only in comparison with the promulgated targets but also in comparison with the past growth momentum and with growth dynamics within the CMEA – throughout the 1960s and for the most of the 1970s Bulgaria maintained the highest *per capita* growth rate in the region. It was clear that the period of crash economic development had come to an end as the potential for growth was exhausted.

In 1979 the New Economic Mechanism (NEM) was adopted, applying primarily in agriculture and aiming to help Bulgaria cope with technological advances, to raise levels of productivity, to improve the quality of goods and services, to decrease subsidies, and to increase the competitiveness of the country's products in the world market. The means to this end were (Crampton, 1987: 198):

- *Decentralisation*, retreating from the pursuit of increasing concentration by giving individual production units and managers more authority and by confining the central plan to such tasks as setting general guidelines and overseeing scientific and technical progress.
- The use of *market forces*, since the NEM reduced the number of plan indicators and established direct links between producer and consumer.
- *Self-sufficiency* in individual units of production, as the higher management and even individual brigades were responsible for losses.
- *Competition*, with widespread election of responsible persons as the mechanism of the envisaged 'mobilisation from below'.
- *Wages* were to become a function of productivity by linking earnings with performance.

Economic performance, under the NEM reforms, showed virtually no growth. Small enterprises did well and grew throughout the 1980s but they could not change the disappointing general picture. A rigid centralised planning system with quantifiable goals was retained, along with the leading role of the party and state bureaucracy in economic matters. While a positive step, the New Economic Mechanism was at best a partial reform, weakly and inconsistently implemented, and did not come close to Hungarian efforts to modify certain aspects of central planning.[19] Although the NEM reforms marked a break with the emphasis of the past policies they did not produce the expected results, and the technological lag grew. Thus, despite the expectations and the enthusiastic initial reports, by the mid-1980s much of the optimism had disappeared and even the party leadership acknowledged that economic growth had slowed to its lowest post-war level.

Additionally in the winter of 1984–85 the country experienced its most severe energy crisis, due in part to the decline in Soviet subsidies and reductions in deliveries of Soviet oil. The situation resulted in regular blackouts of twelve hours per day, a ban on electrical heating in all factories and public buildings, and the curtailment of railway traffic.

> Energy disruptions and very poor agricultural production – mainly because of a severe winter followed by extreme and sustained draught – made 1985 the worst year of the entire Communist period for overall economic performance. The events of that year undoubtedly had powerful effects on popular confidence in the performance of the economic system. (McIntyre, 1988: 115)

The collectivisation process

Of all the changes which took place in the Bulgarian economy, none was so spectacular or fundamental as the collectivisation of agriculture. Gerald Creed contents that

> of all the radical changes in Eastern Europe after the Second World War, none were more closely identified with Communism than the collectivisation of agriculture. If one were to ask any Bulgarian villager about changes in his or her village since the Second World War, one would be certain to hear first and foremost about collectivisation; even older urbanites are likely to respond similarly. The prominence of this event in the Bulgarian historical consciousness is due in large part to the dominance of agriculture at the time of Communist ascension … Thus, for many Bulgarians collectivisation became a metaphor for the Communist transformation in general, reinforcing the political nature of agriculture. (Creed, 1995: 852)

As we have seen, Bulgaria was primarily an agrarian society of small private landowners, who worked the land by traditional methods, with backward techniques and management. The Communists, therefore, considered agriculture as unable to contribute effectively to economic progress through increased productivity or greater production. The scope for modernisation was obviously very limited without integrating the small, dispersed holdings of land into large farms. During the Communist era a series of major changes in the structure and organisation of agriculture took place and that is why a brief description of them is necessary, especially since the changes affected the country's evolution.

Marxist theory always regarded the peasantry as primitive and a hindrance to progress, mainly because of their independent and individualistic attitude and lifestyle, and thus it envisaged the conversion of the peasantry into a kind of rural proletariat. The theoretical objective was total state control of all land and either the creation of state farms (*solhozes*) on which peasants would occupy the same position as industrial workers, that of salaried employees, or the organisation of collective farms (or agricultural co-operatives – *kolhozes*) where most of the land and livestock would be pooled. Theoretically composed of participating independent producers who had pooled their land, equipment and livestock to work together, the members of the latter would derive their incomes from their share in the work of the enterprise during the year. The income of the collective was divided in accordance with the total number of work-days performed by its members.

> Under either alternative method the state planners would be able to dictate the details of production and adjust the levels to the general needs of the economy. In theory, this large-scale farming would be more efficient: mechanised equipment could be introduced, and modern improvements, such as better fertilisers, seed and, insecticides, could be provided. (Jelavich, 1983: 348)

This Soviet model of socialised agriculture was introduced after the Communists came to power. However, the existing conditions in Bulgarian agriculture produced a very different system from that of the Soviet Union or the rest of Eastern Europe. Pre-war Bulgarian agriculture was characterised by relatively even land distribution – actually, the structure of ownership was the most egalitarian in Eastern Europe. Bulgaria was increasingly a land of small farmers, leading to extreme fragmentation, which meant general poverty and the absence of modern methods of agriculture, and there was a strong trend toward co-operation and collective ownership. These conditions were not unfavourable to the collectivisation process under the Communists and, though the collectivisation itself was coercive, the rural population were not totally resentful (as they were in the case of the Soviet Union and other Eastern European countries). Besides, the provision of sufficient capital to newly collectivised agriculture allowed a substantial growth in output. This is not to imply that there was not active and passive resistance to compulsory collectivisation, and in his attitude towards it the Bulgarian peasant was no different from his counterparts in the rest of Eastern Europe.

> Nor does it indicate that in Bulgaria agriculture was viewed as a leading sector deserving more than proportionate investment emphasis, but only that it was not systematically impoverished. While the overall emphasis on heavy industrial investment was high, it was not pushed to such levels that required declining peasant living standards, as happened in the Soviet Union in the 1930s. (McIntyre, 1988: 97)

Agriculture collectives expanded at quite a rapid pace, perhaps faster than in any other East European country, even though collectivisation policy proceeded through several phases and was not complete till about the end of the 1950s. The first phase involved persuasion, during the time when the Communist party was consolidating its power. The collectives' terms of membership in this first phase (1944–47) were relatively liberal and were obviously designed to make membership as attractive as possible and to induce poor and middle-class peasants to join through economic and political pressure. 'Yet, by 1947, only 3.8 per cent of the arable land had been collectivised and this seems to have been accomplished entirely through voluntary means'[20] (Brown, 1970: 198).

These initial steps were followed, commencing in 1948, by a more aggressive policy. Despite measures such as the confiscation of all privately owned machinery, by the end of 1948 the collectivised area accounted for only 6.2 per cent and at the end of 1949 encompassed only 11.3 per cent of the total arable land. But Chervenkov's establishment in power marked the first drive for compulsory collectivisation. Collectivisation was stepped up, and thus by 1950 some 43 per cent of all land had been collectivised and by 1958, it was claimed, more than 90 per cent of the land belonged either to collectives or to agricultural enterprises directly operated by the state. In almost ten years Bulgaria had been transformed from a land of small farmers and became the first Communist country after the Soviet Union to have collectivised its agriculture, having thus built a new pattern of village and agrarian life.[21]

> Collectivisation began by metaphorically transforming the village into an agricultural institution: the co-operative farm. Campaigns were organised on a village basis and, in most cases, activists built upon pre-existing co-operative institutions. A farm often adopted the name of a prior village co-operative or another name of local significance, perhaps even the name of the village itself. With the completion of collectivisation, then, the co-operative became emblematic of the village, reinforcing and enhancing the village's distinctive, quasi-corporate character. (Creed, 1995: 855)

In an attempt to reform agriculture new statutes regulating the collective farms were enacted in 1967. In order to obtain better results from the large amount of new equipment introduced in the late 1950s, farms were assigned more agronomists and were paid higher prices for their products. The ground rent paid to former owners was abolished, minimum wages were guaranteed, and workers were grouped into permanent brigades enjoying some internal autonomy. With these provisions were also ratified extended pensions, health benefits, and other social services for peasant members, well before any other East European regime.

But the process of upgrading collective farms took a more significant and unique turn in the early 1970s when collective and state farms ceased to exist as separate entities and were integrated into a system of giant agro-industrial complexes (AICs), consisting of a number of state and/or collective farms.

> They were to be based on 'voluntarism' – each farm was to decide for itself whether or not to join a complex – and member farms were to retain their legal and economic independence within the complex. The aims of the AIC idea were to increase specialisation and concentration of production and to increase output while lowering costs, thereby making Bulgarian goods more competitive. Another consideration was the desire to stem the flow of people from rural areas by including industrial, construction, and trade activities within the complexes. (Oren, 1973: 168)

The closer association of agriculture and industry was of great importance, as it was planned, in the longer term, to link agro-industrial complexes closely with manufacturing industry and the trade associations.[22] A further task was to raise the urban supply of food without diverting labour back from industry, and this was thought to be achieved by specialisation in agricultural production. The AIC concept was quickly implemented nationwide, and in the period 1970–72 the

800 existing state and collective farms were grouped into 170 very large agro-industrial complexes. Some of them were simply groupings of multiple farms producing the same crop, but others were vertically integrated, including, along with direct agricultural production, fertiliser production, packaging and marketing, agricultural research and possibly retail sales of the finished products. But the agro-industrial complexes were hindered by excessive size (they were by far the largest socialist farms of any type outside the Soviet Union), over-specialisation and planning inflexibility. Because of their disappointing performance, measures to alleviate these faults had been introduced in the late 1970s, with a tendency to divide the agro-industrial complexes into smaller, more manageable, units. At the end of 1982, there were 296 agro-industrial complexes, each averaging 12,400 ha of agricultural land and about 2,660 full-time farmers.[23] Finally, in the early 1980s, the New Economic Mechanism was applied to agriculture, but again agricultural performance remained weak without showing any positive growth. (Of significant influence had been the recurring unfavourable weather in 1983 and 1985.) Nevertheless, it should be stressed that, despite the downward trend throughout the 1970s and 1980s, the Bulgarian Communist leadership did not treat agriculture in the manner of other Eastern European countries. Ensuring a sufficient flow of investment resources, the overall picture of agriculture during the Communist rule was improved and the living standards of those who remained in the agricultural work force were raised.

Foreign trade and relations

In a country as small as Bulgaria foreign trade is always vitally important to economic development. During the Communist era the economy was heavily dependent on foreign trade, being poorly and lopsidedly endowed with raw materials. The foreign-trade sector, used as an instrument of industrialisation, was not profitable. On the contrary, it was subsidised. Foreign trade reflected the benefits, costs and shifts of industrialisation and collectivisation policy. The question was not so much the size as the composition and efficiency of external trade. Yet an examination of the Bulgarian economy indicates that after the Second World War the country followed an autarchic policy in international economic relations. In a centrally planned economy, in order for planning to be operational, the domestic economy should be isolated from the disturbing influence of foreign trade. External trade was a state monopoly under the direction of the Ministry of Foreign Trade and the Bulgarian Foreign Trade Bank. The pattern of foreign trade development in the immediate post-war era was based upon the political and economic isolation of the Communist Bloc from the rest of the world, with, as a further objective, the economic integration and formation of an independent Communist unit. The direction of foreign trade, therefore, clearly shifted from the west to the east, and the increased trade with the Soviet Union constituted the major part of this redirection.

Already by 1949, with the formation of the CMEA, the system of bilateral alliances between the Eastern European countries and the Soviet Union was complete. The members of the council committed themselves to co-operation in the political, economic and cultural spheres and to consult each other on the matter of their foreign policies. 'The original purposes of the organisation were to organise foreign trade in raw materials, foods, and industrial equipment and to further the exchange of technical and economic experience' (Dobrin, 1973: 101). Prevented from trading on any large scale with Western Europe, the Communist countries established strong economic links between each other and the Soviet centre. All countries were dependent on the Soviet Union as the USSR became the major supplier of necessary raw materials, machinery and other industrial equipment, as well as design and technology.[24] During that period the Soviet Union used the resources of the entire region for the restoration of its own economy, exploiting the area through the extraction of reparations, with an unfair system of commercial transactions and offering a limited amount of credit and access to Soviet raw materials. In this frame, the CMEA was not playing a major role in bloc affairs, since the exchange terms were chiefly settled according to political decisions, taking no account of economic factors, such as the relation between costs and prices, and, in effect, the established prices were not related to world market prices, placing suppliers in an unfavourable position. At the same time, CMEA member countries developed specific industries that fitted in the overall bloc division of labour but were not well tied to economic criteria. Nevertheless, the death of Stalin marked a gradual change in this situation.

The great reliance of Bulgaria on foreign trade since the 1960s was reflected in the fact that foreign trade amounted to 67.5 per cent of GNP in 1965, ahead of most other East European economies – and when, for example, for Sweden it was 42.5 per cent, 24.5 for Greece and 19.7 per cent for Japan (Black, 1976: 123). By far the largest share of this trade, as table 2.2 shows, remained within the Communist Bloc. In fact, this interrelatedness with the economies of the CMEA countries was one of the distinguishing features of the Bulgarian economy. For Bulgaria, inter-CMEA links provided a large and stable market for agricultural, food and manufactured exports and a generally favourable source of raw materials and energy supplies. Especially since the 1960s Bulgaria had obtained a well known record of greater dependence on Eastern Europe in general, and on the Soviet Union in particular, than the rest of the members of CMEA. Bulgarian dependence on the Soviet source of supplies of cheap raw materials was in many cases overwhelming.[25] The Soviet Union had also found in Bulgaria a good non-discriminating customer for its machinery and industrial consumer goods. The subsidies also received from the Soviet Union to develop its heavy industry basically from scratch were large, as Bulgaria received indirect raw materials subsidies equal to as much as 12.1 per cent of its GDP. It was a matter of pride to the Bulgarian leadership that almost 80–90 per cent of the technical documentation for the construction of Bulgaria's industrial giants was received from the Soviet Union without any direct payment. Therefore it would be no exaggeration to claim, considering the dependence, the closeness of its relationship with the USSR and the special favours this attitude won, that in many respects Bulgaria was functioning as another Soviet republic.

Table 2.2 Direction of foreign trade, 1960–80 (%)

	1960		*1970*		*1980*	
Trading partner	*Imports*	*Exports*	*Imports*	*Exports*	*Imports*	*Exports*
USSR	52.6	53.8	52.2	53.8	57.3	49.9
GDR	11.1	10.2	8.6	8.7	6.6	5.5
Other CMEA	21.6	20.0	15.4	16.8	15.0	18.0
FRG	5.9	3.3	2.7	2.6	4.8	2.5
Other Western	7.7	9.1	16.5	11.6	12.4	13.3
Libya	–	–	–	–	1.0	3.6
Other Third World	2.4	3.4	4.7	6.1	2.9	9.8

Source: Lampe (1986: 188).

At the beginning of the 1970s, as table 2.3 shows, Bulgaria made an attempt to redirect foreign commerce towards non-socialist countries in the Western developed world and in the developing Third World. Bulgarian trade with the developed non-Communist countries was more important for its quality than its quantity, as those countries were the sole source of supply for a range of products and materials. The developed non-Communist countries were able to supply machinery, equipment, materials and products which were of vital importance to Bulgarian industrialisation. 'This explains why, despite the unfavourable trade balance, its disadvantageous structure, and the attendant financial losses, the Bulgarian government promoted such trade' (Dobrin, 1973: 112). Bulgaria experienced a serious failure, since it was far from making a profit on trade with these countries, as its imports were greater than its exports (see table 2.3).[26] It got into debt and survived this difficult period only thanks to the strength of its economic ties with the Soviet Union as well as by borrowing heavily from the West. Even though Bulgaria had not expanded trade with the West as early as its CMEA partners, since the early 1970s the growth rate of Bulgarian imports from the West was the highest among CMEA countries and well above the average.[27] On the other hand, while machinery and equipment made up the bulk of Bulgarian exports, poor quality made these products uncompetitive in international markets, and Bulgaria was still earning Western currency mainly through agricultural exports. Until 1980 the role of agricultural exports was still the largest of any East European country, as Bulgaria was a primary exporter of agricultural products to both CMEA and Western countries. Yet, owing to industrialisation, Bulgaria was making a transition away from the agricultural exports upon which the country had depended before the Second World War. Accordingly, from a figure over 90 per cent in 1939, in 1968–70 agricultural products represented 35 per cent of total Bulgarian exports; by 1975–77 the figure had been cut to 26 per cent, and by 1981–83 to only 17 per cent (Lampe, 1986: 181).

Table 2.3 Exports and imports, 1985

	Exports		*Imports*		*Deficit (–) or surplus (+)*
Trading partner	*Leva million*	%	*Leva million*	%	*(leva million)*
USSR	7,754.3	56.5	7,849.3	56.1	–95.0
GDR	714.3	5.2	735.4	5.3	–21.0
Other CMEA	2,090.3	15.2	2,198.8	15.6	–108.5
FRG	199.2	1.4	544.2	3.9	–345.0
Other EEC	642.1	4.7	721.6	5.1	–79.5
Libya	619.7	4.5	400.9	2.9	+218.8
Other Third World	1,716.1	12.5	1,552.1	11.1	+164.0
Total	13,736.0	100.0	14,002.3	100.0	–266.3

Source: McIntyre (1988: 79).

While developing its relations with the West, a substantial share of Bulgaria's exports were going to developing countries with which the Soviet Union maintained friendly relations – such as South Yemen, Ethiopia, Iran, Libya, Iraq and Mozambique. The nature of trade with the developing world was the opposite of that with the West, as Bulgaria maintained a positive trade balance and a favourable trade structure. Although during the 1970s the volume of this trade was small, it was favourably assessed for its political and economic significance. In order to promote trade with developing countries, Bulgaria, while receiving credits from the Soviet Union, extended considerable credits and financed some of its Third World customers. As a result, during the 1980s, Libya and Iraq became Bulgaria's chief trading partners outside the Communist Bloc but, as they were not prompt payers, Bulgaria suffered huge financial losses.

The legacy of the Communists

The Balkans, and particularly Balkan political culture, are crucial to understanding and assessing the Communist experience in Bulgaria. The Communist regimes in the Balkan region were much more popular than those in Central Europe. External occupation does not provide a valuable explanation, since there were practically no Soviet troops in the Balkan countries. The Red Army never reached Albania, it merely passed through Yugoslavia in 1944, never to return. It left Bulgaria in 1947 and the remaining few Russian troops left Romania in 1958. Besides, at various points in time, Yugoslavia, Albania and, to some extent, Romania broke away from Moscow. Bulgaria was the only Balkan country that retained close relations with the Soviet Union, enjoying certain economic preferences.

Communism was more successful in the Balkans because, although the standard of living was generally low, socialism had an appeal to the mass of the population, with its guaranteed full employment, free medical services, price controls, social benefits, even slackened work discipline, and corresponded to a primarily egalitarian outlook. In the Balkans, Communism served as

> an overall role model offering simple and clear formulae for transition to modernity – from the village to the city, from family dependence to autonomy, from poverty to mass consumption ... A vast majority of the population thus built their life on the Communist dream of collective salvation through sacrifice and discipline. People felt indebted to the party for having 'given' them work, residence permits, education and so on ... In this respect, Communism was even a greater success than the German or Italian-made totalitarian model of the 1930s which influenced many Balkan countries ... The focus of the general indebtedness, blocking free will and action, was the party leader who combined patriarchic, Communist and nationalist traits. Thus Enver Hoxza became 'Uncle Enver', Todor Zhivkov was informally called 'Pa', etc. The price of this consensus, with few if any dissidents, was external projection of aggression targeting the figure of the enemy which seemed to fit into the regional cultural pattern. (Ditchev, 1997: 7, 8)

In the Bulgarian case, once in control in 1944, the Communists embarked on a programme that transformed the physical landscape of the country, and the political, economic and cultural character of society. Communist modernisation was imposed from the top and relied on an outsize state apparatus – the latter feature is apparent even in non-Communist countries in the region, as in the Balkans the state has much more weight in the sphere of the economy, education and culture than on the rest of the continent. Forced industrialisation and complete collectivisation of the land proceeded faster in Bulgaria than in any other Soviet satellite in Eastern Europe after the Second World War and thus, by the end of the 1950s, Bulgaria became an 'industrial-agricultural' country carrying out a structural shift of labour and capital into modern industry. But considering the pre-war agrarian living standards, for much of the peasantry that formed the new industrial work force it was not a wholly negative experience. The development had been more harmonious than in any Soviet Bloc countries, since it proceeded with more caution. The Soviet Union supported this transformation with supplies of raw materials, machinery and technicians. Above all, the CMEA and the Soviet Union increasingly became the market on which Bulgaria unloaded its agricultural and industrial production. In any case, massive industrialisation, advances in agriculture, the elimination of illiteracy and urbanisation brought about a rapid rise in living standards. Many experts agree that Bulgaria's achievements, at least until the 1980s, were spectacular. For example, the economic historian Derek Aldcroft is quoted by Lampe to the effect that Bulgaria 'has been one of the great success stories of the twentieth century, with the highest rate of economic growth in Europe and a degree of structural change second to none'[28] (Lampe, 1986: 8). The inferiority complex of the Bulgarian people, deriving mainly from the economic backwardness that characterised the country in the past, was put behind them because of this kind of economic development. At the same time Communism, as Karasimeonov points out,

> created a new middle class and intelligentsia loyal to the regime. The Communist Party and the network of its satellite organisations became a much sought-after instrument for achieving a rise in social status and the privileges that accompanied it. The Communists were able to keep their hold over a society still dominated by patriarchal, communal attitudes, a society which had never had sufficient time in its short history as an independent state after 1878 to create a viable civil society and affirm liberal democratic values ... Last but not least the crisis of the system, especially in the economic field, was only seriously felt late in the 1980s, which limited any serious discontent based on material needs. (Karasimeonov, 1996: 255)

Since the country was industrialised, the Bulgarian leadership realised that the methods used to modernise the economy had outlived their usefulness and that further economic growth could come only through structural change. Central planning was not in question, as the country's transformation was tied to it and the goal had been to create greater efficiency, not a market economy. But it was necessary to keep up with new scientific and technological discoveries, to select profitable investments and to give enterprises responsibility for economic growth. Twice Bulgaria sought to address these problems – first, during the 1960s and, second, near the end of the 1970s – but the results did not meet expectations. The problems of industry remained insoluble and affected the whole economy. In the 1970s the standard of agricultural machinery was considerably improved but by the end of the 1980s the equipment had become inadequate, with some 45 per cent either obsolete or worn out, mainly because renewals had been limited and insufficiently effective.

In the late 1970s and especially in the 1980s the economic growth rate started to slow down and it became apparent that the economy was in a deep crisis. The first symptoms appeared as early as the 1970s, with a slackening of technological advance, pricing anomalies leading to the ineffective allocation of resources, and the isolation of the national economy from world markets, which further diminished the competitiveness of exports. The uncompetitiveness of Bulgarian exports affected the balance of payments adversely. As a consequence, in the mid-1980s, Bulgaria's convertible currency debt to foreign commercial banks started to mount appreciably. Foreign debt rose from $2 billion at the end of 1984 to almost $7 billion at the end of 1988 and reached $10 billion a year later, coming second to Hungary among the CMEA countries with the heaviest debt, though Bulgaria was even worse off because of its low level of exports to the West. The economy also began to suffer from energy shortages and the overall downturn in agriculture due in part to the decline in Soviet subsidies and the suspension by the Soviet Union of gas and oil supplies at privileged prices. Moreover, transport failures, an acute shortage of consumer goods, including such basic foodstuffs as cheese, cooking oil, sugar and coffee, and other failures, generated mistrust of the government. The sharp decrease in the production of consumer goods and the poor distribution system caused a shocking decline of living standards.

Obviously, by the mid-1980s, the pressing needs and problems created by the scarcity of both labour and capital, which had plagued the growth of the pre-war Bulgarian economy, had again returned. Despite the reforms, Western experts (Eurostat, 1991: 112) assessed Bulgaria's economic position at the end of the 1980s as follows:

- Gross foreign debt which had risen to $10 billion.
- A deterioration in the international trade structure, particularly in foreign currency receipts from exports, with an increased need for hard currency to service foreign debt.
- For the first time, negative nominal growth of 0.4 per cent in the economy as a whole in 1989 – which meant a real shrinkage of 8–12 per cent, depending on the inflation estimate.
- A decline in industrial production in 1989 to nominal growth of only 1.1 per cent, signifying a real shrinkage in most branches.
- A further decline in agricultural production in 1989, despite good weather and extremely low figures the previous year.
- Low profitability of firms in large sectors of the economy.

Demographic changes had affected the country's socio-economic development as well. Population growth declined from 1.5 per cent in 1939 to a mere 0.3 per cent in 1981. Some measures were being taken to reverse this trend, but by the mid-1980s the demographic crisis had become even more evident. As important, the intense urbanisation to which Bulgaria has been subjected for thirty years precipitated normative social changes. Bulgaria went through 'one of the most rapid and thoroughgoing processes of industry-driven urbanisation in European experience. Urban growth resulted principally from rural migration, which led to a rapid decline in the rural population and sharp changes in all of its demographic parameters' (McIntyre, 1988: 147). A case in point is the official figure showing that the urban population, from 26.4 per cent of the total in 1948, rose to a 70 per cent in 1990. Bulgaria became the most heavily urbanised country in South-eastern Europe.

Even more significantly, industrialisation brought with it increasing environmental pollution, since production considerations were placed above all others. Like most former Soviet satellites, Bulgaria suffered from an ecological disaster as bad as anywhere else in Europe. 'Under the Communist regime, a production-at-all-costs economy promoted short-term output goals at the expense of nature and of human health. The system of party domination, bureaucratic and personal discretion and public corruption aggravated the problem. Finally, the hollowness of apparent legal protections left the environment almost totally defenseless against degradation' (Friedberg and Zaimov, 1998: 83).

The problems which had been building up for decades in the centrally planned economy brought the country to catastrophe at the end of the 1980s.

Intense efforts between 1985 and 1987 brought no results, since the reforms were characterised by contradictions and vagueness. The New Economic Mechanism and its principles were still reiterated but the policy of decentralisation had run into formidable obstacles. The overall deterioration of the economy was accompanied by rampant corruption among the Communist Party *apparatchiks* and the security police. Allegations represented Bulgaria as a transit route for drugs from the Middle East to Western Europe, with drug money used for pay-offs to high-level party and police officials. In addition, the role of the state as the regulator of economic life remained irrevocable and, as before, central planning, price controls and fiscal policy remained the responsibility of the state. Thus, in reality, the state remained the dominant and, in fact, the only actor in the economy.

This illustrates the main problem of the Bulgarian leadership: how to reconcile political and economic reform with the party's continuing role in society. Because Zhivkov always stressed Bulgaria's loyalty to the Soviet Union, it was almost inevitable that he would have to introduce his own version of Gorbachev's *perestroika*. In 1987 he inaugurated the 'July Concept', which, with a wave of administrative and economic reorganisation, called for several steps towards political democratisation. Nonetheless, first because Zhivkov was not clearly committed to political reform, and then because the reforms he initiated were plunging the country into chaos, the reforms proved short-lived. In effect, as long as Zhivkov remained firmly in the saddle Bulgaria continued to operate along the tried and trusted Communist methods.

The fall of Communism was certainly related to the withering away of the omnipotent state and its inability, due to lack of institutional flexibility, to adjust to new problems and to adapt to social change and to new challenges. Still, the collapse of Communism in Bulgaria, as in the rest of Eastern Europe, was largely a result of economic failure, as the Communist regime failed to produce the kind of society it promised, causing popular disenchantment. And this economic failure and inefficiency led to a complete collapse of the ideological legitimation of the Communist system.

As Judy Batt concludes, the reason for the Communist collapse more broadly was

> the failure of the system of central planning to deliver the material abundance promised by the Marxist ideology on which the Communist regimes rested their claim to legitimacy … Declining economic performance affects the political stability of any regime, but in the case of the East European Communist regimes, the problem was particularly acute not only because of the depth of the economic crisis but also because the regimes had been unable to legitimate themselves on the basis of social content. (Batt, 1993: 205)

Vaclav Havel, attempting to explain the collapse of Communism, argued that

> as a system Communism went against life, against men's fundamental needs, against the need for freedom, the need to be enterprising, to associate freely, against

> the will of the nation, suppressing national identity. Something that goes against life may last a long time, but sooner or later it will collapse. (Havel, 1999)

The important issue still to be answered is whether countries, Bulgaria among them, can manage to clear away the 'pollution of the mind' (Vaclav Havel's expression) which had gathered under Communism – the moral, intellectual and political deformity that the contrast between Communist fiction and actual fact had inflicted on individuals and society as a whole. This is an educational, moral and psychological issue which presupposes the development of a liberal, democratic political culture which means the bodies of civil society assuming control over society as a natural result of the struggle of citizens to protect their rights.

Notes

1 In 1878 Russia, winner of the Russo-Turkish war, dictated to Turkey the terms of the San Stefano Treaty, creating a vast Bulgarian state. But under pressure, and in deference to the will of the European powers, who feared that a Great Bulgaria would considerably augment Russian power in the Balkans, the size of the country was reduced by two-thirds under the Treaty of Berlin. This treaty established the conditions that led to a string of Balkan wars, with border disputes and irredentism feeling that persist to the present day. Under these treaties Bulgaria, although a principality within the Ottoman Empire, gained substantial independence. In 1908 the government formally proclaimed independence.

2 Established as a constitutional and parliamentary monarchy, Bulgaria became the fourth country in Europe (after Switzerland, Denmark and France) to introduce universal male suffrage.

3 Nonetheless, as John Bell argues, this modernisation was of a decorative rather than self-sustaining pattern. 'The construction of attractive public buildings, the beautification of cities and towns, their electrification and the installation of telephones, which relied on the importation of both equipment and engineers, little benefited the national economy and still less the peasant who was required to pay for it and who still cultivated his fields with a primitive wooden plow. Many Bulgarians rejected this kind of progress, for it drove home the widening gulf between the urban and rural populations' (Bell, 1977: 12). As far as the educational system was concerned, 'the state's need for educated people in administration was reflected in a considerable expansion of education', with the creation of a good network of elementary and secondary schools so that 'illiteracy, which had been very extensive at the time of independence, was 76 per cent by 1900, 50 per cent by 1920, and almost non-existent after the end of the Second World War' (Dobrin, 1973: 8).

4 John R. Lampe identified three special barriers to Bulgarian industrialisation before 1914. First, the selection of Sofia as the capital for political and military reasons. Although possessing a population of some 20,000 persons in 1878, it was smaller than either Russe or Plovdiv. Located in an upland plateau surrounded by mountains and far from a navigable waterway, Sofia lacked their commercial connections. Russe, Plovdiv and several other towns had a much greater tradition of commerce and artisan manufacture. The second barrier was the location of Bulgarian territory inside and not on the borders of the Ottoman Empire before 1878; the third, the lingering consequences of Ottoman domination after 1878 (Lampe, 1976: 70). On the same issue Cyril E. Black concludes that the high share of state revenue devoted to foreign policy and defence expenditure as well as the populist system of values among townspeople and the peasantry,

which tended to regard industry and foreign capital as undesirable, if not evil, were principal factors in the failure to make more substantial progress (Black, 1976: 122).

5 More than the two-thirds of the proceeds of these loans were going to debt management and military needs. 'The military establishment was the largest single drain on the state's resources, although by the end of the century it was closely rivaled by interest payments on the national debt ... By the turn of the century these two items together accounted for forty four per cent of the state budget' (Bell, 1977: 11). On the eve of the Balkan Wars military expenditure increased even further.

6 The First Balkan War took place over the Macedonian question between the joint forces of Bulgaria, Serbia, Greece and Montenegro and the easily defeated Ottoman army. In the Second Balkan War, Bulgaria, misjudging the situation, fought against the joint forces of Greece, Serbia, Montenegro, Romania and Turkey. Inevitably it resulted in the complete defeat of Bulgaria.

7 The Agrarians, after undertaking radical land reform, expanded the rural school system, extended large-scale support to peasant co-operatives, slashed the military budget and established a compulsory labour service, designed to replace military conscription. Furthermore, Stamboliski's reforms were intended to modernise the countryside and make Bulgaria a 'model of an agricultural state', where the peasantry, allied with the workers and the artisans, would rule. He wanted to cut the bureaucracy to a minimum, to reduce government pensions and to change the taxation system in order to free peasants from supporting the urban population, which he characterised as 'parasites'. Agrarianism retained much of its appeal: Stamboliski's experiment in politics became a powerful myth and has remained so to the present (Pundeff, 1992: 82–3).

8 G. Schöpflin attempts to describe the agrarian life: 'the peasant was characterised by living in relatively small, insular communities, with strict value systems. This generated a suspicion of the outside world, of strangers with different and inexplicable behaviour patterns. Within these communities there tended to exist clear-cut hierarchies which were perceived as unchanging and unchangeable. Overall, the peasant lived in a world marked primarily by the seasons, by a lack of functional specialisation, by low levels of technology and little incentive to improve on this, and by a kind of negative egalitarianism that sought to equalise downwards' (Schöpflin, 1993: 26).

9 Popular affection for the Russians in general and a sense of historical and cultural affinity with the Russian state in particular had not been dulled by the replacement of the Tsarist regime and Soviet rule. Thus a war with the Soviet Union would still be distinctly unpopular with the majority of the population. When, for instance, Hitler and Stalin signed their pact in 1939 Bulgaria was one of the few countries that welcomed it wholeheartedly. In contrast, largely because of its traditional Balkan policy, Britain had never been popular in Bulgaria.

10 Though perhaps not a decisive one, as the BCP had already gained control of the situation, it is worth mentioning the additional advantage for the Communists of the infamous Churchill–Stalin so-called 'percentage agreement' of October 1944 by which the Soviet Union was allocated 75 per cent of influence in Bulgaria.

11 Dimitrov had acquired international notoriety as a defendant in the Reichstag Fire trial, and later headed the Comintern, especially during the period of the Stalinist purges. At that time he became Soviet citizen and, although he would not return to Bulgaria until 1945, he directed BCP strategy from a distance.

12 Besides, as Geremek asserts, 'one useful way of thinking about totalitarianism is to see it as a particularly brutal attempt to settle the conflict between the state and society by utterly subordinating the latter to the former. Totalitarian authority not only undertakes the extreme centralisation of the state, but also strips citizens of their rights and conquers or destroys all those autonomous structures that normally give shape to social life' (Geremek, 1992: 6).

13 'The slogan proclaimed by the Hungarian Stalinist leader Matyas Rakosi, 'He who is not with us is against us,' meant that the party, and hence its leader, 'had the right to absolute and untrammelled power and required no further legitimation for this' (Schöpflin, 1993: 87).

14 This is one of the reasons why the Bulgarian Orthodox Church was deeply divided and marginalised in the post-Communist period.

15 Bear in mind that the Soviet economic system, after the rapid industrialisation and modernisation drive of the 1930s, when a country with a mainly rural economy was transformed into a military superpower, and the extraordinary achievements of wartime relocation and production, was enjoying a quite good international reputation.

16 In 1947, of all industrial enterprises, 83.6 per cent were privately owned, 10 per cent were owned by co-operatives and 6.4 per cent by the state; within less than a year the share of state-owned enterprises had grown to 98 per cent. Indeed, 'on 23 December 1947 trained groups seized the country's 6,109 remaining private enterprises together with all their machinery, property, stocks and accounts implementing a device so as the government paid out in compensation no more than a small part of the value of the property seized. Later that month the remaining thirty-two banks were merged into the central bank and, at the same time, the confiscation of large urban properties put an end to the existence of the Bulgarian private landlord' (Crampton, 1987: 166).

17 The fact that the planners gave industry total priority is illustrated in industry's share of investment: 76.8 per cent under the first Five Year Plan (1949–54), 55 per cent under the second Five Year Plan (1953–57), and 62.4 per cent under the Third (1957–62) (Dobrin, 1973: 20). Actually, after the first Five Year Plan industrialisation drive, the Communist leadership followed the post-Stalin 'New Course' and slackened the pace of investment. Resources were reallocated from heavy industry to agriculture, and even to consumers. But when Zhivkov came to power in 1954 a new heavy industry drive proceeded which peaked during the 'Great Leap Forward' of 1959–60 (Palairet, 1995: 493). Zhivkov subsequently accused Chervenkov of abandoning accelerated industrialisation, leaving himself the historic task of rescuing the economy from stagnation. Zhivkov's reforms and projects were in large measure copied from those of Khruschev in the Soviet Union. And, as Crampton notes, 'the major difference between the Khruschev experiments and those of his Bulgarian disciple was that Zhivkov survived their collapse (even with a struggle) and Khruschev did not' (Crampton, 1987: 183).

18 So, for example, the planning system remained vague; new prices had not been introduced; annual rather than long-term objectives were being set; the supply system had not been changed; in general the bureaucracy continued to attach little importance to profitability as a measure of performance. The absence of any reform of the pricing mechanism and the rigidity of the plan became major obstacles, plus impatience with the piecemeal implementation of the reforms, difficulties in price and target setting and unwillingness to push the initial half-measure concept further (Feiwel, 1977: 101).

19 The Hungarian regime introduced a set of economic reforms in 1968 that rested on three pillars. First, it created a new set of planning principles. In many respects a freer price structure was introduced; managers were encouraged to make decisions independently of the centre and to free themselves from the bureaucratic system; and enterprises were to pay much more attention to quality than before. Second, it involved a shift away from emphasising heavy industry and towards light industry and the infrastructure. Third, it envisaged a new role for agriculture, in which collectives would be very largely freed of restraints on their activities and the individual proprietors (of personal plots) were permitted to sell their produce on the open market. In general, the state retained its monopoly of foreign trade but controls over internal trade were relaxed, and in this way the reforms brought about unprecedented economic activity and a measure of prosperity.

20 Legislation in 1945 made membership voluntary, but once a peasant had joined he was obliged to remain a member for at least three years; all members were to receive wages in proportion to their work as well as the ground rent, which varied with the land contributed. A more stringent regulation in 1946 declared that the members of the collectives owned not actual areas of land but undermarcated percentages of the whole, and thus anyone leaving a collective was to receive bonds, not land, in compensation for the property he had contributed. With the same legislation private land ownership was limited to 20 ha and any privately held land beyond that was nationalised.

21 In Romania collectivisation only got under way in 1952 and was effectively complete by 1962 but not without the use of armed force. In Hungary, even though it was virtually halted as a result of the events of 1956, collectivisation was complete by 1961 but in a more liberal form. In the DDR the first collectives were set up in 1952 and by 1960 embraced about 60 per cent of agricultural land. In Yugoslavia the collectivisation drive begun in 1949 was reversed in 1953, when it became legal to withdraw from a collective and the system promptly collapsed. In Poland collectivisation was always slow and even by 1980 only about 31 per cent of the total arable land was in state or collective farms (Morris, 1984: 87).

22 Indeed, Zhivkov had announced in 1970 that industrial technology and managerial practices should be introduced to agriculture, and that industrial plants should also be built within the agro-industrial complexes. In 1973 as a short-lived experiment a number of agro-industrial complexes were incorporated into industrial concerns to form industrial-agricultural complexes.

23 Apart from the agro-industrial complexes, even from the 1950s the collective farmers, as a form of compensation, were entitled to small private (personal) allotments. The private plot (of 0.2–0.5 ha) was not the same as privately owned land, as it could not be sold and no hired labour could work on it. Particularly in the 1970s, after the adoption of the AIC form, government policy actively encouraged plot production and supported it with measures to raise the scope and efficiency of their exploitation. These plots helped 'to keep the Bulgarian black market one of the smallest in Eastern Europe' (Lampe, 1986: 226).

24 'The co-operation with the Socialist countries also gave economic profits to the USSR. It received from them certain crucial raw materials, such as uranium ore and non-ferrous metals. With their highly skilled workers and talented engineers, some specialised factories operating in the Socialist countries were valuable partners for the Soviet industries' (Tomaszewski, 1989: 222).

25 For example, in 1970 the Soviet Union's contribution to total Bulgarian imports of coal was 100 per cent; of crude oil and diesel oil, 84 per cent; of lubricating oil, 82 per cent; of iron ore, 91 per cent; of construction steel, 79 per cent; of aluminum, 85 per cent; of cotton, 70 per cent; and of wool, 77 per cent (Feiwel, 1977: 77).

26 As a way to balance the trade deficit with the West, Bulgaria promoted tourism through the construction of hotels, restaurants and roads on the Black Sea coast. There was one area of Bulgarian exports, however, that was evidently doing well. In 1982, for instance, exports of arms represented the leading source of export earnings, accounting for 9.1 per cent of the total.

27 Bulgaria's closest trade ties in the West were with West Germany. It was reported that in 1971–75 (full diplomatic relations were established in 1973) trade between the two countries tripled and most of it was on a co-operative basis. For example, in 1975 Bulgaria signed contracts to co-operate with Siemens in the production of telecommunications equipment, medical instruments and automated machine tools; with Lurgi for processing oil shale; with Daimler-Benz for battery-driven trucks and automobiles; and with Krupp for iron and steel, heavy engineering and chemical equipment. It should be remembered too that, in addition to pro-Russian sentiment, the German connection

was a historical strand in Bulgarian foreign policy dating back to the origins of the country's modern statehood.

28 Accordingly, rough calculations by Paul Bairoch indicate that Bulgaria's GNP grew by an average of 4.4 per cent a year throughout the 1913–73 period as a whole, the highest rate of all European countries. For the period 1950–73, in particular, the economy grew by 7.2 per cent a year, compared with the European average of 5.6 per cent (Lampe, 1986: 14).

3

The political landscape

In 1989 Central and Eastern Europe experienced historic and unprecedented changes when a number of apparently well entrenched Communist regimes collapsed one by one. In Bulgaria the historic change occurred on 10 November 1989, a day after East Germany opened the Berlin Wall, when a meeting of the BCP's Politburo and Secretariat accepted Zhivkov's 'resignation'. The major reason for the Communist fall in Bulgaria, as in the rest of Eastern Europe, was undoubtedly the shift in Soviet regional policy and the renunciation of the doctrine of limited sovereignty (the Brezhnev doctrine, adopted in order to justify the Soviet invasion of Czechoslovakia in 1968). This change of policy permitted an unprecedented degree of open dissent and political mobilisation throughout the region. From then on it was obvious that the domestic sources of legitimacy alone (mainly because of the economic failure which has been analysed in the previous chapter) were not enough to sustain the party's dominance. *Glasnost* and *perestroika* paved the way for domestic pressures and created the necessary conditions for political liberalisation and, later, for the movement towards democratisation.[1]

The transition period

Already from the mid-1980s Zhivkov felt he must make an adjustment to the 'new thinking' that had begun to emerge from Moscow. It was apparent that the Soviet Union's reformulated policy was posing a threefold challenge to Bulgaria.

> Firstly, it became clear that the Soviet Union was neither willing nor able to go on propping up the Bulgarian economy, in view of its own desperate needs. Secondly, *glasnost* would mean allowing criticism, although Bulgarian intellectuals had hitherto been kept unusually docile. Thirdly, a Bulgarian *perestroika* would entail the

> grave political risk of demanding real and sustained sacrifices from the Bulgarian people. (East, 1992: 23)

The Bulgarian edition of *glasnost* began in 1987 with the 'July Concept', and one could argue that at that point, the pre-transition period (the decay of the regime) started.[2] The regime's weaknesses became apparent and malignant, and it attempted to overcome the crisis and to enlarge its base of social support, conceding some form of partial liberalisation. But soon after the 1987 campaign against bureaucracy, corruption and inefficiency came signs of a retreat, with the dismissal from the party leadership of prominent reformists, and Zhivkov resorted to repressive measures. Indeed, it could be maintained that Zhivkov attempted to keep *perestroika* out of Bulgaria, expecting perhaps reactionary Stalinist forces to take over in the Soviet Union.[3] Nonetheless, a segment of the nomenclature interpreted the far-reaching reforms outlined in the 'July Concept' as a sign of failure on the part of the ruling elite to control the party and the country, while the Soviet leadership had begun to apply pressure on Zhivkov to push forward with reforms. Though freedom of expression was certainly growing, compared with other Eastern European countries (Romania and Albania excepted) the Bulgarian Communist leadership lagged behind the spirit of the times. Whatever small concessions were made, however, were an attempt to satisfy the limited pressure from below as well as the criticism inside the Communist Party itself. These concessions encouraged the weak opposition forces and the reformist faction in the BCP to press for more effective change, commencing thus a process which Zhivkov could not control.

Public opposition

The context in Bulgaria was very different from that of Central Europe, since there had been no organised opposition to the regime and somewhat less social pressure for change, especially in the countryside. Unlike the ruling parties of other Eastern Bloc countries, Bulgaria's Communist regime, throughout its long reign, was never challenged by dissident forces or political groups. As Zhelev admitted, 'only in Bulgaria nothing ever happened: not a single uprising, not a single revolt or rebellion, not a single political strike or a student demonstration ... Bulgaria can boast absolutely no practical attempt to topple the totalitarian system' (Zhelev, 1997: 293). In this respect, even the few outbursts from time to time were mostly confined to intra-party factional conflict and strife. This is mainly because until the late 1970s the Zhivkov regime was able to prevent the emergence of any counter-elite that might have threatened and opposed the Communist Party. 'Outright repression, a widely accepted parochial political culture, limited national sovereignty, and the clientistic co-optation of most intellectuals into the system prevented the rise of challenging groups similar to those that could be observed in the "national Communisms" of Poland and Hungary in the 1970s and 1980s' (Kitschelt *et al.*, 1995: 145). Although the system contained mounting discontent, in addition, it did not weigh as heavily on Bulgarians as on Central Europeans because they tended to compare their conditions with those of Greece and Turkey rather than with West Germany and Austria. Nor did they hate the Russians as the Poles did, or the Czechs and Slovaks after 1968. On top of all this, the Communist regime, as has been argued in the previous chapter, managed to carry out successfully rapid industrialisation of a country which had been one of the most backward in Europe. Therefore, unlike countries which like Czechoslovakia, Hungary or Poland had a decades-long tradition of opposition to totalitarianism, the Bulgarians on the whole felt rather more comfortable in the egalitarian reality of totalitarian society and in the conservative stability and order of the totalitarian state. The illusion of relative prosperity created by the regime rendered the Bulgarian citizen, who until recently had been a peasant, a mere observer of an idle political reality. That is the reason why the pace of change in Bulgaria was slower than that in most of its Central European neighbours, and why to most Bulgarians Gorbachev's *perestroika* looked like an unattainable dream until the autumn of 1989.

During the second half of the 1980s the fast-deteriorating economic situation, the worsening environmental situation, the regime's massive abuses of human rights (particularly against the Turkish minority) along with the country's growing political isolation in the world gave rise to widespread domestic discontent among people in all spheres of social life with the policies of the Communist Party in power, giving impetus to a fledgling dissident movement. The younger generation in particular began to look to the West rather than to the distant past for a measure of Bulgarian achievement. Between 1988 and 1989 various groups began to emerge. Among the first could be identified the Independent Committee for the Environmental Protection of the City of Russe (March 1988). The roots of this group can be traced in Russe and it was a movement of intellectuals for ecological preservation of that town. This was a spontaneous reaction against the cross-border chlorine pollution from a chemical plant in Romania that had caused lung morbidity to increase by 2,000 per cent in the last fifteen years. Other such dissident groups were: the Independent Association for Human Rights, formed in January 1988; the Club for the Promotion of *Perestroika* and *Glasnost*, organised at Sofia University in November 1988; the Citizens' Initiative, formed in December 1988; the Podkrepa (Support) Independent Trade Union, organised in February 1989; the Committee for Religious Rights, Freedom of Conscience and Spiritual Values, established in March 1989; and the Eco-*glasnost* Independent Association, formed in April 1989. All played an important role in mobilising public opinion, generating criticism, articulating demands for change and undermining the foundations of totalitarian rule (Szajkowski, 1991: 20).

The main feature of these movements, perhaps, as is manifest in their names, was that they declared themselves 'independent'; they conceived of themselves as apolitical, since independence of the only political party was to imply an apolitical stand. But when the system reacted, these movements were driven into politicisation, particularly since it was clear that the solution to the environmental problems of the country, for instance, demanded a political change at the state level. Only then did they change their line of conduct, and the confrontation threshold was crossed in the form of public demonstrations and protests, though even then these were confined almost entirely to Sofia. And only then were the environmental protection demands mixed with or replaced by anti-regime mottoes, and democratisation gradually became the single most important demand. The climax was reached in October 1989, when a series of demonstrations in Sofia (during the proceedings of the Conference on Security and Co-operation in Europe on the environment) were brutally suppressed by the police. Despite the suppression, the environmental movement had managed to unite people from different backgrounds in demanding overall political and social change as well as the awakening of public opinion. 'At the same time, environmental activism provided one of the few avenues for political struggle against the totalitarian regime. Therefore, many used environmental argumentation solely for political purposes' (Koulov, 1998: 159). It was the first time that explicitly politically co-ordinated public protests were carried out.

The role of the intra-party opposition

Despite the growth of anti-regime demonstrations, most of the politically active dissidents in the late 1980s had emerged more as critics and reformers within the ruling party than as active adversaries of the regime. Particularly among the younger members of the nomenclature there were growing demands for reform. For Zhivkov, most problems were surfacing from within the party apparatus, as clearly the governing elite was not cohesive.

Inside the BCP, already since the mid-1980s, a kind of intellectual and technocratically minded opposition was becoming increasingly critical of Zhivkov's monolithic rule and his refusal to follow the changes taking place in the Soviet Union and in other Eastern Bloc countries, especially since images of *glasnost* were reaching the country through the programmes of the first Soviet television channel. Initially, criticism was based on the alarming decline of environmental conditions, but soon this broadened out into a general sense of dismay at the state of the country. But, above all, Zhivkov's rather hasty decision, in an attempt to stress the national identity of his regime, to expel Bulgaria's Turkish (Muslim) minority, which composed up to 10 per cent of the whole population, was what provoked his Politburo colleagues sufficiently to split the leadership, and an anti-Zhivkov coalition came into being.

The Turkish minority, settled in the southern regions of the country, differ from the Bulgarian majority in ethnic, linguistic and cultural as well as religious respects. The enforced bulgarianisation of ethnic Turks by replacing their names with Christian-Slavonic ones restarted in the winter of 1984–85 – the 'Revival Process' – following similar attempts in the early 1960s and early 1970s.

The use of Turkish in public became a punishable offence; traditional Muslim clothing, festive rituals, even Turkish music were banned. The Department of Turkish Philology in Sofia University was closed down. Muslim graveyards were destroyed, and even the names of deceased parents and ancestors were changed in the local government records. All remnants of religious symbols were subjected to annihilation and new, artificially created rituals were forcibly introduced … The entire propaganda machine of the state was mobilised in a smear campaign against the Turks, accusing them of being 'terrorists', a 'fifth column', 'Turkish agents', etc. (Zhelyazkova, 1998: 169).

Apparently Zhivkov tried to stir up nationalism and popular racism in the public consciousness, based on the still widespread fears and resentments rooted in 500 years of oppressive Ottoman occupation. Additionally, in the early summer of 1989, Zhivkov created a more dramatic situation when he ordered the acceleration of the assimilation of the Turkish minority. In response the Turks rioted and demonstrated, and the police reacted by firing on the crowd. Dozens of people were killed, provoking both a diplomatic crisis with Ankara and a potentially explosive situation within Bulgaria itself. In this critical situation, Zhivkov tried to solve the crisis by allowing the minority to emigrate to Turkey. This exodus developed into one of the biggest movement of peoples in modern Europe, since over 300,000 ethnic Turks left for Turkey, earning Bulgaria worldwide negative publicity.

These developments widened the cleavage within the ruling elite. The anti-Zhivkov faction in the top echelons of the party had already become aware of the growing wave of intellectual criticism from below and the widespread discontent, and a *coup* was thought unavoidable if the situation was to be calmed down. Having established that Zhivkov had not had the backing of the Soviet Union, and having seen a major demonstration of popular dissatisfaction, his Politburo colleagues finally withdrew their support and voted for his replacement by Petar Mladenov.[4] Apparently it was the outrage against the Communist regime's oppression of the Turkish minority that offered common ground between dissident groups and public opinion, operating as a catalyst in the disintegration of Zhivkov's regime. The reformist faction among the BCP leadership responded; as a result the old guard lost the initiative and this paved the way for their own demise.

The *coup* was carried out by members of the Communist Party; it was change imposed from the top and not the result of a mass movement from the bottom. That was the main characteristic of the Bulgarian transition: what had brought about Zhivkov's demise was not a popular revolution, as elsewhere in Eastern Europe, but a carefully staged *coup*.[5] One of the key leaders of Eco-*glasnost*, Deyan Kiuranov, has admitted that, despite the Eco-*glasnost* protests, the regime was still in complete control in early November 1989: 'despite speculation to the contrary, the activities of the opposition of the green umbrella were not the direct cause of the anti Zhivkov *coup* … it was essentially an internal party affair. Much as I would like to, I cannot give the opposition credit for the sophisticated palace *coup*'[6] (Linz and Stepan, 1996: 336). Popular demonstrations and organised movements were rather used as a pretext and justification by the party's internal dissent and opposition for taking drastic action. The Czechoslovak type of 'velvet revolution' was impossible, owing to the absence of any dissident movement to organise it. Even the few dissidents who later became the core of the newborn democratic opposition never had the influence to challenge the party's hegemony. In this respect the Bulgarian political reform was more akin to the Soviet *perestroika* (that is, in terms of democratisation theory, a transformation process or transition from above). Those who removed Zhivkov aimed to reform the party from within by creating a new type of democratic socialist party. Immediately after Zhivkov's fall the new leadership pledged to promote pluralism and eliminate the role of the state security forces, promote respect for the rule of law, halt the persecution of the ethnic Turks and allow opposition groups to register legally. Within a week of his deposal, many others of the old generation were ousted from their posts in the party and the state, which set off a wholesale critique of the Zhivkov regime, primarily focusing on extensive nepotism and corruption.[7] Although popular protest and demonstrations had not played as great a role as in other Eastern European countries before Zhivkov's fall, afterwards (at the end of 1989 and throughout 1990) popular demonstrations put increasing pressure on the leadership to speed the pace of reform and their political impact was more significant.

But the BCP still controlled the process of change and

> in contrast to Poland, Hungary, and Czechoslovakia, where the transition to democracy followed a path of inter-elite negotiation or an implosion of the old elites, in Bulgaria the Communists initially managed to hold on to political power by pre-emptive reforms and the strength of their local entrenchment, particularly in the countryside. (Kitschelt *et al.*, 1995: 146)

Only in this way could the Communist Party have managed to maintain a relatively strong influence over the transition process and indeed, unlike other East European Communist parties, the BCP did not collapse (claiming to be the oldest Communist party in Europe). It suffered rather a slow erosion of influence and supporters, but at no point (even after ten years) did it lose its core supporters. The opposition was completely disarmed because the BCP had conceded most of its major demands before it had even had time to articulate them. The November *coup*, even though it came as an after-effect of *perestroika* in the Soviet Union and of the related review of Gorbachev's foreign policy (others have described it as essentially a Soviet-inspired 'palace revolution'[8]), and despite the regime's lack of legitimacy and the condemnation of the overall policy of the BCP, it could still be argued to have mainly been driven by the desire of the Communist leadership to retain power and to ensure its self-preservation. And there is no doubt the BCP elite's support for democratisation was motivated chiefly by a desire to share political power rather than lose it completely.[9] As a result of the *coup d'état*, elements of the corrupt Communist elite were overthrown and the long-entrenched regime began to disintegrate, leaving behind a political vacuum, since the state apparatus was effectively unable to manage the economic and social processes.

To some, what followed after this date was a return to forgotten traditions of democracy, a period of genuine, if sometimes uncontrollable, changes in the economy and in political life. To adherents of a conspiracy theory of history, it was all a grandiose swindle by the old nomenclature and secret police bosses, perpetuating their control over society under a different guise. The truth is that the country experienced within a very short period changes without precedent in its history, and in a completely peaceful way (Pantev, 1996: 22).
Thus, whatever were the reasons behind it, the day of Zhivkov's removal marked the initiation of the second stage of the democratisation process: the transition period and the construction of democracy.

Formation of a plural democracy

Because the country was in a deep economic crisis, internationally isolated, with the national problem complicated by the anti-humane policy against the Bulgarian ethnic Turks, the democratisation process developed in a complex and difficult situation, but in a peaceful manner. Several factors contributed to this effect. Initially there was the common political background of the new political elite, i.e. the Communist Party. Since the newly formed anti- Communist opposition lacked a well educated group of people capable of full participation in politics and government, it had to rely mostly on the more experienced former members of the BCP. Secondly, there was the consensus of the organisationally regrouped ex-political and administrative elite on the question of redistribution of the national wealth, i.e. restitution of the property that had been nationalised by the Communists. Thirdly, there were the 'round table' talks between all political forces which ironed out differences right at the beginning of the transformation. Yet the round-table process was criticised because instead of reducing the power and influence of the BSP, it legitimised and rehabilitated the former Communist Party as a significant factor in the country's political life.

The national round table was an important step in the creation of a democratic constitution as the foundation of creating a civil society and was an important and effective step in the destalinisation of Bulgarian society. The round table, which came to function as a substitute parliament, concluded after dramatic negotiations with a national consensus on common principles with respect to the following: the political system, the economic system, the basic rights and freedoms of citizens, the organisation of state power under the transition to parliamentary democracy, a strong, competent and responsible government, and a call for elections (Melone, 1994: 271).

Finally, the danger of a border dispute and internal ethnic conflict and the need to maintain national sovereignty demanded of the new political elite the adoption, at least in this initial stages, of a non-confrontational peaceful transformation. (The examples of the former Yugoslavia and Albania have shown how critical such an approach was.)

The elimination of one-party totalitarianism does not automatically lead to pluralism and the encouragement of democratic culture, but still, the collapse of the totalitarian system marks the beginning of a period of a possible democratisation and the emergence of a plural model of political system. At this stage of the democratisation process, party and political pluralism was restored – rather quickly – as well as the basic rights and freedoms that helped the revival of civil society. An important element of the democratic transition, at this stage, was the adoption of a new constitution that marked the establishment of democracy. The constitution of 1991, which was modelled on the constitutional tradition of the developed democracies, lays the foundations of a parliamentary, social and law-based state, asserts the division of power and provides for a plural society whose citizens enjoy equal rights and the freedoms normally associated with democracy. The constitution established a parliamentary form of government, with a directly elected President, and a Constitutional Court to oversee parliament's compliance with the constitution. The electoral system is proportional, with a 4 per cent threshold of parliamentary representation. One of the more controversial provisions limits the power of the President to security matters and ceremonial functions. Still, since 1991 the constitution has proved to be a stabilising factor in political life.

The BCP's constitutionally entrenched power monopoly was eliminated, the old elites from the pre-Communist period reactivated their parties, discussion clubs transformed themselves into social movements and young cultural elites abandoned their scientific, artistic and journalistic pursuits, setting up political parties and organisations that borrowed their names, symbols and programmes from Western European political parties (although very often the models taken from the West were unsuited to the Bulgarian reality). This was a quite spontaneous process in which individuals resumed political activity and civil society was slowly reviving against a background of initial enthusiasm and massive desire for democratic changes.

But while the rules of the game were laid down during the transition period, the most important and most difficult stage of the democratisation process is that of consolidating democracy, which means the creation of the necessary conditions to sustain the democratic state and complete the democratisation of the country. What makes the consolidation of democracy so significant is that though the transition period may be complete and a democratic political system maybe established, it is another matter altogether for democracy to survive and become consolidated. And, contrary to arguments that the consolidation of democracy is defined through the ballot box, the experience of Russia or the Federal Republic of Yugoslavia (because arguably these fragile and unstable democracies cannot be considered consolidated despite several election campaigns) suggests that the democratic system, in order to be sustained, certainly takes lot more than that. Embarking thus on the democratisation process, it was evident that in a country like Bulgaria three interlinked but asynchronously evolving processes were required to preserve and strengthen the democratic regime:

- The development of the institutional framework and infrastructure of democracy.
- The development of a democratic culture.
- The development of the economic and social foundations of democracy (the subject of the next chapter).

These ought to be the main objectives of the newly established democratic regime in order to achieve its durability, setting the basis for its consolidation.

Politics in the post-Communist era

The party system

A specific characteristic of Bulgarian political life in this early period is that party formation was a top-down matter of leaderships seeking followings rather than the expression of grass-roots mass demands.

> The newly formed or restored political parties were top-down formations: they usually emerged around certain elites or individual leaders, and seeked electoral support in the course of their political activity along two lines; endeavoring to make voters affiliate with their professed ideology or practical goals; seeking, in the diffused social realm, target-groups which were likely to identify with them. (Andreev, 1996: 27)

In the same period, while the existing nomenclature elite was trying to overcome its negative past and gain democratic credibility, there were, also, political movements that were claiming to succeed political formations of the pre-1944 period, attempting to recapture a legitimacy once held in the past. There were, for example, struggles for the names and the legacy of the traditionally strong Social Democratic and Agrarian parties. These parties, however, did not enjoy the support of important social groups with clearly identifiable interests and they also lacked ideological orientation (apart from strong anti-Communism), practical experience and organisational structures. These 'historical' parties soon discovered that their pre-Communist political heritage and traditions were totally irrelevant in the political situation of the post-Communist era.

Leaving aside a very small number of surviving old members of these parties, the post-Communist parties had to create new identities in a society that was radically different from the past economic and political reality, and moreover in a new international context. In that sense the Bulgarian experience confirms even more than in other countries the conclusion of Berglund and Dellenbrant that all the parties with ideological and historical roots in a distant but glorious past returned to find their constituencies changed almost beyond recognition by more than half a century of dictatorial or Communist rule (Karasimeonov, 1996: 259).

Political life therefore, soon regained most of the features that had characterised it in the past, under former relatively democratic governments, and which are symptoms of a rather immature system of parties and party politics: the existence of a considerable number of parties (more than 200 have been registered since 1989) but only two larger polar political forces which dominate parliament and government. Most of the political parties remain organisationally weak and attract only a few members. Bulgarian politics have been rather elitist, with politicians and deputies shifting parties, splitting parties or starting new ones. Political life has been isolated and distant from the bulk of the population, most of whom view politics with some distaste and its practitioners with considerable suspicion. The prevailing political climate is based on the results of the last four post-Communist parliamentary elections (see table 3.1), which have set the bipolar pattern of political life, establishing the two poles of the political game in post-Communist Bulgaria: the Bulgarian Socialist Party (BSP, successor of the BCP) and the Union of Democratic Forces (UDF).

Table 3.1 Main parties in the National Assembly, 1990–97[a]

	1990		*1991*		*1994*		*1997*	
Party	*Seats*	*%*	*Seats*	*%*	*Seats*	*%*	*Seats*	*%*
BSP	211	47.15	106	33.14	125		58	22.00
UDF	144	36.20	110	34.36	69	28.75	137	52.20
MRF	23	6.03	24	7.54	15	6.25	19	7.50
People's Union[b]	–	–	–	–	18	7.50	–	–
Bulgarian Business Bloc	–	–	–	–	13	5.40	12	4.95
Euro-left[c]	–	–	–	–	–	–	14	5.50

Notes:
[a] The 1990 Narodno Sobranie (National Assembly) consisted of 400 seats, the others of 240.
[b] UDF dissidents and Agrarians.
[c] BSP dissidents.

Although these two political stances have dominated and ruled the post-Communist political scene of Bulgaria their positions on most important political and economic issues were far from clear and have tended to change frequently. This political practice coupled with ideological fragmentation and factionalism frequently produced unusual results. For instance, political parties could not implement their policies even when they were in power, because their own members were not unanimous on any given decision. It should be stressed, however, that among the main features of the transition is that parties across the political spectrum have achieved a consensus on fundamental political issues. Genuine political pluralism, the rule of law, ethnic tolerance, reform and democratisation of the state and state institutions while at the same time reducing its role in the economy, privatisation, encouragement of private enterprise and foreign investment, regional co-operation and European integration have been included in the programmes of all the political parties.

The Bulgarian Socialist Party

After the fall of the Zhivkov regime, a process of erosion began in the membership and social base of the BCP, at the same time as it began a revision of its ideology. Already, from the early 1980s, technocratically minded politicians had emerged within the BCP anticipating the imminent break-up of the Soviet empire and the collapse of the economic system of socialism, calling for market reforms in the economy. Although Zhivkov and the hard-liners who stood for the preservation of the *status quo* surprisingly enough tolerated them, after his fall the reformist political elite was ready to carry out changes.

In the face of a faltering economy, mass strikes, growing political opposition, ethnic strife, and factionalism within the party, the BCP carried through a number of structural and personnel changes and took the first steps to separate the party from the state, declaring also that it would work for the establishment of a political opposition. Some members of the BCP reorganised themselves as separate social democratic parties, generally termed rightist, like the Bulgarian Social Democratic Party (BSDP) and the New Social Democratic Party (NSDP). Taking as a model the democratic socialist parties of Western Europe, the BCP tried to destalinise itself and create a new, modern Marxist (instead of Marxist-Leninist) party, one of democratic socialism. Under the concept of 'democratic unity' it recognised within the party the existence of several factions and tendencies. (The most prominent were: 'Alternative Socialist Organisation', which soon broke away to form its own organisation, 'Marxist Platform', 'Road to Europe', which later formed the party of the Euro-left, 'Democratic Forum', 'Movement for Democratic Socialism'.)

Despite their differences, those who emerged out victorious in controlling existing structures of the BCP renamed it the Bulgarian Socialist Party, thus forming the most powerful and influential political organisation in the country. The BSP claimed legitimacy as a new democratic party, as a party of the social democrats aiming to represent and express the interests of a wide spectrum of people, including workers, the middle class and national capital. The BSP also sought international legitimacy in the form of the Socialist International (of which, however, it is still not an official member) and by creating and maintaining contacts with other European social democrats.

> The elimination of the old guard opened the road for newcomers from the younger generation, many of them well educated and pragmatically oriented, free from the ideological burden and deficiencies of the former leading group. This gave them great advantages over the anti-Communists and explains to a great extent the influence of the BSP and other offspring of the former Communist Party. (Karasimeonov, 1996: 261)

In fact the BSP thrived during the early post-Communist period. Having retained the political initiative during the transition period, firmly rooted in large segments of society, with its vast material, administrative and manpower resources, the BSP also benefited from the fact that it was in control of the key administrative positions. Such was its relative strength that Elster *et al.* noted: 'political and economic elite continuity in Bulgaria was probably greater than in any other post-Communist country of the region, as being a Party cadre was not a liability, but rather an important asset that turned out to be convertible into power and privilege after 1989'[10] (Elster *et al.*, 1998: 262).

The BSP, however, was not united, since it suffered from continual fragmentation and internal struggles. Its ranks included hard-line Bolsheviks, moderate social democrats and technocrats ('enterprise managers'). Apart from the ideological rifts between these groups, the BSP was also the battleground of the newly formed elites (economic, political and media) that emerged from the ranks of the previous politico-administrative elite. The roots of the confrontation can be traced back to the 1980s, when the reform faction emerged in the Communist Party (attempting to adopt a kind of Chinese economic model). Andrei Lukanov, as the reform mastermind, was the leader of the reform wing and the natural leader of the economic elite, who, as he later admitted, along with other reformers stayed in the party waiting for the moment when democracy would become possible, and then toppled Zhivkov and guided the events of 1989. Based on popular support, the economic, reform elite initially took power. Lukanov's model of post-Communist reform was to empower economically the old Communist Party elite and to turn the positions of power accrued under Communism to positions of economic predominance in a controlled post-Communist market economy (the so-called 'Lukanov scheme').

Thus after the fall of Communism, most persons of the old nomenclature, by exploiting their contacts and positions, having access to information and funds, and having the ability to manoeuvre transactions to their benefit, managed to emerge as members of the new elite, especially the economic elite. Being in the best strategic positions when the Communist regime collapsed, the nomenclature members were able to compete successfully for top positions in the new regime. They had the most important assets in the form of the money and personal connections with which to replace defunct organisational connections. This is why the majority of today's *nouveaux riches* in Bulgaria come not from the ranks of the old economic elite but from the ranks of the Komsomol and secret police (Nikolov, 1998: 222).

This new economic elite, dissenting from the old Communist nomenclature, became associated with crime (the 'mafia'), the black market and top-down expropriation of funds. The former nomenclature, having transformed its political influence into economic clout, and having no ideological commitments or restrictions from Moscow's imperatives, dissolved into various groups, each of them forming its own specific interests and political allegiances. During the 1990s a bitter battle among these factions was under way as they competed for a bigger slice of the cake rather than on real ideological-political grounds. Corruption became the rule, and the Communist corporations and their various subdivisions assumed almost total control of the economy and the apparatus of the state. The clientelist party structure facilitated the process of using politics for the accumulation of substantial private wealth. Besides, the political stalemate that followed the 1989 change was such a paradise for crime one could contemplate certain changes but hardly a change of regime. 'These corporate interests stemming from the old Communist Party were the unseen rulers of the country' (Katsanis interview) or, as others put it, Bulgaria seemed to be a country 'largely under the hold of the former regime's inertia' (Elster *et al.*, 1998: 278). After the years of chaos the elevation of Zhan Videnov to party leader and Prime Minister was at first seen as a natural change of generations at the top of the Socialist hierarchy and as a possible return to law and order. But instead of enforcing law and order the Prime Minister himself was involved in a series of economic scandals.[11] The struggle culminated at the end of 1996 when the BSP became an arena of open clashes between various organised interests which had become incompatible.[12] 'There were so many factions that they fought each other and no strategic decisions could be taken because there was no balance' (Dainov interview). The result was the replacement of the hard-line neo-Communist Zhan Videnov by a moderate social democrat, Georgi Parvanov. Despite the leadership change, the division of the party between the reformist and the Marxist factions continues to be visible.

Regarding its political character and programme, the BSP emphasised the necessity of a democratic and humane society, scientific socialism, a plural civil society based on the rule of law, stressing, also, the need for a democratic but strong state. The central objective of economic reform was outlined as establishing a social market economy so that the achievement of economic efficiency and development was linked with assuring social and economic security to all citizens. A social market economy was conceived as a mixed economy where private and state forms of ownership were not only treated equally but also participated relatively equally in the creation of the national wealth. Such an economy was also seen as an open economy which would facilitate participation in the international division of labour, attracting foreign investment and know-how, while at the same time practising selective protectionism to enhance the development of local industry. The party's economic programme pledged a gradual transition to a market economy in which no one would suffer, opposing strongly the shock therapy that was imposed in Poland on grounds of 'Bulgarian specificities' and costliness. Co-operatives were defended but private property was also seen as the base of modern economics. The BSP pledged Bulgaria's interconnection with the wider European economic structures and unconditionally supported accession to the European Union. More debatable has been the issue of NATO membership, as the BSP during the 1990s maintained an anti-NATO stance, being highly concerned with maintaining friendly relations with Russia. (This issue is treated in chapter 6.)

The Union of Democratic Forces

While the BSP was dealing with the legacy of the Zhivkov era, opposition political groups were also being organised. The key element of the Bulgarian opposition, the UDF, was set up in December 1989 in order to bring together the disparate strands of the democratic opposition to BCP rule and was a heterogeneous party coalition, comprising sixteen parties and organisations, formed on a merely anti-Communist basis, trying to cover the whole political spectrum from left to extreme right.[13] It comprised three types of groups. A first category, which formed the liberal centre of the Union, comprised mainly dissident intellectuals and former members of the Communist Party who were opposed to the Bolshevik type of party and to the ruling nomenclature who had been closely connected with Zhivkov. Particularly influential within that group was the Club for *Glasnost* and Democracy, whose leader, Zhelev, became the first UDF chairman. A second group was made up of parties with a long history in Bulgarian political life as they revived traditional historical parties existing prior to 1947 (mainly the Social Democratic Party, the Bulgarian Agrarian National Union – Nikola Petkov (BANU–NP), the Democratic Party and the Radical Democratic Union). Finally, there were new organisations that had been founded shortly before or after the overthrow of the regime, of which the most significant were the Green Party (whose leader Philip Dimitrov succeeded Zhelev), Eco-*glasnost* and the Podkrepa Trade Union.

The opposition developed very quickly as an alternative political force, attracting people with different interests and aspirations, including mostly the intellectuals, the people who had suffered under Communism, young people irrespective of social status as well as ambitious career-seeking political opportunists and even a number of people who had just left the ruling party. Despite its heterogeneous social base, the UDF gained importance in a short time, amid stagnation and fear, in the context of little organisational experience and no mass media of its own, as its newspapers appeared too late and had a limited circulation. Independent radio and television journalists were the main spokesmen for the opposition cause. The one major advantage the UDF enjoyed was that it had been involved in the round-table negotiations, which were instrumental in introducing the opposition to the general public.

The UDF was headed by a National Co-ordination Council, on which individual parties were represented, but at the same time individual parties had their own governing bodies and structures, operating on a central and local basis. This coalition frequently produced conflicts and disputes, and there were constant attempts to transform the UDF into a 'blue party'. Finally, in 1996, Ivan Kostov managed to set out a programme of organisational reform. (His strength stemmed from the fact that, unlike all other UDF luminaries, he was not a member of any of the sixteen parties and organisations that made up the Union.) Until then the nationwide local structures of the UDF were in effect micro-coalitions of the Union's member parties, isolating the UDF from the public at large. (Nobody could become a member of the UDF, only a member of a UDF coalition party.) The change from a coalition of small parties into one party unified the UDF's structure and that was instrumental in redefining the UDF's public image into a more coherent whole and in allowing it to be more convincing. The UDF was then able to both formulate and later implement a governmental programme that was no longer a weak compromise between different party ideologies. Kostov also managed to erect an efficient party machine capable of fighting and winning election campaigns as well as opening up the Union to all possible allies and partners. By that time the UDF had acquired a much clearer Christian Democratic profile and the restructuring immediately resulted in an influx of new people, reversing the old image of an isolated, self-centred, hostile and managerially incompetent party.

Once having acquired this clearer profile, the UDF came up with a coherent governmental platform, which concentrated on the revival of the much needed economic reforms, and for the first time the public saw no contradiction between its ideological character and its programme. The UDF considered private ownership as the basis of economic democracy, while state monopoly of ownership should be eliminated. This would lead to the disestablishment of the ruling party elite from state ownership, which had provided the material basis of Communist dominance of the economy and public life. It called for shock therapy – an immediate and complete transition to a market economy – but did not make clear how it would be effected or how the most vulnerable elements of the population would be protected. From the beginning the UDF considered that the land which had been taken by force at the time of collectivisation must be returned to the rightful owners or their heirs. The UDF advocated that the economic reforms should aim to integrate Bulgaria into the world economy. This meant a structural adaptation of the economy in order to participate in international trade and financial institutions. The UDF has been vigorously supporting Bulgaria's integration into the European Union and NATO.

The Movement for Rights and Freedoms

The third major component of post-Communist party political life is the MRF, established as an almost exclusively ethnic grouping representing and defending the interests of the Turkish minority. That was the main reason why the UDF did not accept the MRF as a member party of the Union, its leadership fearing that anti-Turkish sentiment among the electorate would have negative effects on election results. The MRF was founded by Ahmed Dogan in December 1989 and initially was concerned with ethnic and religious freedom for ethnic Turks and Muslims but always adopted a rather careful approach, avoiding positions and opposing nationalism and fundamentalism.[14] Since the round-table agreements and the ratification of the new constitution, which forbids political parties based on ethnicity or religion (precisely to counter such parties as the MRF), the MRF was registered as an organisation for rights. Based on the 1990 electoral law, which allowed organisations and movements that were not political parties to participate in the elections, the MRF entered the parliament controlling twenty-three seats after the 1990 elections (receiving 370,000 votes) and twenty-four after the 1991 elections. The closeness of the election result in 1991 signalled the rise to political prominence of the MRF, since it held sufficient seats to form a viable coalition with either the victorious UDF or the BSP. Therefore its support made the first non-Communist government possible, and it was the withdrawal of its support that forced the UDF from office in 1992, allying the MRF with the BSP.

During the short period the UDF was in power the issue of the MRF's legitimacy was resolved in the Constitutional Court, allowing it to register legally as a political party.[15] At the elections in 1994 and in 1997 (where the BSP and UDF respectively had a clear-cut parliamentary majority) the MRF's political significance decreased. Its diminishing role is also attributed to the reduced importance of ethnic identity in political life, to economic emigration and the decline in the electoral turnout among the Bulgarian Turks as well as the emergence of powerful MRF splinter groups. In 1994 the MRF won fifteen seats, becoming the fourth major political group. In the 1997 elections, seeking a more adequate political profile, the MRF formed a coalition (the Alliance for National Salvation) with former UDF members, the Green Party, the Agrarian Party, and even with a cluster of monarchist parties with twenty MPs in the parliament. As A. Zhelyazkova commented, 'the fact that such a coalition could be formed with Dogan as its central figure shows how far acceptance of the MRF's participation in political life has come' (Zhelyazkova, 1998: 178).

Moreover, despite its controversial record, the MRF was a major contributor to the marked improvement of the minority's situation. Immediately after the fall of Communism a process started of renovating the identity of the minority. The MRF, taking advantage of the political influence it acquired, managed to reduce tension in the regions of mixed population and, along with the restoration of Turkish names, secured the opening of all mosques, freedom of religious practices and the lifting of the restrictions on the use of the Turkish language and on Muslim publications. Also a news programme in Turkish was introduced on national public television. Considering the relatively positive atmosphere in everyday life in ethnically mixed areas, it can be safely argued that the Turkish minority is fully integrated and represented in political life. The MRF, therefore, played the role of a political and social stabiliser through the influence it exercised over the Turkish minority, and also over minorities that have not been able to produce viable political organisations and gain representation, such as the Gypsies.

Bulgarian politics: disappointment and hope

Bulgarian politics have been anything but a facilitating and accommodating factor for the difficult economic and political transition. Great expectations deriving from political pluralism, competition between political programmes, decisions and actions have gradually given way to disappointment and indifference, since transition seems to have become a chronic state of society. The political dead-ends led to economic dead-ends, which in turn generated further political confrontation, blockage of reforms and more economic decline. Expectations that rapid economic liberalisation would immediately give the initial impulse to a self-regulating market have proved to be illusory. The resolution of the painful economic problems experienced by Bulgarian society is above all linked with active political intervention, since up to now national politics has been a nexus of contradictions which tends to exacerbate rather than mitigate the problems. Political parties tend to be perceived as destructive factors in the political process, as institutions inciting discord and division in society. The generally negative assessment of political parties, and consequently of the parliamentary institution itself, results from their perceived inability to perform the role of intermediaries between the citizens and the institutions, as well as to be a positive factor in the consolidation of the nation.

There is sufficient justification for this attitude. The period from November 1989 to the end of 1997 was characterised by political instability: there were four parliamentary elections and eight changes of government, with the BSP and UDF alternating. Certainly the regular, peaceful and uncomplicated alternations in power in response to election results indicates that Bulgaria, according to Huntington, fulfils one of the 'criteria' of democratic consolidation. Still, from the rise of electoral politics alone no one could conclude that Bulgaria is a consolidated democracy since several other aspects of politics have to be taken into account.

For example, none of the governments elected has put forward a comprehensive reform strategy co-ordinated in time and content. There was no continuity in economic practices and each new government has laid the blame for all adversities on its predecessors, showing an implicit arrogance of power and forgetting their role as temporary representatives of the public interest. The political scene has been pervaded by short-term aims, eclecticism, improvisation and opportunism. The governments' horizons of economic, political and social thinking have invariably been narrow, never extending further than their term in office or going beyond the next elections. There has been unwillingness to assume responsibility for the requisite abrupt economic changes and hesitation in designing and implementing reforms based on economic rationality because, in the short run, such measures were expected to be highly unpopular, thus weakening political support. As R. Daskalov points out, 'the transition has been marked by demagogy as the parties have tried to outbid one another with unrealistic promises while concealing the real gravity of the country's situation from the voters. Terms such as "social protection" or "welfare" have been greatly abused and are devoid of meaning when the state is utterly without resources' (Daskalov, 1998: 20). In sum, delaying hard decisions and shirking responsibility has emerged as a style of state administration, placing politics as one of the main reasons for the failure of economic reform and recovery.

Excessive ideologisation of the governments' political and economic decisions is one more example of the substantial harm done by the political elite that has arisen since 1989. A number of vital laws and Acts were shelved for years without any apparent reason (e.g. mass privatisation) and even when some of them were enacted they were strongly ideologised, having destructive effects. These were political and economic decisions that were driven mainly by the ideology and the political character of the party in office (i.e. democrats versus

Communists) without serious consideration of the possible outcome. Other laws permitted exploitation for quasi-business activities or a plundering of the state sector. Apart from the dissipation of political energy, other problems have also had strategic repercussions and contributed to the unsatisfactory state of Bulgarian politics. For instance, political parties considered the struggle against crime as a police matter of chasing criminals and not as a matter of institutional reform and preventive legislation.

Politicians have proved to be conceptually unprepared for the abrupt change in politics and institutions imposed by historical circumstances. They were obviously overwhelmed by the unique historical challenge with its complexity of economic, political and cultural elements. The failure of economic restructuring, the difficulties in the implementation of privatisation schemes and the institutional reforms demonstrated, in contrast to political declarations, the lack of an overall national strategy during the transition period. So the reforms started without a well thought out strategy and continued for years focusing on day-to-day efforts to find short-term simple solutions to complicated long-term issues. Certainly the dynamic nature of the transition placed certain restrictions on planning and, also, Bulgaria was influenced by unforeseeable external factors with enormous political and economic implications (i.e. the Bosnian war and the Kosovo crisis). However, owing to cognitive limitations and the acute nature of the problems, the new political elite was ill prepared to develop and implement even medium-term action plans to optimise the reform process and make it more manageable. A partial excuse is the fact that many experts from the industrialised countries were equally ill equipped to provide assistance in the management of such a profound transformation. Few would doubt, additionally, that:

> external institutional factors have played a prominent role in determining priorities in Eastern Europe, and that this has reduced the autonomy of the players in the political game. Solutions proposed by international funding bodies are seen by the political elite in Eastern Europe as the only ones appropriate in the circumstances, and those funding bodies are in turn able to make their grants and loans dependent upon certain conditions being met. The economic policies applied in Eastern-Central Europe are part of a dependent modernisation process, in which the relatively backward social, political and economic structures of Eastern Europe are dominated by the Western model of reference. (Coppieters and Waller, 1994: 190)

Reasons deeply rooted in the national and regional culture have also contributed to political instability and institutional inefficiency. With few exceptions the political formations are dominated by the Balkan tradition of factionalism and autocracy. The emergent democratic political elite, since the round-table agreements, has universally adopted confrontational means to attain approbation, with the result that politics has become dominated by destructive and stagnant 'zero sum' games. Political conflicts undermined substantially collective solidarity, instigating extreme individualism.

A particular feature of the non-productive orientation of the political process was excessive harking back to the past. In contrast to the Spanish example, which succeeded in overcoming the authoritarian legacy by consigning it to the past, in Bulgaria that legacy became a dividing line in national politics. This was particularly the case during the first transitional years as a number of dissidents lost legitimacy when it was revealed that they had been police informers under the previous regime (among them a prominent UDF figure, Petar Beron, who was forced to resign). The Bulgarian social scientist E. Nikova described how 'during the whole period of 1989–92 Bulgarian politics remained in a phase of pre-politics or anti-politics. Revolutionary rhetoric was kept alive, together with an anachronistic preoccupation with the past, the KGB, Moscow, and various conspiracies' (Linz and Stepan, 1996: 340). More than ten years after the collapse of the totalitarian regime the Communist past continues to taint political life. For example, while opening Communist-era secret police files was a sensitive issue in all Central European countries in the early transitional years, Bulgaria has not yet turned the page of its Communist past: as recently as 2001 the parliament, amid accusations and counter-accusations of manipulation of the files, approved legislation to reveal the names of former agents and informants of the Communist regime's secret services.

Both expert political analysts and the public at large were quick to realise that many decisions taken by the governing elite have been dominated by private and partisan interests. The widespread expectation that politicians would place national issues and interests at the centre of attention, before party problems and interests, proved to be illusory. Thus, even if it is natural to expect that the intensity of mass involvement in public life and overall interest in politics, which the transition period requires by its nature, should gradually wane, two additional factors contributed to the sharp acceleration of the process. First, the deepening of the economic crisis made Bulgarians overwhelmingly concerned with the deterioration in their living standards. Second, there is great dissatisfaction with the competence of politicians and the nature of political activity, as it is evident that politicians across the political spectrum have lost the confidence of the people. In both cases the effect is the same: mass withdrawal from politics, leading to unparticipatory political processes and to political apathy. This was demonstrated in the 1997 parliamentary elections, where almost 40 per cent of the electorate did not appear to vote, and this trend continued in the 1999 municipal elections, where voter turnout (55 per cent) was the lowest since 1990. Because of the lack of democratic traditions Bulgarians associated democracy with crime, corruption, economic difficulties and low living standards, and there are some who look back with nostalgia. According to *Eurobarometer* for 1996, only 13 per cent of those interviewed were satisfied with the development of democracy while 80 per cent of Bulgarians expressed their dissatisfaction, the highest among all CEECs (European Commission, 1996). Besides, the previous regime had some advantages: virtually no crime and the few things that were available were affordable. Moreover, as Meininger and Radoeva point out, 'the sharp collapse in electoral participation serves as an important measure of the extent to which post-1989 Bulgaria, in failing to find a high level of trust in its new democratic institutions, has undergone a troublesome transition towards becoming a civil society' (Meininger and Radoeva, 1996: 45).

Consequently, the instrumentalisation of politics has already caused large groups of the public to harbour negative attitudes towards political institutions, since their performance does not match expectations. For the majority of the people the basic institutions do not effectively represent and protect their interests and therefore generate considerable discontent and disappointment. They have failed to obtain the citizens' trust when the extent of public trust or even a tempering of distrust is clearly important for democratic consolidation. 'The level of confidence in the basic institutions of the new democratic political system has diminished. Despite some fluctuations, this is a lasting tendency. In 1996 the rating of Parliament, President, government and judicial system reached critically low levels' (UNDP, 1997: 65).

Additionally, this generated a lack of national self-confidence along with a general mistrust of Bulgarian experts and uncritical trust in foreign experts. However, it has to be said that, despite the fact that Bulgarians feel rather tired and disappointed with the political reality, with the competence and morality of the politicians and with their ability to solve social problems, they do not seek alternatives to democracy, as the main democratic principles (human and civil rights, political pluralism, freedom of the press, etc.) still receive broad support.

Institutional inefficiency

The disappointment and lack of confidence in political institutions refers not only to political parties but to the judiciary and the state administration as well. The post-Communist period has been marked by the absence and ineffectiveness of the state and its institutions. That was inevitable, since the reorganisation of the state was not included on the reform agenda. As the Communist system was characterised by the subordination of the state to the party, the dismantling of the Communist regime was perceived as equivalent to the dismantling of the state. The 'dismantling' approach dominated the 1990s and this resulted in a situation where the state administration was exploited by different organised interests, mafia structures and organised crime.

The judicial system and the law enforcement institutions are among the main generators of civic discontent, since they are regarded as major factors behind the 'criminalisation' of society, personal insecurity and the undermining of the law, and, similarly, there is a widespread perception that the public administration is corrupt, incompetent and inefficient. Apparently Bulgarian society is lacking an important element for the construction of civil society and democratic consolidation: trust. Citizens do not trust the government and its institutions, the government does not trust its citizens, and everyone in their everyday concerns is suspicious of everyone else.

Institutional inefficiency is most visible in the management of the crime wave.

> By penetrating government circles through bribery and blackmail the criminal clique has corrupted them and drawn them into their service rather than to the service of public interests. When people begin to seek personal security not from the police but from groups with suspicious activities the circle of institutional decay begins to close in leading to a profound crisis in the moral consciousness of society. (UNDP, 1995: 79)

Bulgaria has been characterised by the operation of semi-criminal 'networks' that, acting together with strategically placed executive officials, have done much to destabilise and destroy the financial, organisational, structural and moral foundations of the state.[16] The growing social crime intensifies the fear in society, breaks the connection between society and state structures and aggravates social erosion. The demoralisation of the whole of society has been the result of the absence of accountability and control, since 'the very line between legal and illegal, between those who enforce law and those who trespass it, has become dangerously blurred and fluid' (Daskalov, 1998: 26). Corruption is a manifestation and a symptom of weak state institutions and affects all levels of the state bureaucracy. Corruption in the state administration and the links between political figures and organised crime lead to the replacement of the state institutions by shadow power structures.

Corruption could be divided into three different levels. The first and lowest could be defined as individual corruption in which the individual customs officer, policeman or minor administrator receives bribes for illegal services. The second level is the so-called group corruption, and that occurs when the abuse of an administrative position is used to establish parallel private structures to gain market share and drain government funds. The highest level is 'lobbying corruption' and this is the phenomenon of using parliamentary channels, the executive and the judicial power to create and pass legislation beneficial to or protective of the strategic goals of certain financial interests. In this way they gain control over key economic areas and social spheres. While corruption existed under the previous regime it was limited in scope, concentrated mainly at the individual level (the first level) and was due to the individual citizen's dependence on officials. The rigidity of the Communist system and the functioning of state bureaucracy gave officials an incentive to exploit their position for private gain. But after the change of 1989, alongside the transition to a market economy, new conditions for corruption were created in the form of organised crime or the mass spread of corrupt ties between private business and the state apparatus.[17] The basic source of corruption is no longer the rigidity of the system but the uncertainty that surrounds it.

Corruption and organised crime acquired great scope with energetic transgressions of the embargo against the former Yugoslavia which created a whole new strata of criminal economic activity and led inevitably to further corruption of the various government agencies designed to implement the embargo (police, prosecutors, judges, customs and excise officials, transport officials).[18] Besides violations of the oil embargo, there has been evidence of arms shipments to Bosnia from Russia, Ukraine and other former Soviet republics passing through Bulgaria. Indeed, for many it is not simply coincidence that organised crime thrived almost simultaneously with the implementation of the embargo. And when the embargo ended in late 1995 the following May the private banks known to be servicing organised crime started to go bankrupt.

The main sources of corruption are economic and systemic, as the system itself provides the opportunities for such practices. A prime cause of corruption is the strong involvement of state administration and bureaucracy in society. As long as the state continues to control most activity corruption is inevitable. The failure of economic transition, the complicated privatisation procedures, the inadequate legislative framework and legislative unpredictability, and the low pay of civil servants, who are prepared to take every opportunity to improve their living standards, created the conditions that allowed corruption to spread. Another source of corruption is the existence of political clienteles and the financial dependence of the political parties on the various economic groups. According to a UNDP report, corruption has been facilitated by two other important circumstances in particular.

> The first has been the demoralisation of considerable segments of society as a result of the abrupt change of world views and moral values as well as of the downfall of the hopes for rapid transition to a democratic society of high material well-being ... The second factor facilitating and spreading corruption has been the weakened state system and inefficient social control. (UNDP, 1997: 26)

Therefore, obviously the state and its institutions have been weakening progressively, while public office is more and more seen as a means of enrichment and, not surprisingly, Bulgarians have little respect for the state.[19] Paradoxically, the perception is still widespread of the almighty state to which all concerns must be addressed and from which the solution to all problems can be expected.

Even more alarming is the fact that social resistance to acts of corruption is weakening, as within only a very short historical period the sweeping scope of such acts has rapidly and rather negatively been reflected in the mass consciousness.[20] This is particularly worrying, considering that corruption has affected even the institutions whose primary task is to combat crime, as there have been proven cases of bribery in the judiciary and the police. According to a survey carried out by the Vitosha Research Institute, in any year 29 per cent of Bulgarians are asked for a bribe by customs officials, 19.5 per cent by the police and 18.6 per cent by doctors in the public sector. Corruption has also penetrated those areas of society that should be putting up a barrier to this syndrome and acting as a positive role model in the dissemination of civil values. For example, there have been numerous press reports alleging that teaching staff of the universities have been expecting bribes and other gratuities from students and parents. It is important to note that corruption has a disproportionate impact on the economically disadvantageous section of society as these are the people who are directly affected when they must pay unofficially for health care, education and civil registrations, and they may also suffer for their inability to pay the necessary bribes. Additionally, state institutions have failed to see the citizen as an equal, as the source of their legitimacy or even as a financial source.

> Given the lack of a clear lead from the top, the institutions of government find it difficult to see themselves as representative [of the citizen] bodies. Institutions of state see themselves as 'superiors' to the citizens, as holders of resources that they can either provide or refuse to provide for the citizens – in short, as 'the Power'. Ultimately, they find it difficult to distinguish between right and might – a fundamental distinction for any functioning democracy. At worst, the citizen is seen as a nuisance; at best, as something of a helpless child that the state, as a 'father figure', may choose to help. (Task Force, 1997: 36)

From all this it is clear that state institutions, starting from a dominant position in spheres of society, have not yet performed their key role in managing the transition towards the market economy and democratic politics and in developing advanced forms of social integration consistent with them. The state and its institutions, mainly because of the lack of strategic thinking and mismanagement, have performed their functions in an incompetent and irresponsible way, without creating the conditions for a sustainable social, political and economic transformation and development. Bulgaria's new democratic institutions have not acquired sufficient authority or respect, since they failed to cope with the severe challenges of the transition. Even worse, by not performing their basic functions, the state's institutions have affected negatively the quality of life of almost all citizens.

The political situation

Following the June 1990 elections (the first free elections for almost sixty years), held after the round-table talks, Bulgaria had a socialist President (Petar Mladenov), a socialist government (under Andrei Lukanov) and a slight socialist majority in the National Assembly, though the level of polarisation meant that no stable government was possible. The results can be largely attributed to the fact that the BSP had the advantage of relatively greater access to the resources necessary for mounting an election campaign, as well as its successful campaign strategy.[21] After the elections, the BSP sought to counteract its political isolation with an alliance policy. The UDF, on the contrary, embarked upon a policy of non-co-operation (indeed, initiated a period of protest and demonstrations) and, since the socialist majority was far short of the two-thirds needed for many legislative decisions, it effectively blocked political progress. Despite its parliamentary majority, the BSP was constantly under pressure and, in fact, this strategy gained the concession of a UDF President, Zhelev, and the eventual resignation of the socialist government. Besides, the BSP quickly lost legitimacy partly because of its inaction in the face of the economic crisis and partly because its reform proposals were contradicting its election platform.

It is evident, as J. F. Brown also argues, that the outcome of the first free elections was not the slow but steady progress toward democracy, with a stable government and a vigorous but responsible opposition, that had at first seemed possible.

> The election had revealed the polarisation of Bulgarian society along social, educational and generational lines – the towns against the countryside, the young against the old, and intellectuals against the workers, particularly the peasants. Such a polarisation is also known in Western democracies. But what was dangerous about it in post-Communist Bulgaria was that factors that might have contained and then reduced it were either too weak or totally absent. Again, the lack of liberal political culture in pre-Communist Bulgaria, the repressive orthodoxy of the Communist period, and then the indecisive way in which Bulgarian Communism was ended sharpened the polarisation. (Brown, 1992: 122)

The 1991 elections produced similar results to the previous elections, except that the UDF, despite having lost a few separatist elements, gained a few more seats than the BSP – hardly a mandate, but still an important political and psychological victory. The UDF formed a government (under Philip Dimitrov) in an unofficial coalition with the third parliamentary party, the MRF. The UDF government was very active in passing significant legislation, such as the laws on the restitution of property and the amendment of the land law to initiate decollectivisation. Still the government did not make substantial progress, particularly in the field of privatisation, and even more the governmental coalition began to disintegrate rapidly. The UDF continued to fracture internally as its unity, based primarily on anti-Communism, was not enough to promote significant political and economic policies. In addition, economic reforms and particularly, land restitution, had severely affected the interests of the Turkish population and the alliance with the MRF began to unravel.

Furthermore, the government's attempts at reform ran into lack of understanding and passive resistance by the state apparatus, and, finally, the UDF found itself between two fires: apportioning blame for the economic catastrophe and having the responsibility for finding a way out. UDF reformers crashed against the unexpected scope of the economic disaster and created the impression that democracy means chaos, insecurity and the constant threat of poverty. The UDF Cabinet was also continually accused of going too far with its anti-Communist stance. The government's confrontational policy could have worked only with a united party and a clear majority in parliament when at the time it had neither.

After its slim electoral victory the UDF government was so obsessed with the past that it gave priority to restitution instead of privatisation and to retribution (or decommunisation) instead of democratisation. Unfortunately, 'backward-looking justice' proved to be incompatible with mass expectations of 'forward-looking' impartiality; the already divided public perceived the strong commitment to retributive legislation as a symptom of non-democratic, authoritarian and even 'Stalinist' trends within the anti-Communist coalition, while the restitution of land and property was viewed as a threat to the effective restructuring and marketisation of agriculture. Thus the 'retrospective' legislation proved to be a major failure for the UDF Cabinet and one of the factors that substantially contributed to its dismissal (Kolarova, 1996: 547, 550).

In brief, the UDF continued to fight against the old Communist Party by taking controversial retrospective measures instead of running the country. By doing so it alienated too many of its own constituencies and supporters (including President Zhelev). Finally, in December 1992, the MRF withdrew its support and the UDF government, the first non-Communist government, collapsed.

New elections were avoided when a coalition of the BSP and the MRF took over with Lyuben Berov, an aged economic historian, as Prime Minister. This technocratic government managed to survive fairly well, given the narrowness of its parliamentary majority. It also attempted to reduce the social impact of the reform measures, retreating from the clearer position of the previous government. (For example, restitution became more of a debate around the practical issues than about the effectiveness of such a strategy.) Having no popular mandate, no reform strategy and no consensus, the government proved to be merely an administration attempting to keep all its backers equally happy, increasingly becoming prey to the direct influence of corporate interests, slowing down the economic reforms and, disastrously, prolonging the economic transition.

Against this background the UDF was criticised for the reform failure and was discredited as it was locked in a downward spiral of internal battles, being incapable of coming up with a coherent programme or vision. Thus it was obvious that the masses would return to the realities and the personalities they knew better, adding, then, to the 'left-wing wave' in the former Communist part of Europe. The BSP benefited most from the problems and the disappointment generated from the transition, and at the elections held at the end of 1994 the BSP again proved the strongest party, but, while everyone expected the socialists to win, few expected them to obtain a clear parliamentary majority – as in fact they did. As Dainov explained:

> by late 1993 people had formed a negative attitude towards all politicians. The politician was a negative figure; someone who would serve his own self-interest, who would possibly steal and was bound to be corrupt. Or a politician was someone who maybe was a positive figure, fundamentally a democratic person but was incompetent in administrating the country. Against this background the BSP created a new image; the image of experience and of good administrators managing to get away from the image of the politician and get into the image of the technocrat. (Dainov interview)

Indeed the BSP managed to reshuffle its leadership, placing it in the hands of young persons who were neither tainted nor deformed by the old Communist practices, adopting a managerial profile. With its consequent promise to improve the economy the BSP attracted the votes of the older and rural part of the population, who reacted against the difficult living conditions brought about by the transition, compared with the previous 'better' standards of living.[22]

Yet once again, and despite its big majority, its promises, its young and technocratic image, and a slight and ephemeral economic improvement at the beginning of its term, the BSP could not fulfil the great expectations vested in it. Not only did the BSP not bring about economic recovery but it prolonged the situation which had characterised Bulgaria since 1989, favouring only criminals and profiteers. The former Communists, who one way or another –with a break of only eighteen months – had held power firmly since 1989, continued the same disastrous policies as in their previous period in office. In addition, there were frequent allegations that the BSP did deals with powerful crime rings and that the former Communist elite exploited privatisation in order to gain enterprise assets. In fact most of the private businesses that had sprung up were run not by a new generation of entrepreneurs but by the old Communist elite (especially those connected with the old intelligence services).[23] These allegations, that touched even the Prime Minister, accusing Videnov of being in the service of shady economic interests, along with the methods applied in the economic sphere that were in effect an attempt to revive the centrally planned economy, had a disastrous impact on the BSP in the presidential elections of October 1996.[24] The Socialist vote collapsed by half and the UDF's candidate, Petar Stoyanov, became President of the Republic.

The loss suffered by the BSP in the presidential elections excited strong dissent among the members of its elite. Some attempted the overthrow of Videnov as party leader and Prime Minister, but even if the latter succeeded in holding his own position it was evident that the government had lost public trust and was incapable of taking any of the crucial decisions needed to stabilise the situation in the country.[25] At the same time the economic position was getting worse. The country found itself locked in the biggest economic crisis since records began. The average wage at the end of 1996 could buy less than the average wage at the end of 1919. And this was a profound shock to the entire nation. As President Stoyanov asserted, 'for the first time since 1989 people and politicians faced up to harsh reality' (*Financial Times*, 1997: Survey). People realised that reform was not a luxury but a necessity and thus, following years of public apathy, took to the streets, demanding elections and rapid economic reform. In the first days of 1997 the largest protest rallies in the history of the country covered the centre of Sofia with a dense mass of demonstrators and the country was in unprecedented uproar. The disastrous failures of successive governments reawakened the public and what had not happened in November 1989 took place in January and February 1997. While it was a *coup* 'from above' that brought down the Zhivkov regime, the BSP government was forced to resign by a *coup* 'from below'.

Public discontent burst out in collective protest against the rampant crime, the racketeering which tortured medium-size businesses and individual enterprise, and the arrogant public behaviour of 'economic' groups. It revolted against the discrediting of the very term 'reform' through the unwillingness or indecisiveness of the government to pursue it seriously. The common denominator of the discontent was protest at the inability of the state to perform its fundamental functions, i.e. it was a protest against bad governance (UNDP, 1998: 15).

The situation resulted in new elections which the UDF won with an exceptional majority and for the first time a non-Communist party won an absolute majority in the National Assembly (137 out of 240 seats). Beyond doubt this landslide signified a sea change in public opinion and an overwhelming public desire for rapid reform and a move to a market economy. Unlike the situation in 1991–92, when the UDF government failed because of lack of experience and lack of public support for the reforms, this time the UDF majority enjoyed an unprecedented basis for reform achievements. Being united and having solved its internal factionalism, having acquired more experience, having regained public confidence, having achieved a unique level of national and political agreement on the reform agenda, enjoying the backing of the international community, enjoying a very secure parliamentary majority, and with its principal political opponent (the BSP) in a state of disarray and hampered by its inability to produce alternative policies, the UDF was in an extremely advantageous position. President Stoyanov described the situation accurately: 'most of the period between 1989 and 1997 we only had the pretence of reform. We deluded ourselves that we could survive without great sacrifices. But things kept getting tougher and we got deeper and deeper into debt. 1997 marked the turning point when we shed our illusions' (*Financial Times*, 1997).

The 1997 elections signalled also the elevation of a new political elite with a more 'pragmatic' and realistic profile. The initial post-Communist period was marked by the dissidents' entry into political life and the removal of Zhivkov's circle, succeeded by ideology-driven elite – radical anti-Communists on the right (Philip Dimitrov) and nostalgic hard-liners on the left (Zhan Videnov). Political life since 1997 has been dominated by people having no association with the Communist regime either as members of the nomenclature or as anti-Communist dissidents. (For example, after the 1997 elections, the two-thirds of MPs had been elected for the first time.)

The main characteristic of political life at the end of the 1990s was stabilisation and normalisation, particularly because it was widely accepted that it was the last chance for Bulgaria to manage the economic and social problems of transition that most of the former Eastern Bloc countries seemed to have overcome. Based on the reformist consensus that emerged both in parliament and among a broad measure of the population, the UDF government introduced a very ambitious four-year programme ('Bulgaria 2001'). The main elements of this programme were: quick economic and structural reforms and the establishment of a functioning market economy, extensive reform of the administrative and judicial system, the strengthening of democratic institutions, the establishment of law and order, the breaking of organised crime, and the acceleration of the process of preparation for EU accession.

The government succeeded in fulfilling several of the key objectives of this programme. The privatisation process received new impetus, a Law on State Administration and a Civil Service Law were adopted with the aim of creating a modern, professional and independent public administration and a significant number of legislative Acts were ratified regulating social and economic issues. Furthermore, the UDF government declared in 1997 that among its priorities was reform of the judicial system, as the endemic corruption and ineffectiveness of the judiciary were evident. While legal changes have been adopted, significant further efforts and resources are needed. The reform is expected to provide conditions for greater openness and transparency, speedier administration of justice, to create internal control mechanisms to prevent abuses of power; and to establish a system for improving the professional skills of those working in the judicial system. This attempt is still in its early stage and no conclusions can be drawn, as the relevant legislation came in effect only in early 2000.

The UDF government managed, with a systematic and a well publicised effort, to crack down on organised crime. The notorious insurance companies were forced to shut down when the government tightened the regulatory framework. The bullnecked ex-wrestlers who terrorised nascent private business and who were involved in trafficking stolen cars, drugs and illegal immigrants, have vanished. Reform of the customs service and an overhaul of the tax system reduced the role in the economy and the influence on the political scene of the shadowy enterprises which dominated business activity in the mid-1990s. Despite these successes, organised crime remains powerful, as became apparent when in 2000 and early 2001 several assassinations and bombings took place in Sofia and other big towns. Although this unusually rapid rise in crime mainly targeted figures from the criminal underground, the population still feels threatened and insecure.

But, while the government has thus far made organised crime the focus of its law-and-order campaign, it has not still addressed the issue of corrupt practices in public administration. On top of that, the clientelist trend in the party system has persisted and the image of the government has been severely dented by allegations of economic scandals involving several of its members. A prime example is the case of Alexander Bozhkov, one of the most prominent figures in the UDF, a former director of the Privatisation Agency, a former deputy Prime Minister, who had been running the campaign for Bulgaria to join the European Union, and who was sacked in June 2000 amid charges of corruption. (Along with him nine other senior officials and politicians have been accused of corruption.) To root out corruption, a national strategy should be implemented consisting of a number of measures in different legal and administrative areas. Decisive further steps, in particular, need to be taken concerning administrative reform because, unless there is an honest and efficient bureaucracy, new laws and regulations will have no significant effect. Such reform should include the liberalisation of the business environment, through the introduction of simpler procedures, in order to stop bureaucrats from over-regulating and to reduce the opportunities for corrupt practices, particularly among mid-ranking officials. According to the 1999 report from the EU Commission, further progress in the fight against corruption is needed in the following areas:

> financing of political parties, strengthening of the legal framework in areas such as public procurement, financial control, liability of Ministers, improving the implementation of measures in areas such as money laundering and creating or strengthening internal and external control structures in the administration and the judiciary. Transparency and judicial control should be reinforced in the privatisation field. (European Commission, 1999b)

In sum, it could be argued that the UDF government, hampered by the magnitude of the reform agenda and afraid of the political cost, did not live up to the expectations. Nonetheless, despite the delays and inconsistencies, it should be noted that the UDF government outlived all previous post-Communist governments and is the only to have fulfilled its mandate. Of itself it is a substantial enough achievement.

Democratic culture

A decade after the collapse of the Communist system, and despite all the above problems, democratisation has at least made some halting progress. A parliamentary democracy has been established and all political actors have agreed to abide by democratic rules, rejecting all alternatives. The constitutional framework that has been created is widely accepted, both by political elites and by the public, as the basis of the democratic regime. Political institutions, despite the problems described above, are seen as legitimate, and the plural party system that has been formed is a relatively stable one, allowing unobstructed alternation in power. The Bulgarians, finally, have consistently rejected extreme political movements and parties and have shown no anti-democratic tendencies in their electoral behaviour. It can safely be argued that, at least from a procedural point of view, Bulgaria has succeeded in becoming a democratic country. Yet the fact that democratic principles have been adopted, and that democracy seems at the moment to be the only formal, openly declared, game in town does not guarantee that this state of affairs will last, especially considering the problems and the deficiencies already described.

Although Bulgaria has achieved the institutionalisation of the new democratic regime, the institutions have yet to gain the genuine legitimacy which is essential for democratic consolidation. If democracy is to succeed, people should believe in its principles and there should be commitment to democratic values, acceptance of the legitimacy of democratic institutions and readiness to deal with political conflict through compromise. The development of a democratic culture comes as a critical condition for the Bulgarian democracy. Certainly the development of a democratic culture is a lengthy process that requires a great deal of time, sometimes even intergenerational change. Nevertheless, several factors have been delaying the development of such a democratic political culture. Incontestably, the failure of the political parties to come to terms with the needs of society reinforced the typical Bulgarian nihilism of the institutions and the state and created a situation where is difficult to involve the public in constructive social activity. In addition, the bipolar political model and the attainment of confrontational policies hindered the development of a democratic culture and the formation of liberal democratic values. The polarisation and the sharp ideological confrontation has even extended to the trade unions, which were very active during the early transitional period but whose political importance has since been in decline. The two major trade unions, Podkrepa and the Confederation of Independent Trade Unions (CITU), progressively lost their political influence as they were ideologically structured in accordance with the polarisation of party politics (the CITU Communist, Podkrepa anti-Communist) and failed to draw a line between political and trade unionist activism. Indicative of the trade unions' loss of political influence is the decrease in the number of unionised workers.[26]

But even the groups that were formed in the late 1980s, promoting human rights, environmental protection and religious freedom or reviving old political parties, in various parts of the country and with thousands of members, did not manage to involve the man in the street in constructive social activity. These groups were not so much the outcome of a social movement as a product of intellectuals, who carried on their activities in defiance of threats and actual persecution but who, it appeared later, also uphold divergent political values and social projections. Citizen attachment to these organisations was not so much a matter of deep psychological commitment and adherence to mutually shared values but an expression of frustration with and rejection of government policy. Hence most such organisations failed to retain their cohesion and unity (e.g. Eco-*glasnost* broke up into the corresponding political party, the National Movement of Eco-*glasnost*, and the Independent Society Eco-*glasnost*) and could not match up to the diverse new challenges of the political transformation.

They did not generally survive to provide the means of participation in the developing post-Communist democracy and failed to provide ready material for the construction of a select range of viable parties. The coherence of these broad movements and their apparent firmness of purpose owed much, it transpired, to the strength and unified character of the Communist regime they opposed, features of the movements that did not long survive the disappearance of their Communist opponent (Lewis, 1997: 455).

The declining performance of the state and its institutions is another impediment to the development of a democratic culture. Indicative of the general enfeeblement of state authority in all areas is its inability to control crime and corruption. In addition, the general mistrust of the state is the reason for the lack of commitment to the public welfare generally, and this explains why private interests tend to prevail over public. Another hindrance to democratic culture is certainly the strong Communist legacy of atomisation and egalitarianism, which is difficult to overcome. Bulgarian society had to put behind it the fact that for almost half a century it had lived without public politics, self-governing institutions, interest groups or rival parties independent of the state, without competing sources of information, with no vibrant civil society traditions, while every visible initiative and active enthusiasm was regularly set up and controlled by the authorities. The lack of the politics of trust, moreover, is another barrier. Because of the lack of a suitable tradition, the lack of trust on all sides, the lack of agenda formulation and the lack of negotiation skills, co-operation and mutual assistance between and among the public and state institutions has been almost non-existent and, even more, the relationship has sometimes flared up into open conflict.

The development of a democratic culture has not been facilitated by the performance of the newly established mass media. Albeit the independent media thrived in terms of numbers after the end of Communism (in 1994, for example, there were more than 1,000 registered independent periodicals for an adult population of 6.5 million, placing the country firmly in the European lead in terms of press pluralism) their services have been anything but constructive. Driven by political and economic interests, the media have been characterised by lack of professionalism or any sense of responsibility, by excessive politicisation, disinformation and the absence of ethical standards. The Bulgarian researcher R. Deltcheva reveals that the vision of reality presented by the media is apocalyptic, negativistic, paranoid and potentially charged with psychosis. Accuracy and integrity were subordinated to sensationalism. The predominance of sensationalist headlines as well as the abundance of reports of scandals, murders, sex and violence, and the high circulation of the newspapers which provide them, suggest that at this stage of post-Communist social development the average Bulgarian is not interested in an objective, informative press (Deltcheva, 1996: 312).

A positive trend is the fact that Bulgarians have not engaged in anti-democratic forms of political participation and chose to reject nationalist agendas, while the situation of the Turkish minority has considerably improved. That is not to say that the phenomena of racism and ethnic discrimination are absent. An acute problem concerns the Roma (Gypsy) minority who represent about 5 per cent of the population and are scattered all over the territory of the country in rural and urban centres. The Roma minority are discriminated against in all spheres of social life (education, employment, housing, social security and health care) and are seriously underrepresented on decision-making bodies. Access to health services remains limited, owing to remoteness from facilities and lack of participation in the normal structure of service provision, and housing conditions remain considerably below those of the rest of the population. Given also that the country's difficulties continue to affect the Roma population particularly, social exclusion is considerable and it can be said that the Roma are the most rejected community, being at the bottom of the social hierarchy. In some areas anti-Roma attitudes among the ethnic-majority population are widespread and the level of prejudice and intolerance is high. The Roma have become a convenient scapegoat for all social problems while sometimes reports by the media use anti-Roma stereotypes.[27] Considering the high level of the Roma population growth rate, which far outpaces national averages, the urgency of improving the status of the minority is apparent. The social situation of the Roma minority was identified by the government as one of the most urgent problems and some steps have been taken to improve their status. For this reason in 1999 the government approved a 'Framework Programme for Equal Integration of Roma into Bulgarian Society' and, although some progress has been made, in general the implementation of the programme has been progressing slowly. Still it is important to note that, although hostile perceptions exist, there has been no violence between ethnic groups.

Notes

1 The significance of the international factor in the initiation of the democratisation process has also been pointed out by A. Karakachanov, one of the Eco-*glasnost* leaders: 'the events which took place in Bulgaria were in fact a repercussion of what had happened worldwide and in Russia ... Left on its own, the ecological movement or any other dissident movement would have been mercilessly smashed if the year had been 1985, for example, and not 1989' (Melone, 1998: 43).

2 Adam Przeworski, as cited by Szablowski and Derlien, gave a more general description of the decay of the Communist regimes in Eastern Europe. 'By the seventies, repression had subsided: as the Communist leadership became bourgeoisified, it could no longer muster the self-discipline required to crash all dissent. Party bureaucrats were no longer able to spend their nights at meetings, to wear working-class uniforms, to march and shout slogans, to abstain from ostentatious consumption. What had developed was 'goulash Communism', 'Kadarism', 'Brezhnevism': an implicit social pact in which elites offered the prospect of material welfare in exchange for silence. And the tacit premise of this pact was that socialism was no longer a model of a new future but an underdeveloped something else' (Szablowski and Derlien, 1993: 307).

3 The statement made by Zhivkov at the 1987 Trade Union Congress is quite characteristic: 'let us duck for cover, lie low and wait and see' (until the turmoil of *perestroika* died away).

4 The *coup* was organised by the Prime Minister, Georgi Atanasov, the Foreign Minister (since 1972) Petar Mladenov, who actually visited Moscow just before the Central Committee meeting, and the Minister of Foreign Economic Relations, Andrei Lukanov. They had also ensured the neutrality of the army, as the Minister of Defence (since 1964), General Dobri Dzurov, an old supporter of Zhivkov, refused to back him.

5 The extent of the care with which the *coup* was staged is further shown by suggestions that the reform faction of the BCP (mainly Mladenov and Lukanov) was involved in secret negotiations with prominent dissidents and particularly with Zhelyu Zhelev. According to Petar Beron, early leader of the opposition and close associate of Zhelev, 'it is now known that Zhelev and the group around him were in touch with Lukanov and company before November 1989 and that they had negotiated the way of doing these things ... We had to support the new trend, the new wave, the so-called reformers

against Zhivkov and his associates. Step by step we needed to push them out of power. It was not possible to do otherwise' (Melone, 1998: 48).

6 Similar is the view expressed by Boyko Proytchev, one of the leaders of the first independent trade union, Podkrepa: '10 November 1989 was a *coup d'état* within the party. In November and most of December 1989 the party still had control of the country. We only made our first public appeal for a strike more than a month after the internal party *coup*' (Linz and Stepan, 1996: 337).

7 Almost immediately after his fall, Zhivkov found himself isolated within the BCP. Almost all his former supporters chose to abandon him and soon after his removal the public began to clamour for Zhivkov to be tried for all that Bulgarian society had suffered under his rule. In a largely symbolic gesture to break with the past, the new leadership decided to imprison him and preparations for a trial began after he had been arrested on 18 January 1990. Zhivkov denied any wrongdoing and demanded immunity from prosecution by virtue of having been head of state. Although his trial began in early 1991 with much fanfare and widespread public support, Zhivkov was tried only on charges of embezzlement. The trial lasted eighteen months and during that time popular enthusiasm gradually diminished as the public's indifference to his fate indicated that they had already become preoccupied with their own social and economic concerns. Still, in September 1992 Bulgaria's long-time ruler was found guilty of having misappropriated $24 million and was sentenced to seven years under house restriction. He became the first former Communist leader in Eastern Europe to be tried in a court of law, found guilty and punished (Engelbrekt and Perry, 1992: 6-8). Todor Zhivkov died in August 1998 at the age of eight-six.

8 In one of his last interviews Zhivkov himself admitted a strong mood against him in the party. 'After Gorbachev came to power I felt that he started to turn the Party against me. Intelligence information appeared that Moscow was leading a campaign against me. I knew that among the people around me there were some that "played" with the Kremlin … Here in Bulgaria there was an enormous army of intelligence officers working against me' (Zhivkov, 1997: 17).

9 That again became obvious in late 1989, when the new BCP leadership faced a series of demonstrations and the then President of the Republic, P. Mladenov, had let slip the phrase, unaware it was being video-recorded, 'We would better call for the tanks'. Eventually this led to his resignation and his disappearance from public life.

10 This was certainly in addition to the economic wealth already accrued during the Communist era. In fact the nomenclature had created a strong financial base outside the country. 'According to data of the Ministry of the Interior, in early 1991 Bulgaria owned more than 250 companies in Germany, Italy, France, Austria, England, India, etc. Those were limited liability and public liability companies, in which about $160 million were invested. Data from 1989 indicate that their turnover exceeded $1.1 billion. The fate of these companies remains unclear' (Centre for the Study of Democracy, 2000: 12).

11 For others Videnov was just the person in the middle, who had no control over these various organised interests around him, ultimately becoming their victim. In his own version Zhan Videnov blames what he calls the 'generation of Gorbachev's *perestroika*'. 'Instead of law and order they created a reality in which corruption thrived on disorder, while the President and the Constitutional Court were given a free hand against the Parliament and the government. Instead of a social state, they engaged in credit blackmail of the republican budget from every side. Instead of a democracy, there was anarchy in the media and in the banks at the expense of the citizens and the government' (Videnov, 1998: 8).

12 At that point Andrei Lukanov became too critical of reform failures and suddenly the former national saviour became the enemy. He was blamed for all that went wrong after 1989, and was ultimately removed by his foes. He was assassinated in broad daylight out-

side his home in October 1996. There is still speculation about the reasons behind his assassination, whether these were political or economic.

13 The central UDF slogan during the 1990–92 period was 'Totalitarianism or democracy'. According to E. Dainov the theoretical basis on which the UDF was formed was very naive. 'The idea was that the UDF covers the entire political spectrum from the far left (left-wing Social Democrats) to far right (revived pre-war authoritarian right-wing parties). It was held together by a single assumption which proved false: that in a matter of months the Communists, who were deemed beyond left or right, would disappear and the UDF would break up, its component parties covering the entire political spectrum of the democratic future. That was the theory, but of course the Communists instead of disappearing won the 1990 elections and since that moment there was a tremendous weakness in the UDF. It was formed as an entire political spectrum party of completely different people, which had to stay together, and this made agreement on an ideology or platform all but impossible, since the only thing the coalition partners agreed on was anti-Communism. This led to disasters in 1994, as the electorate refused to be attracted by anti-Communism alone, without a convincing governmental programme' (Dainov interview).

14 Ahmed Dogan formed the MRF just after his release from prison. Dogan has proved to be an authoritative but very skilful leader and an able political strategist. Indeed, some of the labels attached to him are 'the best Bulgarian politician', the 'iron hawk' and 'the politician who is bored for lack of a match player'.

15 Although the consent given by both the UDF and BSP to the legitimisation of a party based merely on ethnicity could be attributed to the political struggle between the two parties, 'the general feeling in Bulgaria is that the MRF and its leader were "creatures" of state security forces and Lukanov deliberately designed to keep under control the minority and assist the Communists to retain the power' (Katsanis interview).

16 Typical examples of such networks were the notorious 'insurance' companies. A car or a shopkeeper had to subscribe to one of these companies and put the company's sticker on his property so that thieves knew not to steal from it.

17 In this realm research conducted in 1999 by Vitosha Research revealed that 49.5 per cent of Bulgarians consider present-day statesmen more corrupt than the Communist regime before 1989 (Vitosha Research, 1999). In similar fashion a survey conducted by BBSS Gallup in April 2000 concluded that over 90 per cent of Bulgarian voters point out that there is corruption at the highest levels of the state – the ministries and the government.

18 At a Cabinet meeting in 1999 it was revealed that 400 large transactions in various goods destined for Yugoslavia were uncovered during the first embargo on Yugoslavia, depriving the Bulgarian state of hundreds of millions of dollars. The sheer scale of the illegal trafficking indicates the involvement of state agencies and people in the highest ranks of power. It should also be noted that Bulgaria is on the notorious 'Balkan route', one of the major circuits for the transfer of drugs (especially heroin) from South-western Asia, through Turkey and the Balkan countries, to Western Europe. An indication of the scope of drug trafficking is given by the number of shipments intercepted by the Bulgarian authorities. In the first half of 2000 alone, for instance, more than a ton of drugs were seized along the Bulgarian borders (Center for the Study of Democracy, 2000: 30).

19 This came on top of another Balkan characteristic in the Bulgarians' political mentality and that is the rather loose connection between statehood and politics. 'The Bulgarian people never had much respect for state authority, either because the state institution was non-existent during long periods of their history or because, when it did exist, it failed to cope with their problems. Hence the Bulgarians' peculiar democratic spirit: they respect local authorities, steer clear of trouble with local potentates but, as a rule, view the central government and the law as a brake on their initiative' (Pirgova, 1991: 33).

20 According to a criminological investigation from 1996, only 22 per cent of citizens polled definitely expressed disapproval of bribery; 43 per cent would, however reluctantly, have

given a bribe in tackling important problems in life, while the rest would have no compunction whatever. In polls conducted in 1981 and 1984 those rejecting the practice of corruption were 66–9 per cent, those reconciled to it despite their inner resistance 18–19 per cent, and the rest were 10–14 per cent (UNDP, 1997: 24).

21 On the other hand, the UDF carried out an unsuccessful pre-election campaign. 'The UDF entered the campaign with a high level of confidence. Assuming that if the populace were given the opportunity to vote freely it would automatically reject the BSP, the UDF sought to make the election a referendum on the past forty-five years, focusing its campaign on the past. Hence the election results came as a shocking disappointment to the opposition. Due to UDF's excessive anti-Communist aggressiveness, numerous tactical mistakes, weak influence in the countryside, poor organisation and the short time available for the election campaign, the opposition's expectations had been unrealistically high' (Bell, 1990: 428).

22 'In an atmosphere of rural–urban tension the urban intellectual profile of the UDF could not inspire rural confidence. Villagers feared that the UDF's anti-Communist platform would undermine their existing economic arrangements which, although distinct from the co-operative farm system, were still dependent upon it. Given the centrality of agriculture, this was no paranoid suspicion: the intense anti-Communism of the UDF and the close Communist association with collectivisation was a volatile mix' (Creed, 1995: 857).

23 Certainly the economic power of the old nomenclature has been entrenched in other former Communists countries too, but not to the same extent as in Bulgaria. A survey conducted in 1994 revealed that 57.4 per cent of business leaders were members of the BSP, while 19.8 per cent were former members, 19 per cent had no party affiliation and only 1.7 per cent belonged to a non-socialist party (Nikolov, 1998: 220).

24 Videnov was accused of favouring his shady 'circle of friends' and the economic group Orion in a number of economic activities which are still under investigation. Allegedly Orion, backed by the Socialist government, attempted to drown all other private structures of some importance in the country. In this way the Orion group, which united well known figures from the circles of the BSP, came to clash openly with the other economic giant, Multigroup, which is headed by Iliya Pavlov, a former wrestler who married the daughter of the head of military counter-intelligence.

25 Kancho Stoychev, member of the Union for Social Democracy in the BSP, expressed the opinion that 'for Videnov, to be in power meant constantly grabbing greater control over everything and everybody. He imagined the economy and society to be composed of wet clay to be moulded into any or every shape possible. From this point of view, everything seems controllable, and control itself is reduced to increasingly greater capacities to exercise pressure. Because of this, Videnov looked like an old-style Communist without really being one … And for this reason his entire tenure of government was just an effort to take over, subdue and conquer. He waged battle constantly and managed to turn everyone into an enemy' (Stoychev, 1997: 19).

26 A key feature of the trade unions in Bulgaria is that they cover exclusively the state sector of the economy. As they failed to cope with the structural adjustment of the economy and the reform of the state sector, trade unions have been in constant confrontation with the state, behaving in a militant way.

27 The most common stereotypes describe the Roma as lazy, irresponsible, bad parents, thieves and criminals. There are even cases of the media generating ethnic hatred by routinely attributing crimes to Gypsies before any formal investigation has taken place. Furthermore, in May 2000 the weekly *Zora*, which is pursuing extreme nationalist postures, published an open letter addressed to President Stoyanov and signed by a group of intellectuals and artists, portraying the Roma as a barbaric, inferior and dangerous group that poses a threat to Bulgaria's integration into Europe.

4

Economic transformation

Bulgaria is experiencing a unique period in its historical development. It is most evident that the shock of transition was, and still is, considerable. The hesitant euphoria over the expected and possible changes after the autumn of 1989 gradually gave way to sober disappointment. The transition from centrally planned to market economy proved much more complicated than it seemed in 1989–90, much longer than assumed, and demanded a high economic and social cost.

The initial considerations

The task undertaken

Political changes in Eastern Europe triggered the process of marketisation, implying the dismantling of a Soviet-style economic mechanism and the restoration of a capitalist economy, with dominant private property and market-based allocation of resources providing the basis for economic activity. Bulgaria, along with the other former Communist countries, embarked on the reform process with distorted internal and external economic structures, inefficient ownership structures, warped price levels and ratios, an enormous reallocatory role of the budget, low labour efficiency and productivity, large hidden unemployment, a limited centuries-old work ethic and lax labour discipline, isolation from competitive world markets and a heavy burden of debt.

Changing economic models meant the opening up of the planned and autarchic economy, the softening of the tight political control of the economy, the institutionalisation of an autonomous economic system and basically the creation of the very fundamentals of capitalism. The new regime had to break up state monopolies and promote competition; had to built capitalist institutions, banking and financial services as the financial system had to be developed as an instrument of exchange; had to clean up balance sheets and at the same time had to privatise and restructure state-owned assets; had to open the country to world markets, create links with foreign capital and restructure foreign economic relations. A new tax system, new rules governing the state budget, and a whole range of economic legislation had to be created. A change of economic system of this kind required major structural shifts in terms of institutions, ownership, modes of interpersonal behaviour and attitudes to work and the law. Wholly new institutions had to be created that were non-existent under socialism such as a stock exchange, a securities commission, unemployment offices, investment and pension funds and building societies.

> What made a systematic change of European Soviet-style economies particularly challenging was the fact that reformers could not rely on any of the elements of the existing economic mechanism as being adequate to the standards of a market-based system. Their task was to redesign this mechanism but at the same time to avoid a complete economic breakdown following from the progressive disintegration of their economic and political systems. (McDonald and Dearden, 1994: 282)

Moreover, the principal macroeconomic problems, which had to be addressed, concerned the balance of payments and foreign debt, the inflation rate and a tight fiscal and monetary policy, radical reductions in budget deficits through subsidy cuts and tax increases, the introduction of real cost and price signals through free prices and currency convertibility, and incomes and provision for the socially disadvantaged. In view of the country's low living standards, the social price of the transition to a market economy was a particularly poignant problem. Yet only by solving of this range of macroeconomic problems could Bulgaria create the necessary conditions to implement privatisation, restructure the economy and eventually ensure the overall success of the transition to a market economy. In addition, as a result of the collapse of the Eastern European schemes for economic integration (namely the CMEA[1]) the country had difficulty in sustaining its traditional channels of imports of raw materials and energy. Bulgarian industry and agriculture lost markets in Eastern Europe and the Middle East and the attempts to enter competitive new markets have come up against protectionist barriers. The UN embargoes, imposed in connection with the wars in the Persian Gulf and the former Yugoslavia, were devastating for the national economy and no compensation was received.[2] The war in Yugoslavia particularly, and the international community's embargo on Belgrade for forty-three months, isolated Bulgaria from international markets at the very time it was attempting to restructure the economy and reduced its chances of attracting investment. 'Moreover, Bulgaria suffered from the restoration of the image of the Balkans as a dark and savage place, too distant and dangerous for investment, trade, travel, and communication' (Nikova, 1998: 296).

Bearing in mind the enormous task of transition towards a market-type economy that the former Communist countries had to carry out (and despite the national peculiarities which imposed constraints on both short and long-term policies) the primary objectives of the transition were:

- Macroeconomic stabilisation, which was critical in order to eliminate the most dangerous financial imbalances inherited from central planning. Economic stabilisation also implied the initial adaptation of economic mechanisms (such as prices, credit, money supply, wages) essential to the capitalist system.
- Radical institutional reform based on the restoration of private property and market competition. This meant the elimination of the inefficient command economy by privatising the state-owned enterprises (SOEs), by inducing entrepreneurial behaviour and by making enterprises profit-motivated. This kind of change also presupposed the adoption of a new range of legislation and the creation of an appropriate institutional environment. Another important issue was the break-up of state monopolies and their replacement by new enterprises. Closely related to the previous point was the integration of the ex-Communist economies into the international market.

Strategies of reform: shock therapy versus gradualism

Since the collapse of Zhivkov's regime the major political forces have been groping for a way out of the economic crisis. While it was widely agreed that there was no alternative to a market economy, they argued as to whether the transition should be fast or gradual. The main argument among reformers was, from the outset, about gradualism versus shock therapy, and it was a debate more about modalities than about objectives. It was a major debate taking place all over the region. The two approaches suggested very different tactics at different stages of transition: a 'big bang' or 'shock therapy' as in Poland and most of the CEECs or a more gradual shift as in Hungary.[3]

'The main [theoretical] arguments for gradualism were: gradual reforms may be better prepared; and cautious reforms would be easier for the population to accept, thus diminishing the threat of negative social reaction to transition' (McDonald and Dearden, 1994: 286). On the other hand, the case for shock therapy was, in sum, that you cannot be 'half pregnant' and that with gradualism the economy is kept in a state of macro-disequilibrium. We should also bear in mind that the shock therapy model was the official doctrine of the IMF, the major source of financial support to most CEECs. Apart from the economic arguments, there was also felt to be a significant political argument for the shock therapy approach:

> it was expected that the major building-blocks of the market economy could be put in place quickly, while popular confidence in the new governments was at its highest, and before coherent interest groups resisting the impact of the changes could form. In the meantime, it was hoped that relatively quickly the programme would begin to show some positive results, thus demonstrating to the public in general that it was working and at the same time creating new interest groups of people who had gained or could expect soon to gain from the new system. This would then provide the political backing for further steps in the programme. (Batt, 1993: 217)

The implementation of shock therapy meant a significant growth in small-scale, private firms in the service sector, but this did not compensate for the simultaneous destruction of the old heavy industrial sector. These domestic developments, in conjunction with external shocks such as the dollarisation of trade and the loss of Soviet markets, meant rising unemployment and falling real incomes. As several scholars have pointed out, the fundamental shortcoming of shock therapy was its 'neglect of institution building, efficient corporate governance, the development and implementation of the laws necessary for a market economy, the creation of a modern and effective public administration, the development of appropriate social policies, and other tasks which inevitably take time' (Eatwell *et al.*, 1997: 8). Only now has it been realised that in real economic life a shock model of transformation is unfeasible. While a shock change of prices of goods and services, interest rates, exchange rates, trade and currency regulations and a shock abolition of budget subsidies is possible, it is not so with the most important component of the reform: the change of ownership. The same applies to changes in the institutions, the creation of a market infrastructure and the cultivation of market behaviour. Since it is unfeasible in real economic life to attain simultaneously such a profound transformation, shock therapy was bound to be rather equated with a chaotic model of transition as it resulted in economic and social chaos and in a heavier social cost. That is why many economists now argue that the costliest model of reform was chosen and that conceptions of economic reform in Eastern Europe suffered from being too heavily influenced by classical economic liberalism (i.e. Reaganism-Thatcherism), and that a successful reform was impossible without extensive state participation.

Consequently the shock-therapy approach has been attacked on two main grounds: first on the grounds that a radical transformation of the basic structures of a society in a few years is neither realistic nor feasible; second, on the grounds that shock therapy (as it was presented by the Western world) was not the one and only cure for the problems of the post-Communist societies because it did not take into account the historical and cultural characteristics of the different countries. For example, the historical and cultural tradition of Central Europe is very different from that of Russia, Bulgaria or Albania.

The state of the economy

The gravity of the economic problems indicated three main challenges: to stop the downward economic trend and stabilise the economy; to achieve a more efficient use of resources with the minimum social impact; to forge economic relations with the European Union, the United States and the international financial institutions. In order to meet these challenges there was an urgent need for a programme of economic transformation defining the problems, the strategies and the means to attain them.

Although macroeconomic stabilisation is the first and a crucial component in the process of market reforms it is not the only one and some may even argue not the most important.

A critical element in the success of the economic transition is privatisation, since it constitutes the central theme of ownership restructuring. It is important first to understand the repercussions of the privatisation of the state-owned enterprises (SOEs). These include the efficiency gain, the fiscal (price) effect, the immediate budget effect, the future budget effect, and the signalling effect. The gain in efficiency following the transfer of a state-owned enterprise into private hands is obvious, since the state has proved to be incapable of efficient management and since private ownership is the only adequate basis for a market economy. Besides, the state could no longer keep loss-making enterprises under its control, nor did it have the capital to modernise them and make them more competitive. The ageing of the industrial base, for example, had become more evident than ever: in the mid-1990s more than 70 per cent of industrial equipment had been operating longer than twenty years.

The price effect refers to the price at which the enterprise is sold. Certainly this is important for the finances of the government, but its overall macroeconomic significance is negligible. The goal of the economic reform is to create a vital market economy which would lead to sustained growth, higher standards of living and lower levels of unemployment. Hence it is much more important to consider the potential of the prospective buyer in these regards (i.e. the investments which the prospective owner is likely to make) than simply in terms of how much they are willing to pay for the business. These broader considerations have an immediate effect on the budget, which is basically represented by the potential reduction in unemployment (and hence social security payments) and in subsidies. The future effect on the budget comes later when the privatised enterprise starts to function like a normal market entity and pays taxes (as well as the taxes being paid by the employed workers). Finally, the signalling effect refers to the observation by potential investors abroad that the country is moving steadily towards a market economy and thus beginning to represent an environment for profitable investment.

Privatisation has responded to this agenda along three separate lines: cash sales of state assets; mass (voucher) privatisation; and the restitution of land and urban property to the former owners and their heirs. Additionally the flow of foreign capital is crucial for economic growth, and particularly critical for the success of privatisation because of its ability to provide the much needed technical and financial expertise, know-how and access to international capital markets.

Another important aspect of the economic reforms was the agricultural sector. Even if Bulgaria has become an industrial country, with about 11 per cent of GDP accounted for by the agricultural sector, agriculture was still regarded as a priority, mainly for its contribution to social and structural equilibrium, food security and agro-food exports. (For example, during the 1996–97 economic crisis, agriculture supported a great number of households and limited substantially the incidence of malnutrition.) Despite the fact that even before 1989 agricultural output showed a decline, with the winds of change the agricultural sector was seen as a motor of the economy because of tradition but also because of its lower fall in output relative to the industrial sector. The economic difficulties of the early 1990s made access to agricultural produce even more essential than in the past, moving agriculture closer to the centre of urban attention as well. Perhaps this explains the weight attached to agriculture and agricultural reform in the political and public debate. The main features of agricultural reform are the restitution of land to former owners and their heirs, the liquidation of the state co-operatives, and the establishment of new structures adapted to the market economy.

The first attempt, 1991–92

At the time of Zhivkov's fall Bulgaria had already been reduced to economic catastrophe as a result of the inefficient centrally planned economy. In 1990 the economy was characterised by declining production, growing inflation, growing unemployment, a large budget deficit, a staggering amount of foreign debt, energy shortages, collapsed foreign trade with traditional partners and a tangible decline in real incomes and living standards. Bulgaria found itself isolated from international credit markets when it declared a foreign debt moratorium both on principal repayments and on interest obligations.[4] The Loukanov government, at the same time, failed to take any serious measures to prevent the situation deteriorating further, and that was one of the reasons for its resignation at the end of that year. The interim government that was formed took the first steps towards economic reform and these were continued, after the October 1991 elections, by the UDF government. Economic reforms started, though, with a delay of fifteen months after the breakdown of the Communist regime.

In February 1991, in the face of galloping inflation, falling production, black marketeering and empty shops, and at the behest of the IMF and the World Bank (Bulgaria joined these organisations in September 1990), a bold and ambitious 'shock therapy' reform programme of tough economic stabilisation and austerity was originated, adopting market mechanisms. The primary economic reform targets were: financial stabilisation, curbing inflation, money aggregates and budget deficit deregulation; structural reform by changing patterns of economic behaviour through prompt privatisation; and effective economic governance by attempting to follow a coherent general economic policy. More specifically, the components of the reform package included:

> price reform to eliminate the monetary overhang and to correct distorted relative prices (some 90 per cent of prices were decontrolled);[5] the creation of a unified, flexible, and market-based exchange rate and the liberalisation of most current-account transactions; the abolition of almost all quantitative import restrictions and the freeing of enterprises to trade directly with foreign partners without the intercession of foreign trade organisations; the limited growth of nominal wages, so that real wages decline at the beginning of the programme and domestic demand is kept in

> check; adherence to strict nominal targets for the budget deficit and the restructuring of revenues and expenditures to reduce the economic weight of the state. There were three fiscal-policy goals: to reduce the budget deficit to 3.5 per cent of GDP (from almost 13 per cent); to reduce sharply the government debt to the banking system; and to reduce significantly the shares of GDP accounted for by both government expenditure and revenue, largely by a reduction in the redistributive role of the state budget. Price liberalisation would make possible a reduction in subsidies from 16 per cent to 3 per cent of GDP; the subsidisation of enterprise losses would be reduced from 7.7 per cent to 2 per cent of GDP; and export subsidies to former CMEA states would be limited to those under a trade agreement with the USSR. (Wyzan, 1992: 47–9)

The government's economic reform programme, which met with approbation in world financial circles, was in some respects a success, as it did achieve some of the goals it was supposed to achieve.[6] Inflation was brought down to acceptable levels (from 333 per cent in 1991 to 82 per cent in 1992), the monetary overhang was eliminated, prices and trade were liberalised and the lev depreciated at a more normal rate. The measures partially restored the balance between supply and demand, and caused a slight stir in market mechanisms, though there was a marked decrease in consumption. As a consequence, market supplies improved, queues outside shops almost disappeared, the deterioration of the economy slowed and, in addition, contacts with the international financial institutions were resumed. The GDP, which contracted by roughly 25 per cent between 1989 and 1992 (see table 4.1), with the highest declines in industry, indicated that some sectors had begun to show signs of recovery. Yet the continued drop in production, coupled with lack of foreign investment, led to increased unemployment (from about 100,000 or 2.5 per cent at the start of the programme to almost 534,000 or 13.3 per cent by September 1992), a decline in real wages, a further reduction in living standards and growing social insecurity. The struggle to move from a planned to a market economy brought widespread hardship and most of Bulgaria's indicators experienced a sharp contraction. Such contractions have been termed transitional recessions.[7]

Table 4.1 Annual growth of GDP, 1989–94 (%)

1989	*1990*	*1991*	*1992*	*1993*	*1994*
–0.6	–9.3	–11.7	–7.3	–2.4	1.8

Source: IMF.

As far as the structural reforms are concerned, the legal and institutional framework of privatisation was defined in the Law on the Transformation and Privatisation of State-owned and Municipal Enterprises passed in 1992 and with the creation of the Privatisation Agency (PA). The law provided for a wide range of privatisation methods: auctions, tender or direct negotiations, debt/equity swaps, public offering of shares, management and employee buy-outs and sales of separate parts of enterprises. The privatisation law prescribed a fairly complicated procedure for cash privatisation, including specific legal and economic assessments of the enterprise, a decision on the method of privatisation, the evaluation of bids and extensive post-privatisation control of the implementation of investment and debt repayment commitments. The Privatisation Agency was set up to organise and monitor the privatisation process and was responsible for all enterprises the book value of whose fixed assets exceeded BGL 80 million; the line ministries may privatise enterprises with fixed assets of a book value between BGL 10 million and BGL 80 million and the municipalities had the responsibility for enterprises below BGL 10 million.[8] The Czech Republic and some other countries adopted an entirely different approach to the process because state ownership was transferred to the privatisation authorities. In Bulgaria the Privatisation Agency performed its functions mainly in connection with the preparation and execution of privatisation deals for a specific group of state-owned enterprises but the Agency did not exercise ownership rights in them.

Along with privatisation, the government tried to ensure the emergence and development of a private sector in agriculture. For that reason the Law on the Ownership and Use of Agricultural Land (LOUAL), the basis of the agricultural reforms, was passed in 1991 (and amended in 1992). The main provisions concerned the restitution of land and the dismantling of the collective farms. Parliamentary legislation bolstered land restitution as the natural form of privatisation for the simple reason that the former owners had never lost their formal title to land, nor had the land ever been nationalised. As in some other CEECs, the collectivisation of land was not formally nationalisation and thus only a small proportion was state-owned. Land restitution is the process by which farmland is returned to its former owners (based on the situation in 1946) or their heirs. Proof of evidence of former ownership must be furnished by the claimants and in cases where documents are missing, witnesses can help to put forward a claim. Under the 1991 constitution and subsequent enabling laws, those who lost urban or agricultural property through Communist seizures were entitled to seek restitution. Therefore, although restitution is a form of privatisation and although conceptually it is neater than privatisation, its actual implementation can be complex.[9]

Regarding the dismantling of the collective farms the Bulgarian approach relied on 'liquidation councils' to manage the dissolution of the state-controlled collectives and the distribution of their property. Liquidation meant dividing the non-land assets into shares and distributing them among eligible owners, mainly the members or workers of the co-operatives. The LOUAL provided for the forced liquidation of all state co-operatives and the distribution of their non-land assets among eligible owners while the appointed liquidation committees replaced the management of the collectives. Liquidation committees thus were given two difficult tasks: to liquidate the collective by distributing the non-land assets, and to continue to run the collective until the process was complete. The principle behind the distribution of non-land assets was that those people (or their heirs) who had contributed land, labour or other assets to the co-operatives over the forty-five years of their existence should receive some share of the remaining assets.

In 1991 the Foreign Investment Act (FIA) was ratified, creating some of the most liberal conditions for foreign investment in Central and Eastern Europe. Bulgaria had already taken the first steps for foreign investment in the 1980s. Yet owing to the rigidity of price and trade regulations, as well as the state monopoly of foreign trade, the influx of foreign capital was limited. (Only thirty-one joint ventures were created up to 1989 mainly in machine building and electronics.) The 1991 Act granted foreign investors rights equal to those enjoyed by domestic investors, set very low entry barriers, imposed no restrictions on the forms of business activity that foreign legal persons may carry out, offered easy registration, liberal profit repatriation and uncomplicated procedures for buying foreign currency.

Other important legislation passed during the 1991–92 period included the Law on Commerce and the Law on Competition Protection while a securities and stock exchange opened in Sofia. In general it may be argued that, no matter how numerous the mistakes and the inconsistencies of this short period of time Bulgaria made a good start with macroeconomic stabilisation and took some basic measures towards a market economy. This effort was interrupted at the end of 1992, when the UDF lost the parliamentary support of the MRF and a new, technocratic government was formed which failed to push the reform programme forward.

Signs of recovery, 1993–94

The Berov Cabinet, which was the next to attempt to carry on with economic reforms, started as a 'moderate UDF' Cabinet, claiming it would follow the UDF reform programme and be a 'government of privatisation'. The fact that Berov himself was one of the drafters of the UDF programme and had also been economic adviser to President Zhelev lent him some initial credibility. But, without a popular mandate, with the parliamentary majority that appointed him reluctant to provide him with real power (several Cabinet proposals did not received sufficient parliamentary support by the BSP and the MRF), and with the UDF opposition adopting a tough line on the government, this period was characterised by the absence of an assertive economic policy.

> In 1993, GDP continued to contract, albeit more slowly than previously. Real GDP declined by 2.4 per cent owing to a drought-induced collapse in agricultural output. As consumption-driven imports rose and exports fell, the lower real GDP in 1993 was accompanied by a large current account deficit. The weak current account position in 1993 reflected loose financial policies and an appreciating real exchange rate. This policy configuration led to a collapse in the external value of the lev in early 1994. The adoption of restrictive fiscal and incomes policies in 1994 enabled Bulgaria to retain the gains in external competitiveness acquired from the nominal depreciation. With the narrowing of domestic macroeconomic imbalances and

> improved external competitiveness, a rapid and substantial turnaround in net exports was generated in 1994. Thus, Bulgaria recorded in 1994 its first positive growth in real GDP (1.8 per cent) during the years of transition. (IMF, 1995: 1)

Particularly after the signing of the Association Agreement with the European Union in 1993, and the rescheduling agreement with the London Club banks in 1994 (Berov's greatest success during his term), the Bulgarian economy witnessed a revival of moderate economic growth and seemed to be in a process of recovery.[10] This atmosphere of confidence was encouraged by the signing of another stand-by agreement with the IMF which resulted in Bulgaria enjoying in 1995 the highest IMF lending *per capita* of all the countries in Central and Eastern Europe. This agreement was made possible by demonstrating progress on introducing value-added tax (VAT), which came into effect in 1994.[11]

However, progress with the reform agenda itself slowed markedly during 1993–94. In particular, Bulgaria continued to have one of the worst records in completing the privatisation of state-owned enterprises. (Industrial SOEs still accounted for 93 per cent of industrial output in 1994.) According to the IMF:

> Bulgaria's record during 1993–94 in completing market privatisation, particularly of medium and large-scale enterprises, was poor. In 1993, 116 enterprises were privatised, but almost half of these were municipal enterprises – mostly small shops and restaurants. Completed privatisation increased fivefold in 1994 to 555 enterprises, but again the municipalities provided the lion's share (384). (IMF, 1995: 18)

Because the first draft of the privatisation law did not explicitly envisage voucher privatisation, and since direct sales did not prove to be sufficient to ensure quick and efficient privatisation, in order to accelerate the process the necessary amendments of the law were passed in 1994, setting out the main rules for the implementation of the mass privatisation campaign. The ends of mass privatisation were different from those of cash privatisation, as the former had less ambitious economic targets, but the political and social aspects were stronger, since it involved securing the support of the general public. By 1994 a Centre for Mass Privatisation had been created to take charge of preliminary work and the organisation of the process through a Czech-style approach involving the use of vouchers distributed for a nominal fee to the public. A specific feature of the Bulgarian mass privatisation programme was that it combined cash and mass privatisation for the same enterprises, while incorporating several concessions for employees. Two waves of privatisation were scheduled but the first began only in January 1996.

Similar delays were noted in the agrarian reforms. By the end of 1994 formal title had been issued to only around 33 per cent of land subject to restitution; without formal title, individuals could not use the land as collateral, subdivide plots or sell land, which meant that it was still impossible to create a land market. In addition, only 290 of the 2,385 liquidation councils had discharged their functions by the end of 1994, when the intention had been that all of them should have completed their work in 1992. Limited privatisations and delayed restructuring had discouraged foreign investment. Foreign direct investment (FDI) amounted to a mere $540 million in 1992–95 (though in 1994 it recorded a high of $240 million). In addition, bad governance and the political uncertainty encouraged the spread of illegal practices in many parts of the economy.

> Although there were no reliable statistics on this, numerous reports suggested that the tendency toward unregulated, *de facto* privatisation and corruption in state bureaucracies was strengthened. The political commentator Evgenii Dainov described in 1994 the paradoxes of the Bulgarian post-Communist society, in which the roles of the state and the private sector were in many cases the reverse of those in the West, with the state still dominating the economy while private companies had begun to assume responsibility for several aspects of personal and public security. (Engelbrekt, 1994: 22)

In this context even the limited public support enjoyed by the Berov government evaporated and elections held at the end of 1994 were won with a substantial majority by the BSP.

Economic collapse, 1995–96

The signs of economic recovery continued during the BSP's first year in office. In 1995 inflation was reduced to 33 per cent and it was helped by a strong currency: the exchange rate was 66 leva to the US dollar on 31 December 1994, and 71 to the dollar on 31 December 1995. GDP growth in 1995 exceeded forecasts and reached 2.9 per cent, deriving from both higher industrial exports and the rapid expansion of the private sector. At the start of the economic reform process the private sector's share of GDP was only 6.4 per cent, while at the end of 1995 it rose to 40 per cent. (Given the slow pace of privatisation, this was largely due to new businesses.) Official reserves increased to $1,389 billion in 1995. Economic growth had been accompanied by a significant increase in foreign trade. The foreign trade balance reached $500 million in 1995. This moderate growth came from two primary sources: large export-oriented firms, predominantly in the state sector; and a growing private sector that was concentrated mostly in services, trade, agriculture and construction (OECD, 1997: 21). In legislative terms, the BSP government focused on revisions of measures already ratified. The most controversial case was the attempted amendment of the LOUAL (requiring farmers to offer land they wanted to sell to the state first) which was declared unconstitutional by the Constitutional Court. An important Act was the Prices Act, which had no analogue among the transitional economies of Central and Eastern Europe, since it provided for government control of the retail prices of an unlimited number of goods by an open list of government agencies under poorly specified conditions. The Socialists, as M. Wyzan commented,

> in contrast with the former Communists in other East European countries, understood neither the workings of a market economy nor the importance of managing relations with the international financial institutions, particularly when carrying such a heavy load of foreign debt. That their ascendancy coincided with a time of

> favorable macroeconomic performance only reinforced the arrogance of some of their young policy-makers. This set the stage for total economic collapse within two years of their forming a government. (Wyzan, 1998: 109)

The economic growth of 1994 and 1995 soon proved illusory and unsustainable. Whereas the stabilisation policies and the liberalisation of economic activity were gradually achieving some success, the institutional arrangements and privatisation continued to move extremely slowly. Cash privatisation was significantly slowed down. In 1995, for example, out of the 584 privatisation deals planned for that year, bringing anticipated revenue of BGL 14 billion, only 309 were finalised, totalling less than BGL 9 billion of revenue (Minassian, 1998: 339). Bulgaria was making slower progress in privatisation than most other CEECs and, with a high percentage of the economy still run by the state, the economy was suffering from resource misallocation, losses and waste – features of the Communist system. (Of the 5,500 state-owned enterprises operating in 1992–94, 4,100 were loss-making, with the losses amounting to 21 per cent of GDP.) Loss-making enterprises continued to operate not through formal state subsidies but by receiving loans from commercial banks which they were naturally unable to repay. Apparently the commercial banking system was used as an implicit means of subsidising loss-making enterprises. As OECD noted, 'Bulgarian industrial enterprises enjoyed access to commercial credit to a degree that was unprecedented among European transition countries. The availability of soft credit not only weakened incentives for restructuring, but supported various types of rent-seeking behavior that siphoned state resources into private hands'[12] (OECD, 1999: 75).

Delays in privatisation also meant added difficulty in attracting investor interest, especially in light of the East European competition. Foreign investment in Bulgaria was already among the lowest in Eastern Europe. According to estimates, Bulgaria needed at least $1.5billion to 2 billion in investment each year but was getting ten times less. In 1995 foreign direct investment dropped to $110 million – 0.8 per cent of GDP – when the FDI/GDP ratio the same year stood at 14.7 per cent and 9.1 per cent for Hungary and the Czech Republic respectively (Rosenov, 1996: 14). In September 1996 the total stock of foreign direct investment amounted to some $719 million, a figure that was equal to 2–3 per cent of total foreign investment in Central and Eastern Europe.[13]

The failure to implement consistent structural reform, the lack of credibility of governmental policy, combined with a lax fiscal and monetary policy (due to underestimation of the situation) frustrated in 1996 the economic reform and actually erased all the earlier achievements of the stabilisation package. The problems started with agriculture, as the new co-operatives proved unable to secure the minimum grain harvest needed – the 1996 harvest was lower than the 1936 one – and this coincided with an excessive volume of grain exports. As a result, bread queues reappeared for the first time since the last years of Communism. Along with serious delays in addressing problems in the banking sector, the loss-making enterprises, the need to attract foreign investment, and with impending sizable external debt service obligations, these developments limited the scope and credibility of macroeconomic policy and helped to create an exchange rate crisis as the financial markets collapsed. The lev depreciated many times over, falling from 71 to the US dollar at the start of 1996 to 500 by late December. Every single parameter laid down in the 1996 budget exploded in the summer and autumn, as table 4.2 indicates, and the budget had to be redrafted twice before the end of the year. Bulgaria plunged deep into recession and the loss of confidence in the currency quickly turned into a run on the banking system: by September, fifteen banks had been closed.

Table 4.2 Key economic indicators, 1994–99

Indicator	*1994*	*1995*	*1996*	*1997*	*1998*	*1999*
GDP growth (%)	1.8	2.9	–10.1	–6.9	3.5	2.4
Inflation (CPI[a])	121.9	32.9	310.8	578.6	0.96	6.2
Unemployment (%)	12.8	14.7	13.7	15.0	16.0	17.0
Fiscal balance (% of GDP)	–5.6	–6.6	–16.6	–2.9	1.3	–0.9
Current account (% of GDP)	–0.3	–0.2	0.2	4.2	–1.8	–5.3

Note:
[a] Consumer price index, December to December.
Sources: OECD, IMF.

> By the end of 1996, Bulgaria had become the top contender for the title of 'worst-managed country in Europe'. During that year, inflation hit the 300 per cent mark and GDP shrank by a staggering 10 per cent – making Bulgaria a dramatic exception to the general East European trend toward stabilisation and growth. Between January 1996 and January 1997, the average monthly salary fell almost tenfold, from $110 to $12, while the average pension went from $37 to $4 a month over the same period. Bulgaria, a land of peace, actually sank below the economic level of strife-ravaged Bosnia and Albania. (Ganev, 1997: 131)

The deteriorating economic situation had serious political repercussions. The resignation immediately before Christmas 1996 of the Socialist government created severe economic and political difficulties. Street protests were accompanied by a dramatic worsening of the economy.[14] At the start of 1997 the currency collapsed and the exchange rate approached BGL 3,000 to the dollar. Retail sales in the first two months of the year were down 70 per cent in volume over the same period in 1996. In February monthly inflation reached 240 per cent and this short burst of hyperinflation left much of the population impoverished and dependent on emergency foreign aid – 85 per cent of people were below the poverty line. 'This also led to greater differentiation of incomes. While in 1991 the upper 10 per cent of the population disposed of 12 per cent of the incomes and the lowest 10 per cent disposed of 5 per cent of the incomes, in 1996 these indicators were respectively 32 per cent and 2.4 per cent' (UNDP, 1997: 87).

The political deadlock was broken in early February when the Socialist-dominated parliament, driven by the public outcry, finally yielded to demands for the appointment of a caretaker government in order to hold early elections.

The new beginning, 1997–2000

With the ousting of the BSP government, and particularly after the 1997 elections, there was a remarkable return of confidence and economic stability, especially as the exchange rate recovered strongly. The UDF government took office with a substantial degree of support from both the international community and the Bulgarian people, and with responsibility for continuing economic reforms. Working closely with international financial institutions, the government almost immediately introduced a currency board to provide a fixed currency on which to build a stable macroeconomic base, having also a strong social and psychological impact restoring some of the lost optimism.[15] The stabilisation effect of the economic policy implemented, stemming from the currency board arrangement, strict fiscal policy and improved financial discipline in the public sector, ultimately brought about a healthier environment for the recovery of business activity, output and investment. Despite the unfavourable international environment (mainly the Kosovo crisis and the turmoil in the Russian market[16]) the economy by most measures performed better than anticipated. Most of the recovery took place in 1997 and 1998 (particularly in the first half). Thus in 1998 the annual rate of inflation fell to a negligible level, interest rates eased rapidly to single-digit levels, foreign currency reserves increased from $415 million in January 1997 to $2.5 billion by the end of 1997 and to $3.06 billion in 1998, domestic state debt was substantially reduced (its total value, including government guarantees, fell to the equivalent of 22 per cent of GDP at the end of 1998 compared with over 60 per cent two years earlier), real incomes recovered and the country achieved its highest GDP growth (3.5 per cent) in the 1990s. The recovery of the economy was strongly supported by the international community. Hence total international assistance, in the form of official loans and grants, grew from $471 million in 1996 to about $1 billion in 1997 – an increase of 120 per cent. In 1998 this upward trend continued, with contributions in assistance totalling $1.5 billion (UNDP, 2000: 7). Although this trend was reversed in 1999 (the funds declined to $1 billion) the high level of international financial assistance shows the willingness of the international community to support the stabilisation of the economy as well as the country's dependence on international support.

In order to facilitate sustainable growth, the acceleration of structural reforms became the focal point of government policy. Addressing fundamental problems in public finances and in the banking and real sector of the economy, as well as privatisation, were recognised as the key structural issues. The government succeeded in laying the foundations for the rebuilding of the banking and financial sector following the collapse of 1996. Banking supervision was strengthened and the efficiency of the banking sector improved while at the same time measures to tighten tax administration and changes in tax legislation led to higher than expected tax revenue. A number of measures were taken to increase the transparency of fiscal operations and good progress was achieved in limiting the losses of state-owned enterprises. Important reforms of health insurance, social security and the pension system are under way and should further support the market orientation of the economy. The government's strong commitment to accelerate the privatisation process became evident as, following major amendments to the privatisation law, the pace of privatisation picked up notably in 1997 and 1998. In particular 1997 saw a large number of companies privatised as receipts from cash privatisation exceeded those of all previous years combined. While in the entire period from 1991 to 1996 less than 20 per cent of all state assets had been privatised, at the end of 1999 an estimated 47 per cent of all state-owned assets had been transferred to private hands, representing about 71 per cent of the assets subject to privatisation.

Despite the success in stabilisation, the accomplishments of the UDF government in structural reforms and a pronounced strengthening of confidence, major concern continues to be raised by the dynamics of several key economic indicators. GDP recovery became sluggish in 1999, exports slid into decline, the current account shifted to a deficit, expected inflows of foreign direct investment failed to materialise, while the process of privatisation and industrial restructuring showed signs of losing impetus (mainly because of setbacks in the privatisation of larger companies). A striking feature of economic developments during this period was the sharp decline in industrial production. After falling 12.7 per cent in 1998 industrial output was down 12.5 per cent in 1999, with the decline being evident in almost all sectors. Moreover the trade and current account balances shifted from large surpluses in 1997 to larger than expected deficits in 1998 and in 1999. In 2000 this trend continued, largely on account of high oil prices.

Although these negative tendencies do not seem to pose an immediate threat to macroeconomic stability, the economy is still in a critical situation, especially since living standards remain low and unemployment is creeping up to a record high of 17 per cent of the work force, with the trend rising.[17] External debt at the end of 2000 was about $10 billion and, for the next few years, according to IMF estimations, 12–13 per cent of GDP will be needed to service it.[18] The overall drop in GDP for the period 1989–99 came to around 34 per cent. Such a GDP reduction will be reversed only after several years. According to the government's macroeconomic programme, in 2001 the country should regain the level of economic development of 1995 and only by the year 2008 that of 1989.

It should be stressed, however, that, whatever the shortcomings, the economic policies implemented since 1997 represent a significant qualitative break with the past in many respects. Bulgaria still has daunting problems and in order to meet the enormous challenges that lay ahead stronger determination and further commitment are required by the government. In 1999 the UDF government unveiled its updated programme 'Bulgaria 2001', whose objective was the achievement of sustainable low-inflation economic growth as a condition of increasing incomes and improving living standards. Most of the envisaged goals and actions are regarded as realistic, although falling short of the strong and radical economic policy deemed necessary at this stage. The achievement of macroeconomic stability, which came as an immediate result of the currency board introduction, does not itself constitute a real reform. It rather provides the government with a stable economic environment to proceed with economic reforms or, as the OECD survey notes, 'it provides Bulgaria with an important window of opportunity to make up for lost time in structural reform, as the unfortunate delays of previous years impose a heavy remaining burden of necessary restructuring and institution building' (OECD, 1999: 8).

Three key policy areas

Privatisation

Bulgaria has lagged behind most other CEECs in privatisating state-owned property. Significant progress was made in the early years of transition in the drafting of ambitious legislation to facilitate medium and large-scale privatisation. But, despite the declared intention, the privatisation process subsequently stalled, hampered by specific interests, political controversies, administrative inefficiency and low incentives on the part of insiders as in several cases managers of state-owned enterprises created parallel private companies through which they then bought out the state-owned ones. In addition to the attempt to defend their lucrative and special privileges, some managers profited directly from the persistence of state ownership, as it helped access to various subsidies and credits. It is clear that privatisation procedures involved institutions and persons who were interested in delaying rather than accelerating the process. During the 1990s the privatisation results turned out to be a complete disappointment. Bulgaria's record in completing cash privatisation, particularly of medium and large-scale enterprises, was poor. Even the mass privatisation campaign turned into a 'farce' as only a small number of state-owned enterprises were privatised (while, for example, in the Czech Republic during the first wave of mass privatisation, one large and three medium-sized enterprises were privatised per day) and most of them only to the extent of under 50 per cent of their assets (that is, privatisation of only part of the enterprise). Besides, people have not shown any very encouraging interest in it. 'The final data of the first wave revealed that a little over 3 million Bulgarian citizens bought privatisation vouchers (6.5 million people were entitled to them). The deadlines set initially, the list of enterprises to be offered for mass privatisation and the shares for sale had all been the subject of various changes' (Minassian, 1998: 339).

There are several reasons for this delay. Not only did the unusually high degree of political instability massively infringe upon privatisation, but the lack of political will to privatise, the lengthy and complicated procedures which strained the capacity of public administration, the confusion over criteria for evaluating bids, along with basic problems concerning the low level of the wealth of the population, and the low level of development of capital markets, also affected the privatisation process. Other major stumbling blocks had to do with frequent rivalries between the Privatisation Agency and the ministries, poor relations with foreign consultants, the unclear legal status of many enterprises (very few had proper documentation for their properties), the fear that enterprises would be sold too cheap, the inflexibility of the privatisation authorities concerning the prices of the enterprises in the context of the real market conditions, resistance by the state bureaucracy and by the managers of the state-owned enterprises, and the incomplete, unreliable and usually out-of-date information provided by the Privatisation Agency to potential investors.

The bottom line is that privatisation in Bulgaria has suffered severe delay. Ten years after the commencement of the transition process, cash privatisation has not still been completed, and mass privatisation has not really started. Privatisation is only now entering a second stage, involving mainly utilities, such as power, heating plant and infrastructure, while the second wave of mass privatisation is still in progress. The major goals of privatisation were to increase effectiveness, raise the number of proprietors and create and promote competition, yet the emphasis had been on its profitability to the government and not on its speed (the Czech approach). This delay in privatisation had not only an apparent negative economic effect but also a psychological one on society as a whole. The psychological outcome was that people lost their positive attitude and support for privatisation and private property. This is important since, particularly after the economic crisis of 1996, an acceleration of the privatisation process, including sales to foreign investors, could serve as a crucial impetus to Bulgaria's economic recovery and development. To this end, the UDF government, in compliance with the IMF's requirements, embarked on a quite ambitious privatisation programme. In 1998 the number of privatisation transactions concluded by all state bodies was 671 and in 1999 the number was 1,101. The largest share of agreements were signed by the Ministry of Trade and Tourism (428), followed by the Privatisation Agency (218) and the Ministry of Industry (156). The total number of management–employee buy-outs was 539, while foreign buyers acquired thirty-one companies and three detached units.[19] The government also launched an innovative method of large-scale privatisation involving the use of foreign consultants, in the hope that their experience and financial expertise would increase the speed and transparency of privatisation deals, and help to attract foreign investors. In addition, at the end of 1999 almost all urban property subject to restitution had been returned to its former owners or their heirs, involving the restitution of about 25,000 sites. Although after the 1997 elections the political will to complete the privatisation process seems to exist, most of the other factors that delayed privatisation in the past still remain. The success of the latest privatisation drive is dependent on the degree to which the government succeeds in neutralising them.

Foreign investment

The experience of other economies in transition demonstrates that foreign direct investment may serve as a major engine for the acceleration of restructuring and institutional change. But in spite of the fact that Bulgaria was among the first of the CEECs to allow foreign direct investment in its territory, the country has not managed to compete with the other Eastern European countries in attracting it. Thus far, despite quite favourable FDI legislation, Bulgaria has not been able to attract foreign capital and there are several reasons. Certainly the fact that Bulgaria is geographically farther from Western Europe than the other CEECs, its small and poor domestic market and poor infrastructure and communications make the attraction of foreign investment more difficult.

Manolis Katsanis, former President of the Bulgarian International Business Association (BIBA) has expressed this view of the inability to attract foreign investment:

> Bulgaria is a country with a cheap, well qualified and well motivated labour force, in an excellent geographical position (in that it serves as a link between Europe and Asia), enjoying preferential access to the vast Russian market and, with relatively liberal legislation concerning foreign direct investment. On the other hand, as soon as a foreign businessman arrives in the country, the first thing he comes across is the mafia, the lack of firm government, a general feeling of insecurity, the inadequate general legal framework and, worse still, the inability to implement this framework. In such conditions, every investment can only be characterised as risky. (Katsanis interview, BIBA)

Indeed, investors are often faced with a clumsy administration and a leaden bureaucracy that surrounds investment activity. Licensing requirements impose a burden on enterprises while they also create incentives for officials to exploit their discretionary power for personal gain. Tax policies are often unstable and unpredictable. For example, twice within five years long-term tax incentives for foreign investors have been adopted and as suddenly abolished. As a result the planning process of some strategic investors was disrupted. Other factors having an adverse influence on foreign investments relate to: the political instability that produces constant changes in the financial and economic rules and procedures; the lack of long-term priorities and strategy in the reform process; the lack of trust and the unstable banking system; the lack of transparency in business–state relations; and, certainly, the slow progress of privatisation, since a large proportion of foreign investment concerns privatisation deals.

These conditions favour only small investments in trade and services, realising quick and easy profits. Accordingly, as of the end of 1995, 65 per cent of all investments involved less than $1,000, and another 22 per cent did not exceed $10,000. On the other hand, there were thirty-six ventures exceeding $1 million, representing 90 per cent of the total amount invested. As of September 1996 the average value per project was $101,000, almost three times less than in Hungary, Russia or the Czech Republic, and two and a half times less than Poland (OECD, 1997: 127).

According to figures from the Foreign Investment Agency cumulative foreign direct investment amounted to $2.7 billion for the period 1992–99. Over this period about 17 per cent of all foreign investment came from Germany, followed by Belgium ($425.8 million and $373.1 million, respectively). Industry attracted more than half of total foreign direct investment ($1.5 billion), followed by trade ($543 million) and finance ($324 million), while foreign investment in agriculture was equal to only $8.5 million.

Cumulative foreign investment *per capita* of the population remains below the average in Central Europe, though it now compares favourably with Russia, and is at roughly the same level as in Albania and Romania (OECD, 1999: 91). Despite the fact that in 1998 inflows of foreign direct investment failed to meet the optimistic expectations and their recorded annual volume turned slightly lower than a year before, the share of foreign direct investment in GDP was approximately equal to that in the foremost EU applicant member countries. This slowdown was primarily related to the turmoil in international financial markets that provoked the erosion of interest among foreign investors in emerging markets. On the contrary, in 1999 there was a substantial increase in FDI inflows, largely related to the privatisation programme, indicating the increased confidence of foreign investors. This trend continued in 2000 as receipts from foreign direct investment stood at $974.6 million, up 19 per cent from 1999, representing the largest annual amount of foreign direct investment since the launch of the market reforms. Nevertheless, most of the problems mentioned above concerning foreign investments still exist. As attracting foreign direct investment is a key policy objective of the government, with a view to relieving balance of payments constraints and speeding up enterprise restructuring, these problems need to be tackled, and in particular the bureaucratic barriers to foreign enterprise creation need to be removed.

Agriculture

What characterised the development of agriculture in the post-Communist period was the fact that agricultural reform did not manage to secure production, which fell markedly. Farming went through dramatic changes but, far from providing an impetus to the development of other branches of the economy, the reforms resulted in a crisis that set agriculture back twenty or thirty years. Agriculture is still one of the economy's most important sectors, employing about a quarter of the total work force and accounting in 1999 for 17.3 per cent of GDP.[20]

The main issue for agricultural policy in the transition period was land reform. Other issues related to structural change, particularly the privatisation of agricultural enterprises, to prices and to trade liberalisation. But agricultural policy, no exception from the general rule in Bulgaria, has been characterised by short-term measures lacking consistency and continuity, aimed at meeting internal consumption needs in the turmoil of land reform. Technical, bureaucratic and financial constraints delayed the reform process considerably. The general reasons for the marked decline in all the agricultural indicators, according to the European Commission, were:

- The deep crisis in the whole economy, causing a fall in domestic demand and reduced financial resources for agriculture (lack of individual capital, scarcity of credit and limited possibilities of subsidies).
- The fall in external demand, due mainly to the collapse of trade with other former CMEA countries.
- Failure to co-ordinate the process of land restitution and the liquidation of state-controlled co-operatives with the needs of farming, the slow pace of land restitution, along with delays in privatisation, lack of competition on the domestic market and the low efficiency level of the food-processing sector (European Commission, 1995: 28).

Slow progress in land reform reflects mounting political controversy, which, in turn, echoes many practical difficulties with the programme. Indicative is the fact that since 1991, because of the lack of a political consensus on agrarian reform and the many practical difficulties it has encountered, LOUAL has been amended thirteen times. The chosen programme of land reform was very complex, as the restoration of ownership had to pass through different stages and was a time-consuming process. Some 1.7 million claims were filed, on behalf of 54 per cent of the population, covering an area of about 20 per cent more than that planned for restitution.

The character of LOUAL was one of the main problems, as it allowed someone to file a claim without even a proper document or deeds. Thus difficulties in establishing documentation of previous ownership have been more complex for land than for urban property, since many deeds had been lost and claims significantly exceeded the acreage available. The process is further complicated by the fact that there were more claimants than there were landowners in 1946. At that time some 850,000 landowners possessed plots, and there were twice as many owners or their heirs with claims, with obvious implications for farm size and fragmentation. In general, the whole process of land restitution and liquidation of co-operatives was complex, cumbersome and extremely demanding of local administration, requiring a considerable range of technical and financial support. At the end of 1999 restitution was close to completion but actual legal titles had been issued for only about 25 per cent of the land and there is still no functioning transparent market in land. Agriculture is still suffering from the absence of market mechanisms, poor distribution systems, low quality of produce, lack of investment and the fragmentation of production and commerce.[21] As a result, around 40 per cent of arable land remains uncultivated.

The question is why Bulgaria and the countries that based their agrarian reform on restitution decided to 'look backwards thereby burdening themselves with the mammoth task of identifying who owned how much land in the 1940s and 1950s and who are the heirs of the original owners, to check the legitimacy of their claims and to re-register their ownership' (Davidova and Buckwell,

1997: 7). It is difficult to judge to what extent morality was the deciding factor but it is certain that the size of the constituency for restitution and the desire for an expeditious return of land to private ownership and management also weighed heavily. Besides, it should be noted that the ownership of the land never ceased to be in private hands: only the use rights had been expropriated. This restricted the possible policy choice and practically left no alternative for the post-Communist governments but to recognise the private ownership. This is evident from the fact that there was no real political controversy concerning restitution itself, as even the former Communists agreed on it. The controversy was centred on the way it was implemented.

So the pre-reform situation dictated the nature of land reform in countries like Bulgaria. However, the monumental task of restitution was much more difficult in Bulgaria, as the circumstances were more complex, mainly because agriculture was fragmented, with many small landowners even before the Second World War. An additional burden came from the whole political situation in the country with its structural and financial difficulties. The costly, energy-demanding and time-consuming process of restoring property rights to where they were fifty years ago was not compatible with the need to preserve and promote efficient production structures. As is very widely believed now, restitution, representing historical justice and equity, was put before efficiency and economic progress.

Appraisal of the economic reforms

The economic reforms and the economic restructuring initiated in the early 1990s affected all economic sectors and social groups. In the course of the 1990s there was a substantial drop in production along with a drastic decrease in living standards. Apparently the economic transition in Bulgaria has in no way been successful, falling far behind the example set by the Central European countries. But while the model of reform in all CEECs had the same origin, how can this economic differentiation be explained, with some countries making faster progress (particularly the Central European ones) whereas others lag behind (particularly Bulgaria and Romania). For certain, the legacy of the old regime was not the same in every country, and in this respect Central Europe had the advantage of more favourable initial conditions: an earlier start to economic reform, fewer distortions in the economic structures, comparatively smaller external and internal debt, higher credit and investment rating with the world financial community, less dependence on the Soviet Union and more active contacts with Western countries, better adaptation to the requirements of Western markets, a more advanced market infrastructure from before Second World War, geographical and cultural proximity to Western Europe, a powerful lobby in the industrialised countries, and a more skilled and disciplined labour force. Additionally, despite a less dire legacy, the reforms in Central Europe started more cautiously and stayed that way. In Bulgaria reforms were accepted and applied almost mechanically while the Central European countries adhered more closely to their specific conditions and demonstrated a higher governance culture in the conception and implementation of the reform process.[22] Economic reforms were presented in Bulgaria, from the start, with several weaknesses and mistakes, inevitably bringing the economy during the winter of 1996 to the brink of collapse.

The strategy

Although in Bulgaria the shock therapy reform model was adopted only for eleven months, the country followed a mixture of economic measures that was a rather poor combination of both shock therapy and gradualism, lacking consistency and continuity (for instance, rapid liberalisation of prices and restitution of land and urban properties but, on the other hand, mass privatisation never really came into practice).

> The combination of a primitive market economy with a still existing state-centralised economic system produced sad results. The implementation of free prices and an over-liberalised currency regime, while the state still possessed more than 80 per cent of the industrial enterprises, was not productive. This led to combining the faults of both systems in a knot. (UNDP, 1997: 93)

The structural, social and administrative reforms that applied in Bulgaria were only partial and though the centrally planned economic model was abolished neither a viable economic environment was created nor macroeconomic stability and growth consolidated. It seemed that the political elites just followed the course of events, absorbed by current events and related concerns, mainly because of the lack of strategic thinking and lack of political will. Or, as Dainov put it, Bulgaria 'had the shock but without the therapy' (Dainov interview).

Reforms have been characterised by the inactive role of the state and its ineffectiveness in the management of the economy. For example, the transformation of the banking system from one central bank with various specialised branches into a central bank and independent commercial banks demanded strong control over the emerging commercial banking system. Yet from 1990 to 1997 none of the governments succeeded in implementing efficient policies to prevent Bulgaria from reaching the stage of almost complete collapse of the banking system. The reform process was guided by the assumption that market forces would provide the conditions of their own integration in a spontaneous, fast and efficient manner, and it was further assumed that market integration would become the basis of the whole social system. On the contrary, this kind of economic transformation could be accomplished only by a 'strong' state. The intervention of the state was especially needed when the shock of change became more obvious. According to the UNDP,

> the disassembling of the centralised system requires privatisation of production capacities, reduction to the minimum of subsidised and inefficient enterprises, and the implementation of direct production investments on behalf of the state. That means not an elimination of the regulatory role of the state, but establishment of a favorable institutional environment for the implementation of the reform, namely modern legislation, control on the currency turnover, reasonable budgetary policies. No transformation is possible without the regulatory and supportive role of the state, as it is the state that must determine the rules of the transformation.[23] (UNDP, 1997: 94)

This was not the case in Bulgaria. After the rapid liberalisation of prices and foreign trade, producers were left unprotected, while they had to learn the skills of working in free market conditions from scratch. The same applied to the state-owned enterprises that could not function effectively as real market actors. The social security system also proved to be equally unprepared to cope with the tensions of mass unemployment and mass impoverishment.

The transition became all the more complicated as the transformation lacked clear objectives. The state lacked a concept and strategy of economic development and there were no short or medium-term national targets and priorities, no vision and no clear idea of the ways and means to attain them. The economy was left to its own momentum of market automatism. But even the concept of the market economy was used with meanings varying from socialist market economy, through social market economy to neo-liberal market economy, with each of these types presupposing a different approach to transition, a different distribution of the burdens and different outcomes of the reform process. The lack of such a strategy ultimately undermined the credibility of policy makers as people lost confidence in their ability to manage the problems of transition and have so far incurred criticism, disappointment and negativism.

The implementation

The lack of co-ordination, a piecemeal approach to the problems and the inadequate assessment of the actual conditions in the country produced unreal expectations and measures not adequately planned. So, for example, the overestimated expectations of the economic team that launched the economic reforms in early 1991 led them to believe the negative consequences could be quickly overcome.

> The development of a short-term programme in co-ordination with the so-called structural reform in progress would have allowed a much better and deeper understanding of the bottlenecks and the possible ways and means to solve these problems. The typical features of Bulgarian economic development in the past had been neglected too. The fact that it was more tightly tied to (compared with other East European countries), as well as more heavily dependent on the former USSR's economy was ignored. The outcome, therefore, was a macroeconomic policy which aimed at short-term objectives and did not take into account the latent short and long-term consequences. For this reason most of the unwelcome results proved unexpected and not officially foreseen. (Minassian, 1994: 343)

This does not mean that various instructions from the World Bank and the IMF have not shaped the actual course of policy. In fact, soon after the implementation of the reforms, the authorities commenced negotiations with the Fund and various guidelines were drawn up.[24]

> Doubtless, the IMF disciplined the process of outlining and structuring macroeconomic policy in Bulgaria. The Fund's missions turned out to be management courses for senior government officials. At the same time they transplanted the standard IMF wish to present the desirable for real, its cult for certain unattainable parameters, and its propensity for ambiguous justification of policy failures. (Avramov, 1994: 17)

Additionally, institutional restructuring and structural reforms were considerably delayed not only because of incorrect assessment of the situation by the ruling elite, but above all because of their lack of competence and skills. The main error was the underestimation of the relation between macroeconomic stabilisation, the difficult initial conditions at the beginning of the transition and the very slow progress of the structural reform in privatisation, the loss-making enterprises, the banking sector, the taxation and the promotion of foreign and local investments. The outcome was the rather chaotic sequencing of macroeconomic regulation activities.

To these has to be added the excessive ideologisation of many of the economic decisions. The policies of restitution of agricultural land and the liquidation of all existing collective farm units, that formed the main theme of the agrarian reform, provide a good example of the strong influence of ideology in the reform process. 'The strong ideological commitment to destroy the basis of Communism in the countryside meant that other available options for reforming agriculture (i.e. changing pricing policies, and providing the right incentives for producers without radical changes in asset ownership or in farm structures) were not given serious consideration' (Davidova, 1994: 12). Another example is provided by the BSP; while in office, sharp attacks against international financial institutions, such as the IMF and the World Bank (on the grounds that they infringed the country's national sovereignty), were an indispensable component of the BSP's political rhetoric, attempting to prove the party's determination to distance itself from the West and to conduct 'independent' policies. As a result the financial assistance from these institutions was frozen.

The picture of chaos is completed by the magnitude of the grey area of the economic underworld which, no matter how accurate they may be, statistics cannot embrace and describe. Observations in the country suggest that a certain amount of economic activity is not declared, since private entrepreneurs conceal taxable income and evade taxes on a massive scale. Hence, for example, in 1994 the private sector generated about 23 per cent of GDP, employed more than 30 per cent of the labour force, but contributed only about 5 per cent of taxes. These undeclared activities benefit only a small part of the population and weaken the role of public authorities and represent a loss of budgetary resources

(UNDP, 1995: 77). The damage from economic crime, such as the black market, unpaid taxes, currency speculation, deceit, theft and smuggling, illegal trading, arms dealing, violations of the import and export regulations and the sale of low-quality goods, has soared.

More serious are the manoeuvres of structures with vested interests that attempt to appropriate public goods or to consolidate former advantages, such as monopolistic situations. This sorts of 'enterprises', which are thriving, are not productive and their only real capital is the power they have among the political parties, the government and the state. This power produces the capital and the latter increases the strength of the ruling elite. But even more destructive is the fact that these structures are hindering the emergence of normal market conditions, of authentic market actors and of normal market behaviour, and even more they are affecting the subsistence problems of ordinary people. And still the gap between laws and their implementation is significant and has had a negative effect on stabilisation policies and restructuring.

This inability to enforce rules means that economic structural reform, supposedly a fundamental change in economic responsibility and decision making, can fall prey to special interests, corrupt individuals and organised crime. Some of the most serious problems with inflation of the prices of basic goods and falling output can be traced directly to the activities of criminal groups which are able to create and enforce their own 'market' rules and, as long as they remain unaffected by government sanctions, are able to make reforms irrelevant. As a consequence, the vicious circle of economic uncertainty and an inhospitable climate for private-sector development, stemming from corruption and an inadequate pace and depth of structural reforms, have combined to yield a disappointing economic performance during the 1990s. Therefore, economic development will depend heavily on strengthening the institutions and lowering the level of corruption.

Bearing in mind this context, and the great post-1989 expectations nourished by the irresponsible fostering of illusions, the Bulgarian people developed – so-called – 'reform fatigue'. Soon after the initiation of the reform process the country's economic state started to suffer from the typical problems of a market economy, and the first tangible results ordinary people could see from the transformation were previously unknown levels of unemployment, inflation, erosion of incomes and shrinkage of consumption, social and personal insecurity, crime, corruption and economic differentiation. Consequently the initial euphoria vanished fast and whereas in early 1991 even the most unpopular measures could have been accepted as a solution to the economic deadlock, since then a substantial change of attitude has occurred. The mishandling of economic reforms added to the fatigue and frustration, unleashing powerful destructive processes without giving rise to others sufficiently distinct and constructive. The expected and inevitable income differentiation turned into a dramatic social polarisation as Bulgarians had yet to adjust to life without the egalitarian habits of the Communist period when people had a certain security, guaranteed work and a wide range of welfare benefits. Business activity dropped below the admissible critical minimum and left large social groups without an income. Social, educational, research, medical, cultural and other services, which people were accustomed to at a high level during the Communist period, have been commercialised without the appropriate economic and institutional conditions. The alienation which existed under the totalitarian regime, and which disappeared during the euphoria, returned redoubled as the individualist approach to survival grew without observing the interests of other members of society.

Poor economic performance caused economic inequality as there are wide differences in living standards and social cohesion is threatened by strong regional variations in poverty levels. The Roma minority in particular are one of the social groups which have suffered the most severe economic deprivation during the process of transition from a socialist to a market economy. Poverty in Roma neighbourhoods is around 85 per cent, or almost two and a half times the national average, and the depth of poverty (i.e. how far the average poor person falls below the poverty line) is significantly worse for the Roma population. Indicative is the fact that 50–60 per cent of citizens receiving public assistance are Romani. Roma households typically display several characteristics associated with a high poverty rate, including a high birth rate, low educational attainment (including substantial illiteracy) and high unemployment. Apart from their vulnerable political and economic situation, most Roma live in social deprivation and isolation, since they have generally been among the first to become unemployed and, given their low skill level, have found it difficult to find re-employment.

Although the deterioration of living standards was not a feature of Bulgarian society only, as in all the post-Communist states the social cost of the transition was high, Bulgaria was hit harder than most.

> … the deep economic crisis, the decomposition of the old social structures, the transformation of social relations, the uncertainty of the present and the unpredictability of the future contributed to the formation of a mass crisis of consciousness. It characterised the way of thinking and acting in broad segments of the population. This consciousness has been marked by the dominance of material values, minimisation of expectations, limitation of personal goals and aspirations and by resignation and passiveness. The problem of individual survival turns into an existential one. This leads to a closure into the narrow frames of everyday life, to personal and group isolation, to social alienation and to distancing from macro social processes. (UNDP, 1997: 59)

The outcome

A decade of transition has left Bulgaria with a legacy of a negative economic growth and declining living standards. The failure of economic reform can be attributed to four major factors. First, conditions at the outset were less favourable than most of the other former Communist countries. Second, macroeconomic stabilisation policies have been inconsistent and, combined with uneven implementation of the reform programmes, resulted in poor economic performance. While more recent gains in macroeconomic management and stability are encouraging, progress remains tenuous, subject to reverses, and deeper enterprise restructuring and new investment will be needed to sustain productivity improvements. Third, structural reform policies have been weak; trade liberalisation, privatisation, institutional and enterprise reform, competition policy, financial sector development and social reform policies have made disappointing progress. Finally, regional conflicts in neighbouring former Yugoslavia have disrupted normal economic activity, further exacerbated the uncertain business climate and made access to Western European markets more difficult. It is apparent that Bulgaria has not taken the complete step towards a free-market economy and has made the task of economic reform much more difficult and urgent than in most of the other CEECs. It is no surprise then that, in general, economic progress during the 1990s lagged behind that of the Central European economies (although progress has been greater than in the Commonwealth of Independent States).

The Central European economies, based on more resolute and coherent reform programmes, a better-developed institutional framework, dating in part from before the Communist era, and more stable political conditions, are now nearly 10 per cent larger than their pre-transition levels. The transition recession in these countries lasted for some three to four years, and the decline in output was about 15 per cent of the 1989 output level, on average. At the other end of the scale, in Bulgaria the decline was greater and, as has been mentioned, it will take several years before economic activity recovers to pre-transition levels. It is important to note that the Central European economies also experienced high persistent unemployment, but the rate has broadly stabilised since the mid-1990s at a significantly lower level while in Bulgaria registered unemployment continues to increase. Real wages declined throughout the 1990s, whereas in the Central European economies they fell less in the initial transition period and had risen above their 1990 level by 1997. The explanation of the fact that during the 1990s some countries did better than others lies not in the choice between big bang or gradualism but between a coherent reform programme and wasted opportunities. In contrast to Central European countries, Bulgaria wasted most of the 1990s as the reforms lacked a sense of purpose and nervous governments sought to spare the population the pain of restructuring but instead condemned the majority of the people to a worsening of living standards.

It is obvious that whereas the Central European countries are in the vital stage of a 'second generation transformation' that will determine what kind of societies the new democracies and market economies will become as well as the path of EU enlargement, restructuring and institutional development in Bulgaria are not yet complete and thus, in its current state, Bulgaria has rather to be considered as a case of failed transition. More than ten years after the fall of the Communist system, structural reforms aimed at establishing a market economy have no more been realised than they were at the beginning of the transition, since the economy is still state-dominated and has a fragile financial system. Most important, Bulgaria has made little progress in establishing the legal and social institutions that underpin effective markets and provide the predictability, fairness and transparency required for private investment. It is clear that delayed reform has disrupted the economic system of the past without replacing it by a well functioning market economy with all its associated economic and social benefits. On the contrary, the way reforms were introduced and implemented over the 1990–97 period has undermined the belief in market economy and democracy as viable systems for the economic and social development of the country. The low level of economic security led to a tendency to equate political security with economic prosperity and social security. Therefore the long delay in achieving what Bulgarians were promised, and especially any new failure in the socio-economic sphere, may threaten the popularity and stability of the democratic regime, leading to alternative political solutions.

In addition, certain groups, particularly the socially disadvantaged, do not see in political activity any means of protecting their interests. Under these conditions there cannot be an active and vigorous civil society, at least in the long run. Unless Bulgaria manages to establish normal market conditions, that will allow a relatively even and unrestricted distribution of political, civil and socio-economic rights, the organisations of civil society will not have the necessary social space for them to develop, and the legitimacy of democracy will continue to be fragile and questioned. The more optimistic view is that after the deep crisis of 1996, with the introduction of the currency board that brought economic stability, and with the support of the international community, Bulgaria has the potential for sustained economic development. What is still uncertain is the political will.

Notes

1 Most frequently the dissolution of CMEA is presented as an external shock to the countries of Eastern Europe but they dissolved the organisation voluntarily. Certainly it was not the best possible scenario, as was illustrated by the fact that soon afterwards the problem of regional co-operation arose once again.

2 Bulgaria lost $2.5 billion as a result of sanctions against Iraq and Libya and, as of mid-1995, had lost $8.5 billion as a result of the Yugo embargo. This latter loss was in large measure because 60 per cent of Bulgaria's exports to Western Europe, mainly fruit and vegetables, were formerly trucked via the ex-Yugoslavia (Strong *et al.*, 1996: 28). Numerous appeals to the international community and various attempts by successive Bulgarian governments to secure compensation met with no response.

3 Hungary constitutes a notable exception mainly because, having made great strides in the last few years of Communist rule, the reforms were so much more advanced that shock therapy was inappropriate.

4 When Bulgaria's foreign debt hit $11 billion in 1990 payments were suspended. The main reason usually cited was the drop in exports and Bulgaria's worsened export standing with the OECD member countries. Against the background of the total depletion of

the country's foreign reserves, it was precisely that move which deprived a large number of businesses of vital imports and the country ran acutely short of some raw materials and fuels.

5 Only the prices of goods accounting for 10 per cent of the total turnover of retail and wholesale trade in 1989 were subject to state control: electricity, heating, petroleum, butane and propane gas, and coal. But in order to bring the prices of these energy products into line with world levels, the state introduced enormous increases. Thus the prices of foodstuffs (such as flour, oil, butter and other dairy products) climbed fivefold to sevenfold, while the cost of public transport rose by 1,100 per cent.

6 Western observers viewed the stabilisation programme as having been reasonably successful. Anup Singh, head of the IMF mission dealing with Bulgaria's case, visited the country twice in 1991, pronouncing the reforms to be sound and administered in a consistent manner. As judged then by the international financial community, Bulgaria was making progress – something that only very few people in the country could feel, because although the shops were stocked with a greater variety of goods, people were still unable to detect the benefits of a market economy.

7 This contraction produced a cumulative fall in GDP of 27 per cent from 1989 to 1993, slightly larger than the real GDP decline experienced in most other transition economies: Czech Republic 21 per cent, Hungary 21 per cent, Poland 12 per cent (IMF, 1995: 64).

8 These figures are according to the 1992 evaluation. Since then the threshold book value that determines which companies are to be sold by the various institutions has been changed several times. In 1997 the government, aiming to reduce the number of privatisation projects within the domain of the Privatisation Agency and to ensure that the Agency will focus on the privatisation of large enterprises of strategic importance to the economy, increased the threshold for enterprises sold by the Privatisation Agency to BGL 1 billion.

9 More scholars explicitly treat restitution as a form of privatisation. Yet others, like S. Davidova and A. Buckwell, argue that since the largest portion of land in most Central European countries was still, formally and legally, owned privately by whoever owned it pre-collectivisation, it is not possible to privatise something that it is already privately owned. 'The use of the term gives a wrong flavor, suggesting that through the land reforms in CEECs there is a privatisation of something (land) that is not public. The word loses its meaning if it is not used to describe a transfer (sale) of publicly owned assets to the private sector ... The case for calling it restitution is that the use rights of privately owned land had been expropriated from the owners during the Communist era, so returning these rights to the owners (or their heirs) ... The argument for calling it privatisation is that the use right had indeed been held publicly, therefore passing it to private hands is indeed privatisation' (Davidova and Buckwell, 1997: 5, 9).

10 The debt agreement was a fundamental political and economic decision of the Bulgarian state with far-reaching favourable consequences. Thus when a debt settlement was reached in 1994 (involving $8.7 billion of Bulgaria's total $12.5 billion foreign debt) the country was reintegrated into the international financial community. However, economists were quite sceptical of the country's ability to handle the terms of repayment. In spite of the substantial relief, debt service still represents a serious financial burden.

11 The introduction of VAT did not produce the expected results, as the level of collection remained a constant problem for the budget. As Garabed Minassian shows, 'the country found itself living in a situation of a paradox – its tax rates ranked among the highest in the world, while the degree of revenue collection (as part of the GDP) was among the lowest. In 1993, for example, central government budget receipts equalled 18.4 per cent of GDP. In April 1994 a VAT of 18 per cent was introduced and the proportion rose to 24.1 per cent. In the following year, although tax rates remained unchanged and positive

GDP growth was evidenced, the indicator fell to 22.7 per cent. In 1996 VAT was raised (from the second half of the year) to 22 per cent and tax collection was reported to have come to 21.1 per cent' (Minassian, 1998: 342).

12 According to the OECD, problems in the banking sector were central to the crisis in the economy. Despite serious efforts by the government to adapt a legal and regulatory framework for the banking sector, largely similar to Western practice, a spiral of 'bad loans' (non-performing loans) and refinancing has taken enormous toll of the economy underlying the financial crisis. The position of the banking sector continued to deteriorate at an alarming rate during the ephemeral economic recovery of 1994–95 owing to lavish expenses, economically unwise lending by many commercial banks and corruption. The proportion of the bank's sound loans was decreasing, while the proportion of doubtful and bad loans was growing fast. By the end of 1995, excepting one large bank, the aggregate capital base of the banking sector had turned negative, over 70 per cent of all commercial banks were classified as problematic, and losses were rapidly accumulating. Furthermore, new credit went to the private sector (in a very small number of big loans), which had no better a record of debt service than the state sector. For the OECD this is a clear indicator that commercial banks were operating under distorted incentives, contributing to the failure of 1996 (OECD, 1997: 7).

13 In *per capita* terms Bulgaria was trailing all countries except some of those of the former Yugoslavia and the former Soviet Union. Furthermore, CEECs can fall into winners and losers as far as their share of foreign investment is concerned. For instance, while in 1996 foreign investment in the whole of Eastern Europe amounted to $12 billion, two-thirds of this amount went into only four countries: Poland, Russia, Hungary and the Czech Republic.

Table 4.3 Average monthly wage through 1996

Period	*Lev*	*$*
January–March	8,723	118
April–June	10,728	92
July–September	14,323	74
December	17,920	37

Source: *Insider* (1997a: 7).

14 In fact the crisis was unprecedented not only in the history of the reforming ex-Communist countries but also in the history of Bulgaria. By the end of the year basic foodstuffs had gone up four or five times since January. The price of bread increased sevenfold, fresh milk increased in price by five times and the increases for meat, cheese, sugar, rice and flour-based products were similar. Fuel and heating also went up fivefold. At the end of 1996 the average wage was far below the cost of adequate nourishment of an individual in Sofia.

15 As of 1 July 1997 the lev was pegged to the German mark at 1,000 BGL to 1 DM. On 1 January 1999 the euro replaced the German mark as a peg currency. Note that Bulgaria redenominated its curreny in July 1999, dividing it by 1,000. The unit of currency is now called the 'New Bulgarian Lev'.

16 By June 2000 direct Bulgarian economic losses from the Kosovo crisis were reported to be BGL 136 billion. Losses in transport and industry were highest, while the impact on tourism was less. The main reasons were the increase in transport costs due to the disruption of traffic through the Federal Republic of Yugoslavia and the contraction of regional trade. The economic crisis in Russia affected Bulgaria mainly through trade.

17 Unemployment edged up to 17.86 per cent of the work force in December 2000, and in actual numbers 682,792 people were jobless. It should be noted, however, that unemployment data need to be treated with caution, as many registered unemployed work in the informal economy.
18 The burden the external debt imposes on the economy is shown by the fact that for the period January–November 2000 payments to service foreign debt stood at $1.113 billion. Bulgaria repaid a total of $633.1 million of principal and another $479.8 million in interest.
19 The reason for the large number of management–employee buy-outs is that the privatisation law provides them with preferential terms. Management and employees are given the right to put up only 10 per cent of the purchase price in cash, the remainder being paid in instalments over ten years, while other buyers have to pay immediately.
20 In 1996 agriculture provided as much as 12.5 per cent of GDP while in 1997 the figure increased to 23.4 per cent. Although this jump was mainly related to a sharp decline in industrial production, the situation of the agrarian sector has improved. For instance, the average annual income of an agrarian worker in 1999 was three times higher than in 1996.
21 With the exception of the wine trade, which has succeeded in penetrating Western European and US markets, agricultural exporters rely heavily on the Russian market, as they are unable to meet the quality standards of Western markets. Bulgaria thus falls far behind in the competition with countries such as Poland, Romania, Hungary and Turkey.
22 Compared with Central European countries, reforms in Bulgaria have been carried out carelessly. A characteristic example is pricing policy. All Central European countries launched a rapid and massive deregulation of prices. Yet several groups of goods and services remained with their prices set or controlled by the state (mainly energy resources, water, public transport fares and the rents of state and municipal housing). Thus in Hungary the prices of 10 per cent of goods and services were state-controlled and in Macedonia controlled prices included milk, car insurance, etc. Even advanced countries like Greece and Austria regulate the rents of state, municipal and old private housing. The Bulgarian government relinquished this function in 1991.
23 This line of argument was adopted by the BSP while it was in power (1994–97) but somewhat differently. The Socialists were advocating that because the country was in a crisis it needed a strong state to get out of it and, once out of the crisis, reforms would be brought in. Hence the BSP took measures favouring a strong state (such as the reimposition of price controls and budgetary subsidies) but at the same time halted the reform agenda.
24 According to Roumen Avramov, those guidelines were 'exerting political pressure in the Fund's name and presenting IMF conditionality as an exogenous factor for economic policy; cultivating moderate optimism over the second stage of any IMF programme, which imbues it with the necessary positive touch; a 'soft manipulation' of figures (similar to the former relations with the planning authorities) in two directions: a subtle adjustment of aggregates (GDP) so that they meet the conditional fiscal parameters, and shelving unsolved problems for the next calendar year' (Avramov, 1994: 16).

5

The 'rebirth' of civil society

In 1989 the notion of civil society was used by Western scholars as well as by the various opposition movements in Eastern Europe to explain developments in the Communist camp. It is not surprising, since the aspiration to civil society was born of the social condition of the Soviet system, as the autonomous and mass-organised social sphere was exactly what people most lacked and most desired. The content of the notion, however, was rather luminous and simple, as it came to express the end of the monopoly of state power, the monopoly of political and social organisation, the monopoly of truth and information and all the characteristics of Communist society. Civil society thus became an ideology, a political programme and a slogan and was presented as the main opposition to the Communist regimes, providing democratic credentials to those who were claiming to be part of it. Civil society was even seen as the driving force behind democratisation, having the role to challenge state power and gradually dismantle totalitarianism. Yet in Bulgaria that was not the case, since civil society barely existed and certainly was in no position to challenge the regime. Instead the Communist demise is attributed to a combination of reasons which have been analysed in previous chapters. Democratic transition, nevertheless, signalled the resurrection of civil society, which had to take place under unique historical circumstances of political and economic transformation.

In the post-Communist period the failure of political institutions to handle the reform process along with the shock of economic transformation had severe effects on the behaviour and the mentality of the Bulgarian people, who, once again, entrenched themselves in the family, leaving the larger social stage in order to survive the period of hardship. A declining economy, lower living standards and the everyday struggle for survival under conditions of poverty, high unemployment and inflation left their negative imprint on the development of civil society. There is no doubt that such a change in socio-economic and political life as that attempted by the Eastern European countries was bound to be reflected in all spheres of life, affecting even a citizen's mentality, behaviour and his or her own nature. Society experienced an acute crisis of values, since the old ones like equality and collectivism were invalidated and there were no new values to replace them.

> Under the new conditions of an emerging market economy and the necessary stage of accumulation of capital, the system of values proclaiming the superiority of the spiritual over the material, which had for so long at least outwardly governed society, was inverted to a degree practically obliterating the significance of anything which cannot be priced. (Deltcheva, 1996: 305)

While in the past the path to social success was relatively clear, the case now is that success is increasingly identified with material wealth. Poverty and wealth are perceived to be randomly affecting people, bearing little relation to factors such as intelligence, hard work, education and skills. Most people feel underestimated, deprived and disoriented in a society in which individual effort and capacity do not offer greater chances of success. The process of creating a market economy and capitalist structures, then, weakened the elements of civil society that were developing already under unfavourable conditions. The fact that the collapse of the Communist system only brought about a worsening of people's material conditions and a widespread social crisis certainly had a direct effect on the participation process and discouraged political involvement.

One of the most important and difficult of the tasks undertaken in Bulgaria is the transformation of the nation into a society in which the citizens not only expect the state to do certain work but also expect to become an integral part of that state. Following the demise of the Communist system, the active role of the state in society was reduced and other sectors of the community were called upon to fill the void. As more power has devolved to local communities, people must be given opportunities to be active participants in society, to shape that society, and this is exactly the role of the non-governmental organisations (NGOs): to provide these opportunities to people to become citizens, to bring citizens into active engagement with public life, to encourage citizen activism and to facilitate civil co-operation. A widely accepted NGO definition is that of an organisation

> which is formally constituted, non-governmental, self-governing, non-profit (i.e. not organised chiefly for business purposes), not overly partisan (in a party political sense), characterised by some degree of voluntary involvement and may be membership or non-membership based. This is a broad scope including international, national and grass-roots organisations; special interest organisations, networks, service providers and public service contractors; funding, operational and advocacy NGOs; professional associations, community associations, co-operatives and membership organisations of the poor, and many other categories. (Clark, 1995: 600)

The significance of such organisations is enormous for a democratic society because they foster democratic principles, they encourage civil participation, they educate and sensitise the public as to their rights and entitlements, they strive for the creation of a more sustainable environment, they close the gap between governmental programmes and public need by seeking to influence state policy, they help to set the political agenda, to realise this agenda or to thwart its implementation, to nurture the beliefs and actions of individuals, to change the attitudes and practices of governmental and local officials and to serve as a check and balance to state power. These purposes are best served when such organisations have a broad popular base and their activities are not embraced by just a narrow circle of people. Civic associations of this sort usually promote grass-roots participation and deliberation, and most frequently have a purpose oriented to what they take as the wider public good. Furthermore, as Clark indicates, NGOs have achieved importance for various reasons:

> their ability to reach the people especially in inaccessible areas; their capacity for innovation and experimentation, which are difficult for official agencies; their representivity – often having close links with poor communities; and their skills of participation. Moreover, their resources are largely additional, and they not only 'fill in the gaps' but serve as a response to failures in the public and private sectors. (Clark, 1995: 595)

In a country like Bulgaria, where people are still learning to practise democracy and civil society is in an embryonic form, these associations gain even more importance. Particularly since replication is one of the most powerful mechanisms for the dissemination of civil activities. 'Once collective action has proved successful in one field, its practice is likely to spread. Organising and administration skills become more widely held, and the level of trust and sense of community – so crucial to a viable civil society – increase' (Hadenius and Uggla, 1996: 1624). It is becoming evident then that an examination of how successful the NGOs have been thus far in Bulgaria would give a rather clear idea of how viable civil society currently is and of its future prospects.

The general setting

The third sector in Bulgaria includes organisations of various origins, backgrounds, motivations and functions covering all possible fields of action; there are organisations left over from the previous regime, organisations associated with the 1989 developments or others that were established after the democratic change; organisations operating on a national, regional or local level; grass-roots organisations, research centres, political foundations, professional and business associations; NGOs working on the promotion of local civil initiatives, decision making and policy advice, human rights protection, youth, environmental protection, classic charities, local government, information provision, security and international affairs.

Amid such a diversity it is extremely difficult to come up with even an approximate estimation of the number of NGOs in existence. More than 6,000 are legally registered, yet this figure is not reliable. The difficulty of establishing a relatively accurate figure of the number of NGOs is mainly due to the fact that the legislation under which the NGOs are registered (the Persons and Family Act) dates from 1933. This legal framework, which never ceased to be active during the Communist period, is quite inclusive and broad, as it treats all types of organisations in the same way. For example, charity organisations are treated exactly the same way and under the same regulations as tennis clubs. Under these circumstances it is no surprise that, by the end of 1996, the majority of the registered NGOs were in sports, leisure and entertainment (21.8 per cent), followed by professional and branch associations (19.2 per cent). The proportion of associations and foundations in culture and the arts was way behind (10 per cent), along with those in social security and welfare (9.5 per cent), education and research (9 per cent), environmental protection (6.9 per cent), health care (4.1 per cent), human and minority rights (4.1 per cent) and international co-operation (3 per cent) (Task Force, 1997: 13).

Still, the lack of a legal clarity is only one of the reasons for the confused situation in the third sector. It is widely accepted that several organisations, registered as NGOs, serve as fronts for profit activities (even for illegal trade) or have been established by businesses to dodge taxes. That was the case particularly in the early 1990s when there were businesses, that took advantage of the legislation that allowed the NGOs to import goods without paying customs dues, discrediting the whole NGO sector.

> In the early 1990s, tax legislation – and lack of practical experience – led to massive abuse of NGO status. A number of Foundations became notorious for using legal loopholes to engage in tax-free and duty-free business, mostly imports of alcohol, tobacco products, household electronic goods. Serious misappropriation of funds also took place. Since 1993 this wave of bad publicity – which gave the very word 'foundation' a troublesome ring – has been retreating following not only the tightening of legislation, but also a change of practices in the NGO sector.[1] (Task Force, 1997: 44)

But if it is difficult to estimate their number, it is almost impossible to identify accurately how many of the registered NGOs are active. Arguably, there are a lot more registered organisations than there are active ones. It is estimated that the organisations which actively operate are no more than 400–500 while the others exist more or less on paper. The phenomenon of fewer active than registered NGOs can be seen in other countries, though certainly not to the same extent. In Bulgaria this differentiation could be explained again by the lack of an adequate legal framework and by the fact that the overwhelming majority of the NGOs operate not on a professional level but on a project basis. Therefore the operational basis of the NGOs itself makes it difficult to estimate their number, particularly the number of really active ones.

As the primary role of the NGOs is to stimulate citizen participation by providing the public with opportunities to undertake civil initiatives, NGOs need a broad popular base. The findings of a survey on popular attitudes to NGOs, conducted in late 1996 (and compared with a similar one conducted in 1994), are indicative of the level of integration of NGOs into public life and of the extent to which people generally trust them and of the reputation NGOs have managed to earn themselves. Unreservedly favourable perceptions of third-sector related concepts ranged between 13 per cent and 25 per cent, and completely unfavorable ones between 4 per cent and 5 per cent. There was an overall decline in negative attitudes, and a growth of positive attitudes to NGOs over the period in question between April 1994 and December 1996, a tendency which has continued since. Foundations were the most negatively perceived, mainly because foundations were associated with past disclosures of unlawful business operations, while the politically loaded terms 'political party', 'trade union' and 'artistic union' have been discredited in the public consciousness. On the contrary, charitable organisations enjoyed the highest rate of approval (Centre for the Study of Democracy, 1998).

A more favourable perception of third sector related terms was characteristic of the younger respondents, students, town residents, and those from the higher income groups. On the other hand the socially disadvantaged, such as older respondents, non-working retired and handicapped persons, those living in villages and respondents from the lower income groups displayed a more negative attitude towards the NGOs. The third sector still did not appear to be very prominent in public consciousness, in fact it was largely unfamiliar to the general public. Of those surveyed, 72.6 per cent failed to name a single organisation. Of all respondents (1,561) only ten listed four names, and three actually named five third sector associations. As a result of the low public awareness of the activities of charitable organisations, foundations and civic associations, only two in 100 respondents had ever turned for help to such organisations. There has been, however, a noticeable rise in optimism and confidence in the potential of NGOs. Students, the employed and town residents were most confident that NGOs were capable of influencing decision making in key areas for the country. Young people were the most supportive and believed to the greatest extent in the competence and resources of NGOs. Respondents generally saw the best opportunities for real influence and positive action on the part of NGOs in spheres and activities in which the state was no longer in a position to maintain its position – notably, in social and environmental issues. Nevertheless, the ability of NGOs to address major social problems, especially in the areas of health care, education, public order and transport, was limited (Centre for the Study of Democracy, 1998). The findings in general suggest that there is a favourable environment for fostering broader third sector support, which could be achieved by NGOs through more effective steps to inform the public of their activities and by having greater transparency to their activities.

Bulgarian tradition

This favourable environment is reinforced by the Bulgarian civic tradition dating back to the nineteenth century (something very typical of many of the countries in the region), particularly since tradition is one of the factors that affects the level of civic association development and the degree to which the NGO potential is realised. In Bulgaria prior to Communism there was a tradition, in self-help initiatives and charitable activities, which can be traced back to the time of Turkish domination and national revival. In that period, with the absence of any official institution and particularly with the absence of a state and a central government, local communities created social groups in the form of self-organisation. That was the so-called *chitalishte* (literally, reading room), where community centres, that had all the characteristics of civil associations, were preserving the culture, the national identity and religion. The establishment of this kind of social club in Bulgarian communities was widespread. It is widely recognised that the cultural and educational revival that led Bulgarians to question Turkish domination and later to national independence, would have been impossible without personal initiatives and the *chitalishte*. The *chitalishte* could stage lectures, meetings, theatrical and musical performances, debates and other social events, promoted charitable activities and introduced European ideas to pre-modern Bulgarian society.

The educational and cultural role of the self-constituted communities was significant.

> The Bulgarian school owes its existence and development to personal initiative revealed either by individual Bulgarians, or by private Bulgarian communities ... In Bulgaria, schools were founded and supported by generous individuals, wealthy benefactors, parish communities, and various cultural organisations ... Personal initiative was responsible for every line of work connected with education, i.e., literature, printing-presses, publishing enterprise, etc. (Mishew, 1971: 365)

An illustration of this statement is the foundation of the Bulgarian Learned Society (later renamed the Bulgarian Academy of Sciences) which was founded in the years of Turkish occupation (1869) outside the Bulgarian lands (in Romania) in the absence of a Bulgarian state. It was created by ardent Bulgarian patriots and its expenses were met by voluntary contributions from individuals and the Bulgarian communities in Romania and Russia.

The *chitalishte* had also a central role in promoting individual participation in social activities and influenced the modernisation of the patriarchal and amorphous Bulgarian society. The writer and activist Stilian Chilingirov pointed out in 1911:

> Not only did *chitalishte* play the role of a cultural-educational institution, but also of a club, where every Bulgarian, regardless of status, could share his views on public issues of local and national importance, discuss ways and means and make decisions for common activity and struggle. However, the *chitalishte* greatest achievement was elsewhere: as a national civil club, it united the population around one ideal – that of public interest, local and national; fostering national awareness, encouraging the strive for public and personal freedom, the Bulgarian *chitalishte* was the source of a huge public wave which swept spiritual slavery; it made the nest where the democratic spirit of Bulgarian society grew. (UNDP, 2000: 16)

It has to be pointed out, however, that, although civic initiatives acquired importance during the era of the national revival (in the absence of a central authority), ever since the establishment of the state the activities of these organisations and associations has remained limited, since the direct intervention of the mechanisms of state in public life was extensive and, as has been argued in Chapter 2, the centralisation of public affairs characterised pre-war Bulgarian society.

After independence, therefore, despite the establishment of civic organisations such as trade unions, chambers of trade and industry, youth organisations, co-operative unions, charities and professional organisations, civil society remained ineffective. That is particularly true considering that these organisations never eluded the indirect control of the state and the palace and their efforts were never meant to win autonomy from the respective state institutions. The trend of centralisation reached its peak during the Communist period that followed, and hence whatever tradition these organisations created was destroyed after 1944. It is apparent, given this past experience, that local communities have the ability to, and potentially could, play a crucial role in developing civil society activities. The loss of the tradition of civic initiative and voluntary civic participation has emerged as the most serious problem of the transition from totalitarian regime to democratic society. Reviving the pre-war civic traditions is perhaps the greatest challenge for post-Communist Bulgaria.

The conditions

The formation of the NGO sector commenced in 1989, immediately after the fall of Zhivkov's regime, so that by the early 1990s several NGOs were already operating in various fields of activity and in various parts of the country, though mainly in Sofia. With no experience of how to run an NGO, with only marginal financial and technical support, with no real knowledge of what civil society is or its potential, these NGOs managed to survive, and even to achieve their objectives, because they were based on the willingness and determination of the people to contribute to and work for the democratisation of the country. The excitement and the enthusiasm about the working of democracy was evident in various forms of political activity such as electoral participation, civil protests and the existence of a remarkably high number of political parties and independent media. Moreover during this period the NGOs were in a position to influence the political process to some extent.

This situation, nevertheless, changed as the country's political and economic problems took their toll and left a negative imprint on the further development of the NGOs. By 1993 Bulgarian people had realised that not everything about democracy is ideal; in particular the high social cost that accompanied democratisation discouraged involvement and any commitment to further change. Instead of creating more favourable conditions for the development of civil society, as had been largely expected, economic reforms, as they were implemented, at least in the short term, had the opposite effect. The reforms introduced inequality to a society that, as has been suggested, felt rather comfortable with the egalitarianism of the Communist era, thus disturbing people's traditional social notions and positions. Nascent civil society had to function in an atmosphere of social erosion, facing threats from sources of incivility such as poverty, unemployment and criminality. As people responded by retreating once again to their private sphere a new atomised society was created, reluctant to engage in civil activity and leaving no room for the development of civic organisations. As a result the number of newly founded NGOs decreased. While the deep legacy of alienation, along with political instability, the redefinition of the role of the state and its inadequate performance, the limited dimension of the private sector and the economic hardships of the post-Communist period drove Bulgarian people away from political participation, the developing civil society has to reverse this trend by promoting citizen activism. Better understanding of how the political and economic conditions affected the development of civil society is provided by examining the environmental movement, which was very active in the transition period.

The environmental movement

As has been discussed, the Communist legacy on the environmental front was one of the heavier burdens of post-Communist Bulgaria as rapid industrialisation was accomplished with little thought for the impact on the environment.

> As a result of shortsighted industrial development policies, in 1989 forty-one per cent of the population of Bulgaria lived in regions with poor air quality. Emissions of sulphur oxides were nine times greater than the world average while emissions of nitrogen oxides were twice the world average. Forty-seven per cent of the total length of rivers in Bulgaria was contaminated with pollutants from power stations, and with industrial, agricultural and domestic waste. In the 1980s about 1.2 million hectares of arable land were damaged by water or wind erosion, acid rains and salination. About 48,000 hectares were polluted with heavy metals up to levels far above permitted concentration. 1.1 million persons lived in areas where the level of environmental pollution was as high as in the most polluted regions of Central Europe. (UNDP, 1995: 61)

Such was the Communist legacy of extensive industrialisation that it is expected to take decades and considerable resources to restore the environmental balance. At the end of the 1980s public discontent with the grave environmental problems the country faced and with the totalitarian system as a whole led to the establishment of the Committee for the Ecological Protection of Russe and the independent association Eco-*glasnost*[2]. These organisations played an instrumental role toppling the Communist regime as environmentalism provided a channel for political struggle. A number of NGOs such as Green Balkans and the Bulgarian Society for the Protection of Birds subsequently emerged.

After the change, and despite the adversity of the transition period and the general economic crisis affecting the country, in early 1992 the government adopted a National Environmental Action Plan with the main objective of supporting the implementation of a national environmental policy by providing financial assistance to municipalities, companies and research institutions.[3]

This was the period when the environmental NGOs were influential and the contribution by both NGOs and various Green parties was significant and extensive in the drafting of this legislation. Further examples of such influence include the Environmental Protection Law, the Solid Waste Law, the Local Government and Local Administration Law and regulations on the collection, transportation, storage and neutralisation of hazardous wastes. Yet the situation was bound to change.

After a flourishing period for the environmental NGOs following the political changes in Bulgaria, both in Sofia and throughout the country, there has been a noticeable decline in public interest and involvement in environmental problems, paralleled by the stagnation of the environmental movement. The environmental organisations, consequently, although they were among the first to confront the Communist regime, gradually lost their wide public support. At the same time the changes in the political and economic arena brought about other priorities, pushing environmental protection into the background while mass preferences favoured economic growth even at the expense of the environment. Under conditions of rising unemployment and declining living standards only a few people would prefer long-term environmental results to material benefits, while the majority would like environmental conditions improved but only after the resolution of economic problems. Although the environmental situation has shown improvement in some respects (particularly in the worst-hit areas), this partial improvement is due mainly to the decline in production and not to the introduction of technologies which are friendly to the environment or the elimination of the main generators of environmental hazards. The poor and lower income groups are especially vulnerable to environmental degradation, as they depend to a larger extent on natural resources for their livelihood and usually live in closer proximity to degraded areas. Such an example was put forward by Clement Mindjov and derives from a village in southern Bulgaria: 'living conditions were affected by pollution and people started to demonstrate, demanding the closure of the factory that was responsible. A year later the same people started to protest, asking for the reopening of the factory so that they could have their jobs back.' 'If it is a choice between bread and environment people prefer bread' (Mindjov interview). Similarly, the coverage the environmental issues received in the media has decreased while business sector attention to environmental protection problems is also marginal. A report produced by the United Nations asserts:

> In the conditions of a grave economic, political and cultural crisis environmental protection and reproduction have been relegated to the outskirts of public interest. The state environmental policy is being formed and implemented practically outside the range of vision even of the citizens who take an active part in political life. The arguments in favor of or against nuclear power stations, the unequivocal demands for closing down hazardous metallurgy and chemical productions that happened every day in the early 1990s, are but a memory today. Compared to the daily concerns of making a living and job preservation environmental issues have

> become a luxury that can well be ignored. The environmental movements which used to be among the motive forces of social changes have gradually lost their wide public support. This does not mean that environmental issues have been forgotten. On the contrary, they are widely believed to be a major problem facing the country, being even more important than national security and inter-ethnic relations. But in late 1996 by their intensity as matter of public concern, they lag far behind inflation and crime. (UNDP, 1997: 69)

This situation is directly reflected both in the difficulties experienced by existing organisations, some of which were forced to disband, and in the emergence of new organisations. Therefore, in spite of the NGOs' strong and ambitious programmes, the post-Communist period has been marked to a great extent by lower activity and apathy, and by the constant search for the minimum financial resources necessary for the movement's sustainability. Nevertheless, at the end of the 1990s there was some kind of an attempted revival of the environmental movement. New environmental NGOs were formed and more people, particularly young people and students, have been involved in their activities. This element of attractiveness to young people not only somewhat regenerated the environmental movement but rendered environmental activism as 'one of the most promising avenues for the emergence of a stronger civic engagement among Bulgarians' (Meininger and Radoeva, 1996: 49).

Barriers to civil engagement

In order to assess the role and the position of the third sector it is essential to examine the problems and the impediments that are still limiting its further development. Many of the factors which have influenced the performance of the NGOs lie outside their own control (government policies, for example). There are several problems and barriers the NGO community is called upon to overcome and the most critical of them are described below.

The financial constraints

The lack of sufficient financial resources has been unquestionably the major problem for the NGO community ever since its formation, as organisations are usually obliged to function with low budgets. Even if this kind of financial barrier were true of any NGO, in any country of the world, the reasons for the problem in Bulgaria are rather specific. In general, the NGO sector in the developing countries of the world, particularly in the early stages of its development, has four major sources of financial support: the state's assistance, donations and sponsorships by the private sector, its own fund-raising activities (membership fees, entrepreneurial activities, etc.), and financial support from external sources. In Bulgaria the first three fund-raising sources have been almost non-existent.

While the third sector is still going through its formative stage state assistance is a more than crucial component. Nevertheless, the state's support for the third sector thus far has been no more than trivial. In terms of figures, the percentage of NGO financial support that comes from the state is not more than about 1 per cent, when generally in Europe the percentage varies from 30 per cent to 40 per cent.[4] Bulgaria, in fact, is the only country of the whole ex-Communist Bloc which has not set up special governmental funding for NGO activity. Apparently the third sector is not included in the state's budget. Although to some extent the absence of any meaningful financial assistance from the state is understandable, bearing in mind the difficulties of the economy, the main issue has been misunderstanding between the state and the NGO community. Activists often perceive state funding as a way for the state to supervise them. On the other hand, the state has been unwilling to provide the third sector with any kind of support, and, even when it has done, has tended to regard it more as a way of controlling the organisations than of assuring the standard of the services they provide.

> Most Bulgarians still think that civil society develops somehow on its own once the external obstacles are eliminated; civil society is popularly regarded as some sort of natural state of society once the latter breaks free of authoritarian or totalitarian diktat. It is still far from clear that civil society presupposes consistent development and elaboration of procedures and rules of relations with the state and other agents of society. (Task Force, 1997: 38)

The situation is not largely differentiated concerning the assistance provided to the NGOs by local government. Although it has shown more willingness compared with the central authorities, local government lacks also the necessary resources and financially is dependent on central government.

Given the absence of state assistance to the NGOs, most of the burden would normally have fallen on the private sector. Yet there has been no business funding to speak of, and though there have been cases of the private sector financing NGO activities it is not an established and regular practice. Owing to the unresolved economic problems the private sector cannot afford to sustain the organisations of civil society. This became more evident during the economic crisis of 1996–97, when indigenous businesses disappeared from the donor community, and only a small number of enterprises which had hard-currency revenue remained active in this field. The lack of interest by the private sector in assisting NGOs is also explained by the lack of incentives, since tax reductions for donations by companies practically do not exist. In addition the absence of any tradition of giving means that there is a very shallow base of local support for assisting civic organisations.[5]

The scarcity of financial resources could be solved, to a certain extent, by taking on self-supporting activities. But such activities have not been exploited and civil organisations have not yet become self-reliant. Certainly, there are organisations that have managed to incorporate business activities but such cases are the exception, since self-supporting activities are still practised on a very limited scale. There are two main reasons for this limitation.

The first is related again to the legal framework and to the ill defined taxation policy for NGOs, as the profit any civil organisation generates is taxed like that of a commercial company. Such is the situation that there are cases where NGOs prefer not to declare a profit. The lack of clear-cut regulations not only leads to serious difficulties in accounting and taxation for NGOs but also creates preconditions for various ways of 'bending the law'. Actually, the only opportunity NGOs have to conduct business activities and to finance non-profit through for-profit activities is to register a limited liability company to act as the market agent of the organisation. This scheme, however, in order to be sustained, should be based on a clear division of labour, perfect accounting and separate management and therefore can be implemented only by a small number of organisations.

The second reason is lack of proper experience of how to run a civic organisation and how to develop supporting activities. The majority of the organisations are unfamiliar with the concepts of marketing, resource development, fund raising and long-term planning. The lack of experience also explains the fact that the overwhelming majority of the NGOs operate on a project basis, a financial source that is very uncertain and is not permanent.

Non-existent state financial support, inadequate financial assistance by the private sector and the inability of the NGOs to develop, to any significant level, self-supporting activities render the international organisations almost the sole source of financial assistance (around 95 per cent of the NGO sector's total budget). Foreign donor support is of vital importance for the survival of the third sector, and, particularly after the economic crisis of 1996–97, it seems that the international donor community will have to continue to play the key role in supporting Bulgarian NGOs. Indeed, without external financial support it would be extremely difficult for the NGOs to survive and most of them would cease to exist.[6]

Evidently the international donors' assistance has thus far carried the burden of sustaining the NGO community. The priority of the assistance is held by areas such as human rights, conflict resolution, the environment, democracy building, the transition to a market economy, NGO networking and information exchange, poverty prevention and community development, assistance to socially disadvantaged groups. Still the main principle of the donors appears clear: the stimulation of citizen participation and to empower citizens to defend and represent their own interests.

The impact of external assistance

Despite the strong significance of international donors' assistance to Bulgarian NGOs, it does not always produce the desired results, as the relationship between foreign donors and the local NGO community in particular has not been developed on an ideal basis.

External actors were taken by surprise by the momentous events of 1989 and when they reacted their efforts were mainly concentrated on restructuring the state and assisting the new political elites, not on rebuilding civil society.

Hence during the early 1990s there were only a few international organisations operating in the country, and even fewer were those which had a real knowledge of the country.

While foreign missionaries needed quick and visible results to justify their intention to work in Bulgaria, the local NGOs needed longer-term and process-oriented activities to prepare themselves for adequate and effective operation in the new environment. Time pressure, and the need of resources did not allow local NGOs to work on establishing sound concepts and rules for their existence, relevant visions and strategies, coherent missions; most were tempted to give up and place the responsibility for working out third sector missions, objectives and strategies on the shoulders of the donors. The donors, not receiving enough feedback and contribution from their local partners, got used to developing their grant-making programmes, policies and practices themselves, in an anonymous environment physically far removed from the local Bulgarian situation (Task Force, 1997: 96).

As a result, co-operation between NGOs and foreign donors was not built upon a real partnership on a strong and long-term basis. The Bulgarian activists tended to regard foreign donors only as a means of acquiring the necessary subsidies while the latter looked on the former only as amateurs who needed guidance, models of operation and supervision. The Bulgarian NGOs used to expect, rather passively, the support provided by international institutions, while the strategy and the vision of the latter were often neither sought nor critically evaluated. Besides, the suggestion that very few organisations could survive without external assistance shows the apparent failure on both sides to establish co-operation of a sort that can be self-sustaining over the long run and even when donors' support eventually dries up. Under these conditions, external assistance is more likely to generate a structure of dependence that can deteriorate into a clientistic pattern.

The donor–NGO relation was not reframed even after the development of an in-country based grant-making sector, since most of the grant makers were not prepared to carry out a structured consultative process with individual NGOs on basic questions of the future development of the third sector. Therefore it is clear that the donor–recipient relationship in most of cases did not evolve into a sound partnership.

The absence of a proper developed partnership and a joint strategy between the international donors and the Bulgarian NGOs produced some distorted results. Donor policies in Bulgaria continue to suffer from a lack of information, and though they have greatly improved their understanding of the situation, there are cases where international donors are still funding projects with a distant relation to Bulgarian reality and with little correspondence to local conditions. There are several NGOs implementing projects without any scope and purpose merely in order to gain the funding that allows them to remain operational whereas foreign organisations are coming with their own agendas (sometimes at the expense of local issues and concerns), expecting fast and short-term results. There are donors that are just transferring known techniques, as they tend to stick to what is known to have worked elsewhere. Instead of attempting to apply existing, contingent knowledge to the given Bulgarian social structures and relationships, donors tend to replicate models and practices already arrived at in other environments. This tendency starts at the level of overall programme design, and runs through guidelines and priorities to the frameworks of monitoring effectiveness and efficiency, rendering the NGOs passive objects of transformation.

Perhaps what has most characterised the external support of Bulgarian NGOs is the fact that it has not yet managed to create an enabling environment for the long-term future of these NGOs. Indicative is the fact that there are several organisations without a specific mission and well defined goals and target groups in order to tailor their activities to the flow of the available funds. This practice certainly entails the danger that fields of activity that do not fit into the donors' agendas may lose out at the expense of more attractive areas. The obvious result is the existence of opportunistic organisations, with no mission other than winning donor funds and with no role in the democratisation process.

Furthermore, donor policies, in comparison with Central Europe, have been characterised by the absence of large grants and concentration on small-scale grants, with ambivalent results.

> On the one hand, they give opportunity to increasing numbers of organisations to have access to resources; on the other hand, organisations become overburdened and frustrated by the necessity to carry out extensive reporting activities, to fund-raise permanently by developing ever newer (and, as a rule, over-diverse) projects and by the lack of opportunities to plan and follow their own strategic objectives. This situation has led to the recognition that longer-term support was necessary for longer-term and better profiled results. (Task Force, 1997: 100)

The need for flexibility and innovation on the ground runs against the limited, logically framed and measurable outcomes favoured by many donors, while the requisite continual dialogue about objectives and strategies has often been substituted by a simple specification of outputs and targets and evaluations by overseas consultants. While indigenous grant-making organisations, established to provide for the management of foreign private or public subsidies, know the country and its people better, international donors situated abroad do not have the necessary knowledge and more easily can be driven to wrong decisions.

To ensure that civil society has a positive impact on democracy's prospects, and in order to make the most of their influence, NGOs need some kind of co-operation among themselves, and certain forms of alliances and compromises.[7] Nevertheless, the lack of sufficient sources of funding has created an unco-operative atmosphere among the NGOs, since the competition for funding has been strong, and occasionally unfair, in a way that seems unlikely to foster collaborative relations on which successful policy alliances are built. Competition for limited resources has often led to rivalry and secrecy about NGOs' activities instead of co-operation and information sharing, while the urgent need to succeed in order to maintain funding has provoked avoidance of risk taking and even overstatement of project impact. In addition, the lack of co-operative attitudes, the lack of trust and tolerance among societal groups, indicates inadequate knowledge about the whole spectrum of civil society issues, both in terms of institutional development and in terms of potential achievements. Even co-operation between donors has been limited and weak – occasionally they have been caught up in complex political or corporate contests – and there has been a tendency for them to separate territories of influence. This whole situation has resulted in what has been described as the absence of a sense of community.

In spite of these negative aspects, the impact of the external assistance on the growth of the NGO sector has been more than significant. The considerable growth of the third sector is demonstrated by the establishment of hundreds of operational NGOs, the growth in the number of regional and community-based initiatives, the establishment of several in-country grant-making organisations, the numerous studies and publications, seminars, workshops and conferences, the smaller or larger-scale projects and programmes carried out, the information and resource centres, and so forth. The third sector is more organised, more professional, more systematic, with a better institutional infrastructure established in Sofia as well as in other parts of the country and with a much better fund-absorbing capacity in regard to assistance provided from donors. There are examples of practices of civil participation, especially at local level, and there are strong thinktank NGOs which are influential in setting the political agenda, initiate public debate on key issues, stimulate institutional and behavioral change and encourage initiatives to remedy some of the most acute problems facing Bulgarian society. It is evident that the level of the third sector has been raised, primarily because of the external donor support it has received.

In this respect, the generally unco-operative atmosphere has started to change as activists more and more become aware that co-operation and work in partnerships is a better way to overcome their problems and to achieve their goals. This is a critical development because, apart from being merely a web of autonomous political and social organisations, civil society should interact more or less responsibly within an agreed set of rules. Otherwise the result is cacophony and political paralysis that leaves society susceptible to new forms of demagogy. For a civil society to develop, thus, it is necessary to establish such arenas in which civil organisations can express their views, negotiate, co-operate and co-ordinate their efforts. An example of such a forum is Coalition 2000, an initiative of a number of Bulgarian NGOs aimed at combating corruption through a process of co-operation among governmental institutions, NGOs and individuals.[8] These kinds of initiative acquire more importance given the virtual failure of the Union of Bulgarian Foundations and Associations (UBFA), created in 1992, to establish some kind of nationwide co-operation. The UBFA has not yet managed to become an attractive centre of membership, as it has been accused of being created by former Communists with the aim of controlling the sector, and has been also criticised of politicisation and of failing to meet the needs of the NGO sector. The UBFA can potentially play a prominent role if it manages to overcome its past ambiguous reputation and bureaucratic problems to become the arena for expressing views, exchanging information and formulating a code of ethics and a common strategy.

Civic organisations and the state

Though the essence of civil society and civil organisations lies in their autonomy from the state, yet this autonomy is often relative. Direct co-operation between the state and civil organisations is a constant requirement, while in order to influence public policy and to perform as effective policy actors civil organisations need to relate to the state. The state, moreover, not only should provide the space in which the autonomous civil organisations can act, but it should also provide the proper institutional structures, such as formal and informal channels of influence, arenas for interaction, and a facilitative legal and administrative framework. The work of NGOs cannot be conducted independent of contacts with institutions of state authority and local government. In Bulgaria, nevertheless, given the absence of vibrant civil society traditions, along with the political stalemate, the lack of open representative government, and the attitude and practices of the state bureaucracy, NGO–state relations are clearly fraught with difficulties and conflicts.

As in the case of individual citizens, NGOs are usually seen by the state authorities as a nuisance, as amateurs or even as organisations carrying out anti-governmental actions. (That was especially the attitude of the BSP government of 1995–96.) Consequently the interaction of civic associations and state institutions is not taking place on an equal basis. NGOs are seen, by the state, as being in an inferior position in a power hierarchy, with no legitimate right of participation in policy debates. On the other hand, civic associations tend to perceive the state and its institutions as distant and hostile, as well as a source of potential privileges, and as a result tend to act in an antagonistic fashion. The NGOs have not been active enough in raising the awareness of government officials of the need to be more open and more active in developing a social partnership – a partnership that would not consider NGOs as subordinate to governmental ideas but as equal and reliable partners. 'Ultimately, neither the citizens nor public authority have demonstrated the habits, inclinations and skills of communicating within a democratic construction of power and society. Here the legacy of the Communist period mingles with that of the preceding authoritarian paternalistic model of development' (Task Force, 1997: 37).

The relationship with the state and its institutions remains a very difficult one, sometimes even a conflicting one. The mutual misunderstanding, the paternalistic tradition, the lack of trust on all sides, along with the Communist legacy, was hardly the ideal basis for such a relationship to be built upon. In addition, the state has not formulated a clear policy towards the NGO sector and still there is not the general framework needed to nurture working partnerships and to regulate civil society organisations in an open, supportive and favourable manner. Although there are a few cases where NGOs and state institutions have managed to work together, this co-operation was primarily based on personal relations between individuals on both sides. Yet this personalised approach (of personal relations and personal allegiance) is not compatible with democratic practices, since NGO–state interaction is not principled, institutionalised and codified in rules.

Nonetheless, following the strong NGO involvement in controlling and monitoring aid distribution during the widespread charity effort around the country (1996–97) and also the central role which civic associations had in the national protest which overthrew the Socialist government in 1997, both the President and the UDF government pledged a new openness and responsiveness to civic organisations. The NGO response to the collapse of living standards revealed the pivotal position civic organisations can have in society and exposed them to the centre of attention. It was the first time that the organisations of civil society were seen as agents able to bring about social and even political change, challenging the dominance of the state. As a result, most ministries have set up working groups to address issues with NGOs, giving various organisations the opportunity to propose ideas and suggestions for the improvement of current legislation. In this context, it seems imperative for the NGO sector to become more active in reforming the governmental mentality and practice, to become closely involved with institutionalised forms of co-operation and interaction with the central government, as well as with the parliament and the party political establishment.

Co-operation between the NGOs and local authorities has been somewhat more positive and with a tendency to improve. This is not surprising, since local administration is closer to the citizens and their problems and is usually more ready to act in consort with autonomous groups, since it does not have the resources to implement decisions without local support. It should be stressed, however, that Bulgaria is still characterised by a very centralised system which tends not to provide adequate resources and not to confer enough autonomy on local communities. A more decentralised structure would facilitate the activities of the organisations of civil society better, as most likely they would enjoy increased influence.

Civic organisations and the media

In the post-Communist period it has become obvious that the media's fundamental agenda is entirely compatible with the third sector's and thus they should be seen as natural allies and partners. While the media want to secure the public's right to information, the NGOs want to involve and empower the citizens in the decision-making process and ultimately in the solution of the problem. Both communities want to keep society informed, to keep civil society autonomous from the state, to eliminate unlawful organised interests and to increase the sense of citizenship. Aside from the largely common goals and aspirations, civic organisations, as organs of socialisation into the practice of democracy, should not be alienated from the public sphere. Thus it is obvious that the importance of the media is enormous if NGOs are to access the public and mobilise the existing human potential. Especially since the Bulgarian public is receptive and would welcome more information on NGO activities.[9]

Crucially, then, even though over the years closer interaction has been evolved between the NGOs and the media, it should be noted that most frequently this interaction has not been conducted in a beneficial manner. This is a twofold problem: on one hand, the media have not been so interested in publicising civil society activities and, on the other, the NGOs have not yet developed the necessary skills to promote their own activities via the media.

The tone of the media during the post-Communist period (particularly up to 1995–96) has been uninformative, apocalyptic, disaster-promoting and with the overall message that nothing is achievable. An analysis published as late as 1996 typified the attitude of the media:

> By constantly reading about the horrors around him, the individual falls into a state of victimisation which provides him or her with psychological comfort. Inherently not ready for impulsive action, the Bulgarian finds an excuse for his or her passivity and is thus saved from his or her otherwise destructive guilt complex. Helped by the press, he or she begins to believe that any attempt to achieve anything is doomed to failure and would only bring about more misfortune. The media know this psychological need of the individual and stimulate his or her emotional reactions, at the same time paralysing him or her for action by insinuating that there is no point in action. (Deltcheva, 1996: 313)

Such messages were, obviously, completely counter to the proactive and achievement-oriented principles and practices of the NGO community. The NGOs, accordingly, were not offering the kind of stories that the media would be interested in and media coverage of their activities was marginal.

Notwithstanding these comments, it is still clear that the situation during the second half of the 1990s evolved in a direction more favourable to the NGOs. Along with a rapid improvement in media professionalism, the approach of the media became more informative and more positive, which created an opening for the NGO community to publicise its activities better.[10]

Additionally, specific reference should be made to the local media. The gradual emergence of local media, which largely do not imitate the scandal-mongering approach of some of the national media and are more susceptible to civic participation in the solution of local problems, has created the proper climate for local NGOs to promote issues of citizen participation. The interaction, thus, between NGOs and local media is taking place on a stable basis and with better results. Given also the coincidence of general message and goal, it is not surprising that local NGOs and local media have been progressively establishing links and ways of co-operation.

The second part of the problem of the low level of co-operation between the mass media and NGOs lies with the NGOs themselves, since it is widely accepted that they lack media planning and public relations skills. Indeed, activists have been resistant to the idea of using standard techniques of profile enhancement. Given that the third sector is still in its developing period, it is quite understandable that activists may lack the experience, the managerial skills and the technical expertise needed to run an organisation as well as the knowledge of how to promote their activities. The acquisition of such experience and knowledge is obviously an ongoing process and hence only towards the end of the 1990s did NGOs came to realise that they should not be alienated from the public and they needed to attract the attention of the media in order to ensure the involvement of citizens, to widen the network of social subjects acting voluntarily and to achieve their integration into society. Despite this progress, the NGO community is still very far from presenting a common message, a common approach and a community image to the media. In this context, the capacity of the third sector to achieve its objectives, to become an actor in the process of change and become a legitimate representative of the general interest remains limited.

The prospects

Post-communism revealed that the task of reviving civic traditions was extremely difficult for Bulgarians and hence the conditions for building a dense intermediary sphere of organisations, a strong autonomous social sphere, remained structurally weak and the initial expectations proved to be simplistic, overestimating the strength of civil society in the country and in the region. The further advance of democracy depends to a large extent on people's understanding of democratic principles and of the fact that democracy and democratic consolidation are not a process which is distant and far from their own existence and instead involves the participation and engagement of citizens in political life. Indeed, since the mid-1990s Bulgarians seem to be leaving their passivity and indifference behind and becoming increasingly aware of their citizenship. The widespread demonstrations of 1997, when thousands of people stood up for their rights, though they were the products of economic despair, manifested to everyone what active citizens can really achieve. This case of spontaneous collective protest, that was an expression of disappointed people urging better management of the economy, better living standards and faster economic reforms, could be described as the bursting upon the scene of civil society. From this point of view, it could be argued that the events of 1997 were a turning point toward the evolution of a civil society.

Still, our discussion of the third sector revealed several types of problems and various weaknesses. In spite of the fact that civil organisations have not yet managed to become an integral part of public life (on the contrary, they sometimes even acquired a negative reputation) there has developed a rather favourable environment for fostering broader third-sector support. It could even be suggested that a more dynamic phase seems to have commenced for the

NGO sector, especially since more young people are engaged in civil activities, particularly in the environmental field. This view is strengthened by the fact that, despite the destruction of the pre-war civil tradition by the Communist regime, there is the potential for the young to build upon. Despite all the problems, the level of the third sector, ten years after the Communist breakdown, without any doubt has been raised, and in many ways the situation has improved. It is obvious that the third sector is still in its formative stage, combining characteristics of both maturity and immaturity. Still, the beginning of the second post-Communist decade represents a more promising picture for NGO potential and for a more vigorous civil society.

There are at least three powerful elements that could hinder the further expansion of voluntarism and civil activism. The first of these potential impediments concerns the creation of a solid legal base and of a more favourable policy setting. A legal framework has to be in place defining the civil rights of the NGOs and chartering a transparent fiscal policy that will minimise legal restrictions, eliminate bureaucratic delay and provide tax concessions in order to encourage indigenous donations and income-generating activities. Yet this does not mean that an uncontrolled policy environment would benefit the third sector, as in that case there would be an increased risk of unhealthy and even corrupt NGOs (as happened in the past) which would taint the sector as a whole. The purpose of such a legal framework should thus be to nurture NGOs' growth and to provide new perspectives for their sustainable development but with all the safeguards against corruption and malpractice. A step in a positive direction is the new NGO legislation that came into effect in January 2001 after several years of campaigning on the part of the NGOs. The main component of the new legislation is the distinction between organisations according to their activities as well as the introduction of the principles of transparency and public control in fund raising and the spending of funds.

Second, even if the legal issue is resolved, relations with the state could remain a problem. Despite the fact that the totalitarian state has been dismantled, there is still deep-rooted mutual distrust between civic organisations and state agencies. In this realm, the central government and the NGOs have to take more steps to establish lasting patterns of co-operation and institutionalised forms of interaction, initiating a genuine partnership and collaborative relations. Certainly such relations are based on mutual respect and are conceivable only when both parties share common objectives and look to complementary rather than competing activities. The state can no more replace civil society and its organisations than the latter can replace the state and its institutions. In this realm, the government's initiative in setting up NGO units and NGO consultative committees in the most relevant line ministries improved the quality of state–NGO relations as it enables both the government and the NGOs to plan their programmes in the full knowledge of the activities of the other. It should be stressed, nonetheless, that the state–NGO relationship is sector-specific, as, for instance, there is more room for interaction on a significant scale regarding the alleviation of poverty than in tackling environmental issues. Still there are arguments that closer links with the state may weaken the legitimacy of the NGOs as independent and autonomous actors in society. Although this approach is not completely unjustified, since civic organisations are always vulnerable to nepotism and paternalism, total autonomy makes it impossible to maintain channels for demands and control. Besides, the experience of other countries shows that where the interaction is high the climate is most favourable for the NGOs to achieve their goals. As Clark indicates, 'it appears that where the voluntary sector is not only sizable but also where it interacts with the public and private sector it is able to achieve a significant multiplier effect on its own efforts' (Clark, 1995: 594).

Moreover, in a polarised political system, the autonomy of civic organisations may be threatened, as there have been already attempts by political parties to benefit from the improved public appeal of the NGOs. On the other hand, this is also an opportunity for the NGOs to achieve fundamental changes in the distribution of power and the allocation of resources. This issue reflects an unresolved dilemma for the NGOs of how to engage in the formal political process in order to gain access and influence decision-making and achieve their objectives but without becoming embroiled in partisan politics. Although neither antagonism between civil and political societies nor the isolation of these two spheres promotes democratic consolidation, the relationship between civic organisations and party politics should be applicable only if it is compatible with the cause of a civil society.

The third potential impediment to the flowering of NGOs is the inadequate development of managerial and professional skills as well as the development of a culture of civility in society at large. With ten years' experience behind them, it is time for the NGOs to abandon their self-isolation, concentrating on resource budgeting and on particular projects, and to attempt to improve their external communication techniques, targeting the state authorities, new NGOs, local communities, the media and thus closing the gap between them and the public, claiming thus a wider legitimacy. The NGOs should improve their management and they should implement projects that are effective and well targeted, ensuring popular participation. Obviously, a major obstacle will continue to be, at least in the coming years, NGOs' limited resources. Yet the NGOs should change their clientistic attitude and fund-chasing habits by developing diverse financial resources and reserve funds. Foreign donors should also start granting more permanent financial support for institutional development and not only in the form of project funding. Besides, foreign donors, apart from improving their grasp of the local political, social and cultural context of their funding activities, should provide the NGOs with the proper training programmes, sharing their knowledge and experience and investing in the development of human resources. That is because unless NGOs manage to mobilise domestic support for civil initiatives their sustainability will continue to be in question. A note of concern is the possibility that the very large NGOs may come to dominate both resources and ideas to such an extent as to act as a barrier to pluralism and diversity of opinions and approaches, characteristics on which the concept of a viable and healthy civil society is based. In this respect, the role of the UBFA is crucial, given that it manages to become the undisputed and legitimate representative of the third sector, facilitating hence the emergence of new civic organisations.

Even more essential, NGOs should ameliorate their strategic planning and they should develop such channels and methods as will open up an interface with the citizens and promote the emergence of civil society attitudes and practices as guarantees of democracy. The NGOs should also demonstrate the advantages of citizen participation, the ways citizens should express and defend their own interests, and the potential of civic associations to become a driving force of societal transformation. This is an illustration of how the NGOs can assist the revival of a civic culture and particularly of the potential NGO role in overcoming the Communist legacy of the atomisation of society by building up areas of communal activity and by recreating horizontal relations between people. Civic culture must be built up in the everyday traditions of trust and civic engagement, and is not a top-down process. In other words, unless the culture of society as a whole supports civic organisations as a kind of informal school for civic initiatives it will not be possible for them to succeed.

Notes

1 Occasionally there are still scandals in the media concerning NGOs. A case, for instance, that in 2000 acquired extensive publicity concerned a well known foundation that was financially supporting a specific political party.

2 It should be mentioned that during the 1970s, when the environmental movement emerged on the world scene, the National Committee for Nature Protection and the Committee on Environmental Protection were established mainly in order to demonstrate that there was freedom and pluralism within the Communist regime.

3 The NEAP was based on the Environmental Strategy Study carried out with the assistance of the World Bank and the US government (USAID and the US Environmental Protection Agency). 'The Environmental Strategy Study (ESS), carried out in 1991–92, laid out the principles for environmental policy, reviewed the country's main environmental problems, and proposed a number of recommendations in response to these problems. It concluded that past economic and management policies were a major cause of environmental degradation so that market-oriented reforms would produce environmental improvements. The ESS outlined the institutional, legislative and regulatory reforms required to implement its recommended policy, stressing a decentralised and participatory approach to environmental management and the importance of establishing a balance between a "command and control" approach and market mechanisms' (Mindjov, 1995: 25). The 1992 legislation, however, had several weak points, particularly since some of its provisions were rather general requiring further regulations.

4 For example, 'the five largest development NGOs in the UK all show a significantly rising trend, with levels of dependence on government grants oscillating between 18 per cent and 52 per cent in 1994, up from between 7 per cent and 15 per cent ten years earlier. Levels of dependence are much higher in continental Europe and in North America; for

example, it is common to find government grants making up between 50 per cent and 90 per cent of the budgets of major NGOs in Scandinavia, the Netherlands and Canada' (Edwards and Hulme, 1996: 962).

5 In contrast, in Hungary, where the NGO sector is well understood and well supported both mentally and financially, legislation allows citizens to assist NGOs through their tax returns, as anyone can direct a small percentage of their tax payments to an NGO of their choice.

6 Bulgaria is certainly not a unique case, as the pattern is more or less similar in many Third World countries. 'It has been shown that, in the case of El Salvador, external funding for autonomous organisations was given *en masse* during the process of reconstruction and reconciliation in the wake of the civil war. This certainly furthered the establishment of a great number of organisations. Yet, a critical evaluation shows, many of these groupings are unlikely to survive a cutback in aid. This entails a risk for the newborn democracy, as failed projects and frustrated hopes may turn conflictive' (Hadenius and Uggla, 1996: 1637).

7 Arguably poor co-ordination, disagreement, and open conflict among its constituents would endanger a democratic civil society. The example of the Philippines is characteristic. 'In the Philippines, there are more than 20,000 registered NGOs, which ought to indicate a most viable civil society. Yet the NGO sector is highly fragmented, very politicised, and in many respects, given their numbers, spectacularly unable to advance a progressive social agenda' (Hadenius and Uggla, 1996: 1627).

8 Coalition 2000 was started in March 1997 as a result of the initiative of the Centre for the Study of Democracy and a number of other Bulgarian NGOs with the support of USAID, and was officially launched in April 1998.

9 Various polls reveal that around a third of the public would welcome more information on what NGOs do; another third would like to be provided with more information on the larger goals of NGOs and their larger mission. This indicates that a large majority of the public would like to be provided with more information on NGOs (Task Force, 1997: 45).

10 The change of tone by the press was exemplified when a fifteen-year-old Roma boy was violently murdered by skinheads in May 1998 and the press reacted with fierce denunciations of racism. It was not the first incident of skinhead violence against Roma in Bulgaria, but it was the first to generate more than dry indifference on the part of the media, and commentaries highlighting the racist nature of the murder went on for a week in the mainstream newspapers.

6

International relations in the post-Communist era

The changes in the course of the Bulgarian foreign policy after 1989 have been as profound as the shifts that have occurred in political and economic life. During the Communist era Bulgaria earned for itself the reputation of the most faithful Soviet satellite and had no need to formulate its own foreign policy objectives. Zhivkov characteristically declared after Khrushchev's visit in 1962 that the 'political watch dial is exact to the second with the watch of the Soviet Union … Our watch is working toward Moscow time. This is a matter of great pride for all Bulgarian people' (Jelavich, 1983: 369). Indeed, the essence of Zhivkov's policies was to make Bulgaria an inseparable part of the Soviet Union, or, as he liked to put it, to make them share a 'common circulatory system'. This kind of relationship with the Soviet Union was certainly beneficial for both sides. As has been previously discussed, Bulgarian industrialisation, which radically transformed the country, was possible only because of the substantial support received by the Soviet Union in terms of both financing and raw materials. Bulgaria also, after consecutive defeats in the Second Balkan War, the First World War and the Second World War, found in its alliance with the Soviet Union the necessary security cover to guarantee its interests. The Soviet Union, on the other hand, found in Bulgaria the only devoted ally in a region where it traditionally had an interest (even from the days of the Russian empire).

The dramatic events at the end of the 1980s shattered these earlier patterns, and brought an end to the division of Europe and the bipolar security order that had characterised East–West politics for the previous forty years. The end of the Cold War, the break-up of the Soviet Union, the dissolution of the CMEA and the Warsaw Pact meant that Bulgaria had to seek a new identity, and presented a totally new situation with unfamiliar opportunities, challenges and problems.

To a large degree the agenda of Bulgarian post-Communist foreign policy is determined by the need to find solutions to the main issues connected with the irreversible political changes that have occurred in international relations as well as in the field of security in Europe. The main goals of foreign policy are to establish the most favorable conditions for the country's economic development and the reinforcement of its national security. To this end, the priority in foreign policy is accession to the European Union and in parallel and complementary mode is the process of integration into NATO. Bulgaria's integration in the European community of democratic countries became an undoubted strategic objective, forming the basis of a national consensus among the political forces and society in general. That is not to imply that there are no differences between the two major political parties (the UDF and BSP) in the conduct and priorities of foreign policy. For instance, while the UDF has been a fervent supporter of integration with NATO, the BSP considers that no European security formula is possible without Russia and regards the traditional relationship with Russia as more important.

Despite controversies and differences in the formation of foreign policy, Bulgaria has consistently sought to develop ties which would bring it into full European partnership. For Bulgarian society, EU and NATO accession is an indivisible part of the political and economic transformation of the country that will guarantee its social, economic and national security. On a regional level, Bulgaria has sought to develop good bilateral relations with all its neighbours and has worked to promote regional stability, security and co-operation in South-eastern Europe (the region embracing Albania, Bosnia and Herzegovina, Bulgaria, Croatia, the Federal Republic of Yugoslavia, the former Yugoslav Republic of Macedonia and Romania). Such relations also aim at finding solutions to problems accumulated during the years of transition, and especially those relating to the conflict in former Yugoslavia.

The quest to join Europe

Since the fall of the Berlin Wall, joining Europe, or a 'return to Europe', has become synonymous with political, economic and social reform in the former Communist countries. At first glance, joining Europe refers to the process of securing entry to the European Union, which has emerged as the central institution of post-Cold War Europe and to which almost all the states of the region are committed. Ten ex-Communist countries are in entry negotiations, others either have or are seeking co-operation agreements with Brussels in an attempt to facilitate and consolidate reintegration into the world economy. On a deeper view, joining Europe means embracing Western values such as democracy, respect for human rights, a free-market economy and reaching Western standards of living. Along with the European Union, NATO, already joined by three Central European countries (Poland, Hungary and the Czech Republic), has emerged as the other basic instrument of European integration. As relations with the European Union and NATO have developed in a different manner, let us examine each in turn.

Bulgaria and the European Union

The greatest challenge the European Union had to face in the 1990s was the one that was least expected: the need to respond cohesively and effectively to the collapse of the Communist regimes in Central and Eastern Europe and to prepare to extend its membership eastwards. While the prospect of building a 'new Europe' was welcomed almost unanimously, the short and medium-term problems were immense and came at a time when the Union was already grappling with serious internal issues and a growing queue of applicants for membership. As the European Union lacked a strategic concept to cope with this historic challenge, the initial reaction was rather slow and cautious, basically restricted to financial and technical assistance, and improving trade relations. The contacts between the European Union and Bulgaria were initiated in August 1988, when the two parts established diplomatic relations, and in May 1990 a Trade and Co-operation Agreement was signed. The same year Bulgaria joined the Phare programme (Polish and Hungarian Assistance for the Reconstruction of Europe), which was designed to provide know-how and technical support and became the main instrument for assisting the whole area of Central and Eastern Europe. Although an innovative concept, Phare was not an adequate response, and it was only in 1993 that the European Union managed to devise and implement a common and consistent policy towards CEECs. The starting point was the criteria of membership, formulated by the European Council in Copenhagen in 1993, and the Association Agreements (or Europe Agreements), which together identified a path for integration into European structures.

THE CRITERIA

At the Copenhagen European Council the European Union for the first time committed itself to eastern enlargement. Henceforth the question was no longer whether the Union would take on new members but when and how. With the document *Towards a Closer Association with the Countries of Central and Eastern Europe* the European Union agreed that accession would take place as soon as the candidate countries were able to assume the burdens of membership and meet the political and economic conditions required. The conclusions of the European Council in Copenhagen defined the criteria for EU membership. The first of the Copenhagen criteria contain political conditions: stable institutions, democracy, the rule of law, respect for human rights and the protection of minorities. The economic criteria are formulated in the implementation of two general conditions: the existence of a functioning market economy and the ability in the medium term to withstand the competitive pressure of market forces in the Union. The candidate countries must also be able to take on the obligations of membership, including the ability to adopt the *acquis communautaire* (the body of laws, customs and regulations) and adherence to the aim of political union. The Copenhagen council linked the process of enlargement with institutional reform, adding, in an ambiguous statement, that the Union's capacity to absorb new members and to maintain the momentum of integration is an important consideration in deciding upon eastward enlargement. Thus even if candidates fulfil the membership criteria they can still be turned down if EU member states have not agreed on where European integration is heading or conclude that the European Union is unable, or unprepared, to absorb new members.

Certainly the Copenhagen council provided the framework for the development of relations between the European Union and the countries of Central and Eastern Europe, and the criteria gave the Union the means to exert pressure on candidate countries to carry out reforms. Yet no specific timetable for membership was set, while some of the conditions are unclear and vague (for example, as to what constitutes a market economy or what political union actually means).

ASSOCIATION AGREEMENTS

The European Union opened negotiations on the Association Agreements with Czechoslovakia, Hungary and Poland in December 1990, but it not until the time of the August 1991 attempted coup in the Soviet Union that the Commission declared its intention to expand co-operation with Bulgaria and Romania. 'Geopolitical concerns seem more important in this decision than a positive appraisal of Bulgaria's and Romania's fulfilment of the criteria for concluding Europe Agreements' (Smith, 1999: 97). In March 1993 Bulgaria signed an Association Agreement with the Union that came in effect in January 1995.[1] The Association Agreement structured the relationship between Bulgaria and the Union, provided a framework for integrating Bulgaria into the Union and created institutional mechanisms for political dialogue at ministerial, parliamentary and official level on a wide range of issues of mutual concern. Under the agreement Bulgarian legislation has to be progressively approximated to the *acquis* while economic co-operation is extended to a wide variety of areas. Even more significant, the agreement envisaged a ten-year period of progressive movement towards a free-trade area. On that account, a complex system of trade liberalisation measures was set up using different methods of dismantling tariffs and quantitative restrictions for various groups of products, with the Union opening its markets sooner than Bulgaria. There are sectors, however, defined as 'sensitive', which are excluded from the process of trade liberalisation, since the agreement provides for a slow pace of abolition of custom duties and quantitative restrictions on the part of the European Union. The major industrial exports of Bulgaria (steel and non-ferrous metals) and particularly agricultural products still face substantial tariffs and non-tariff barriers (as is the case with the Association Agreements signed with the other CEECs). This protectionist stance adopted by the EU countries, in an attempt to control (or delay) the real increase in trade flows from Central and Eastern Europe, has been widely criticised and condemned by the associated partners. While CEECs have reoriented their trade toward the Union and away from the former CMEA countries, they still face significant barriers in penetrating EU markets.[2] The weak Central and East European economies pose no real threat to the far better developed EU economies and, in fact, what these countries need most is the stimulus of free access to

European markets instead of financial aid. For example, Bulgarian agriculture, which has been hit severely by the transitional crisis and has to function under free-market conditions, is in no position to compete with heavily subsidised EU agricultural produce. In this context the cost to Bulgaria of implementing the agreement has been higher than expected and has revealed how EU policies are influenced by powerful domestic lobbies. Despite these limitations, the Association Agreement became the primary link between European Union and Bulgaria and generated a significant growth in the volume of trade between the two. The European Union became Bulgaria's major trading partner as the EU share of Bulgaria's overall foreign trade gradually rose from about a third (34 per cent) of the total in 1994 to more than 50 per cent in 2000.[3]

AGENDA 2000: ACCESSION PARTNERSHIP

Following the implementation of the Association Agreement and the drafting of the White Paper, which makes recommendations for the integration of the associated partners and maps out the route to the alignment of legal and administrative structures with the Union's, Bulgaria applied for full EU membership in December 1995. Furthermore, in July 1997, the Commission presented a voluminous document, entitled *Agenda 2000: For a Stronger and Wider Union*, consisting of recommendations for the Union's financial framework for the period 2000–06, proposals for the development of EU policies and the strategy for enlargement, recommendations for the strengthening of the pre-accession strategy as well as the Commission's opinions on the ten applications from the CEECs. On the basis of the opinions, the European Union inaugurated accession negotiations in March 1998 with the Czech Republic, Hungary, Poland, Slovenia and Estonia (plus Cyprus). The former Communist Bloc's less economically developed countries – Bulgaria, Latvia, Lithuania, Slovakia and Romania – along with Malta, were invited to begin negotiations on accession in December 1999. From *Agenda 2000* it became obvious that since not all the applicant countries would meet the membership criteria at the same time and, since the institutional framework of the Union could not cope with an extensive enlargement, the accession of the CEECs will take place in waves. Bulgaria reacted to *Agenda 2000* with almost no surprise, as the economy had just gone through a deep economic crisis. Despite disappointment and concern at being left in the slow lane, both the government and the public acknowledged that Bulgaria had made limited progress on reforms.

The second key event in 1997 came in December when the European Council decided that the Accession Partnership, launched in March 1998,

> would be the key feature of the enhanced pre-accession strategy, mobilising all forms of assistance to the candidate countries within a single framework. In this manner, the EU targets its assistance towards the specific needs of each candidate so as to provide support for overcoming particular problems in view of accession. The purpose of the Accession Partnership is to set out in a single framework the priority areas for further work, the conditions applying to assistance and the financial means available. (European Commission, 1999a)

The Accession Partnership requires each candidate country to adopt a 'National Programme for the Adoption of the *Acquis*'. The programme should outline the country's strategy for accession, including how to address the partnership's priorities and the timetable for achieving the partnership's objectives. Both the Accession Partnership and the National Programme are revised on a regular basis, to take account of progress, and to allow new priorities to be set. In May 1998 the Bulgarian government presented the first version of its National Programme in which it acknowledges that membership of the European Union requires

> significant changes in the Bulgarian economy and legislation. Without these changes, Bulgaria will find it difficult to achieve integration and accession will not bring with it the full benefits. Unfortunately, in recent years, as a result of mistaken state policy decisions and inaction, Bulgaria has begun to fall behind in the introduction of a market-oriented economic policy, land reform, privatisation and the development of a dynamic private sector. (Bulgarian Parliament, 1998)

PHARE

Following the publication of *Agenda 2000* and the acceleration of the enlargement process which ensued, Phare was redirected to reflect the changes in Central and Eastern Europe and re-focused on preparing the candidate countries for accession. Working in the context of the Accession Partnerships, during the period 2000–06, Phare support will focus on two main areas, institution building (around 30 per cent of Phare resources) and investment (around 70 per cent of resources).

> Institution building is defined as helping the candidate countries to develop the structures, strategies, human resources and management skills needed to strengthen their economic, social, regulatory and administrative capacity in order to be able to implement the *acquis* and to prepare for participation in EU policies such as economic and social cohesion. Investment support will take two forms: investment to strengthen the regulatory infrastructure needed to ensure compliance with the *acquis* and direct, *acquis*-related investments; investment in economic and social cohesion through measures similar to those supported in member states through the European Regional Development Fund and the European Social Fund (European Commission, 1999a).

The Phare management system was reformed in 1999 to improve its efficiency and transparency, increasing the emphasis on management. The new regulation allows the Commission to supervise the implementation of the assistance while previously this was the responsibility of the authorities in the partner country. This possibility will be reviewed on a country-by-country, sector-by-sector basis and introduced gradually. Furthermore, since January 2000, alongside Phare, there are two other programmes to assist the applicant countries of Central and Eastern Europe in their pre-accession preparations: the Instrument for Structural Policies for Pre-accession (ISPA) which finances large-scale infrastructure projects in the fields of the environment and transport, and Special Accession Programme for Agriculture and Rural Development (SAPARD), which supports agricultural and rural development.

Certainly the transfer of know-how, technical assistance and financial resources provided through Phare during the last decade of the twentieth century was welcomed by the CEECs as an important factor in reducing the cost of transition. While the overall impact of the programme has been positive, the implementation of Phare has encountered problems and the European Union has been criticised for several reasons. First, because of the difference in scale between Phare and the funds made available for the reconstruction of the Mediterranean economies prior to accession. Phare has also been criticised for being overly bureaucratic, cumbersome and centralised and for the extensive involvement of Western consultants who usually do not know the local needs and demands.

Even more significant, Phare has created winners and losers among the CEECs, with some countries receiving much less financial assistance than others. For instance, the Phare programme during the period 1989–99 allocated EUR 865.5 million to Bulgaria while a total of EUR 1.03 billion went to Hungary and a total of EUR 2.05 billion to Poland. It should be noted, however, that the absorptive capacity of Bulgaria has been low and inadequate. Inconsistent governmental policies, political controversies, inefficient administration, lack of functional financial infrastructure and the underdeveloped NGO sector have a negative effect on the utilisation and efficiency of EU assistance. In an attempt to improve the efficiency of Phare, the government in 1998 introduced a National Fund (at the Ministry of Finance) through which Phare assistance is channelled, with overall responsibility for the financial management of funds. Indeed, Bulgaria's performance regarding the implementation of Phare has shown improvements, particularly as transparency has been increased and the dispersion of funds has been reduced (absorbing capacity increased from about 40 to 60 per cent). But still the main difficulty is lack of co-operation and co-ordination.

> Although implementation of the Phare programme in Bulgaria is generally satisfactory, the authorities need to improve their capacity to assist the Commission proactively and strategically with programming and developing priority projects. This is particularly the case in areas that involve inter-ministerial and donor co-ordination, and collaborating with business and civil society. Phare programming and implementation should be more closely integrated with ministerial policy making and administrative structures. Efforts are needed to reduce staff turnover and provide adequate resources for the contracting, technical and financial aspects of project implementation. (European Commission, 2000)

The problems and prospects

Despite the problems described above and in previous chapters, Bulgaria has made considerable progress in preparation for EU membership. The European Union, acknowledging this progress, initiated accession negotiations in March 2000. Of course, in order for Bulgaria to meet the Copenhagen criteria substantial effort is still needed. In its 1999 opinion on Bulgaria's application for EU membership, the Commission concluded that:

> Bulgaria fulfils the Copenhagen political criteria. However, further efforts need to be undertaken to strengthen the rule of law and protect human and minority rights, particularly of the Roma population, where recent government decisions need to be followed by concrete measures with appropriate financial resources. Particular attention needs to be paid to the fight against corruption and improving the functioning of the judicial system. Bulgaria has continued to make progress in establishing a functioning market economy but further steps are needed and it is not yet in a position to cope with competitive pressure and market forces within the Union in the medium term.[4] (European Commission, 1999b)

It is clear from the report that Bulgaria does not yet qualify as a functioning market economy. Moreover, Bulgaria has taken appropriate steps to deal with some of the Accession Partnership's short-term priorities (such as to adopt economic reform strategy, ensure macroeconomic stability, adopt legislation concerning financial services, taxation, competition, organised crime and corruption) while dealing with other issues demands more time and it is expected to be several years before the necessary measures are implemented (measures in the field of the environment, energy, agriculture, transport, employment and social affairs). In terms of the harmonisation of legislation, Bulgaria has maintained a good pace of alignment with the *acquis*, and in fact ranks second only to Hungary. Bulgaria still faces, however, considerable difficulties in the implementation of this legislation and thus is considered to be unable to take on the obligations of membership in the medium term.

There is a feeling in Bulgaria that the country's progress towards meeting the criteria for EU membership is not yet fully recognised and is somewhat underestimated. This belief has been reinforced by the European Union, despite pledges to treat all applicants equally and on the basis of their performance in relation to the Copenhagen criteria. The first instance was the linking of the opening of accession negotiations with the closure of the Kozloduy nuclear power plant, and the second, excluding Bulgaria from the Schengen Agreement on visa-free travel.

In the context of achieving and maintaining a high level of nuclear safety, the Union has asked for the closure of candidate countries' nuclear power plants, which are deemed non-upgradable to international safety standards at reasonable cost. In Bulgaria's case, the European Union asked for the adoption and implementation of a realistic timetable for the closure and decommissioning of the four units of the Kozloduy nuclear power plant. Moreover the Commission stated that the opening of accession negotiations would be conditional on reaching agreement, before the end of 1999, on acceptable closure dates. Finally, in November 1999, agreement was reached as the Bulgarian government committed itself to the definitive closure of units 1 and 2 before 2003 and to the early closure of units 3 and 4 before 2006 at the latest. The issue of the Kozloduy nuclear power plant, nevertheless, acquired political significance as 'public opinion strongly opposed conditioning the invitation to Bulgaria to negotiate accession on its progress in closing these units of its only nuclear power plant' (Economic Policy Institute and CSD, 2000: 112). Considering the significance of Kozloduy to the Bulgarian economy, as it produces about 40 per cent of the country's electricity, this treatment was seen by both the public and the political elite as unfair, while Brussels were portrayed as issuing dictates on Bulgaria.

The thorniest problem in relations between the European Union and Bulgaria came up in 1995, when Bulgaria and Romania were the only EU associate members excluded from the provisions of the Schengen Agreement on free travel. The visa restrictions on Bulgarian citizens were kept in place because of EU concern about the security of the borders and illegal immigration. Yet the visa restrictions became a burning political issue and one of the most sensitive, with an impact on national confidence and pride that was interpreted as evidence of unequal treatment.[5] The visa restrictions became an issue of geostrategic importance for the government and a matter of dignity and self-esteem for Bulgarians. 'For most Bulgarians the "Schengen List" was proof that the EU cared nothing for their progress toward political democracy and regarded them simply as drug dealers and a source of unwanted immigrants' (Bell, 1998: 313). Additionally, Bulgarians who wished to acquire a visa had to go through lengthy and cumbersome procedures, face the long queues outside the EU embassies, humiliating interviews with consular and customs officials – and frequent were the cases of corruption involving the staff of the embassies, generating even more negative publicity. It should be stressed that the visa issue also had symbolic significance, since the removal of visa requirements would have been the first visible sign, with an impact on everyday life, of European integration. In December 2000, when it was clear that Bulgaria had met all the security requirements, including replacing passports and other identity documents to prevent falsification and strengthening border controls, the Council of Ministers formally decided to waive visa restrictions fon Bulgaria and Romania.

Whatever these problems, the overwhelming majority of Bulgarians continue to support EU membership. 'In November 1998, seventy-six per cent of those surveyed were in favor of Bulgaria's accession to the EU. In April 1999 the percentage was practically the same – seventy-five per cent' (UNDP, 1999: 5). Yet if the European Union continues to mishandle such issues it may give rise to an extremely euro-sceptic public opinion and political elite. The result may be the same if the accession of Bulgaria is delayed. The expectation and the plan of the government is to complete membership negotiations by 2006 and, given that the pace of economic development continues with (at least) the current speed, it is a target which seems realistic. Nonetheless, the date of Bulgaria's admission is also dependent on internal developments in the Union as well as on the implications of the first wave of enlargement. Bulgaria, for instance, should be prepared for a number of CEECs to become EU members while it is still negotiating. The European Union has agreed that the most advanced candidates could close accession negotiations in 2002, preparing the way for accession as early as 2003 or 2004. Still the composition of the first wave is not finalised and depends on individual progress. Malta and Slovakia in particular are considered to have caught up with the first-wave applicants, while, on the other hand, Bulgaria and Romania are regarded as the least capable, among the applicant countries, of assuming the obligations of membership.

Apart from debate about the date of accession, EU membership should be treated by the Bulgarian political elite as a process and not as an aim in itself.

> The really important part is the process of change preceding the act of accession. Its direction and speed are equally important. The integration agenda should be concentrated on domestic efforts, aimed at reaching a level of development (political system, institution building, structural reform, economic growth, changing patterns, legislative framework, etc.) corresponding to the requirements of membership. (UNDP, 1998: 89)

Because EU membership has been recognised as a national goal by all political forces the political debate in Bulgaria has focused on progress in meeting the EU criteria and not on what membership will actually entail. That is perhaps why the overwhelming majority of the public which supports EU membership does not have enough knowledge of the Union and the short and long-term implications of accession. As Bulgaria moves closer to the European Union political debate should not be limited to the issue of 'when' but a general discussion in society should be stimulated, involving the state, business and the third sector, on the costs and benefits of membership as well as on the practical aspects of integration.[6] Only in this way will the public feel that, even if the country is involved in lengthy negotiations, it is still participating in European integration.

Bulgaria and NATO

As a military alliance NATO's chief task up to 1989 was to guarantee Western security based on collective defence, by countering an external threat emanating from the Soviet Union and the Warsaw Treaty Organisation. The revolutions of 1989 not only toppled Communism but also created a security vacuum in the region of Central and Eastern Europe and unleashed a set of dynamics which left NATO with the paradox of less threat but also less peace. The crises in the former Yugoslavia highlighted the changing nature of the security agenda in Europe and, at the same time, demonstrated that, irrespective of the mistakes and weaknesses of the Western policies, NATO remains the most reliable security and defence body in Europe. It is not then a surprise that NATO membership is seen by the CEECs as the only guarantee of their security. At its summit in Rome in 1991 NATO announced the formation of the North Atlantic Co-operation Council (NACC) with the aim of extending co-operation to the countries of the former Warsaw Pact and building a genuine partnership between the alliance and the countries of Central and Eastern Europe. But the first major step in the evolution of a close relation between NATO and the CEECs came in January

1994, when NATO adopted the US initiative Partnership for Peace (PfP) which attempted to offer an orderly process towards eventual membership for the countries wishing to join NATO (albeit such membership was not guaranteed).

Although in the post-Cold War period Russia has not been the most active player in the construction of the new European security architecture, the importance of that great country to the evolving European security system is assessed as pivotal. Since 1992 Russia has repeatedly declared that it opposes the expansion of NATO to the area of Central and Eastern Europe. Following intense negotiations, a NATO–Russia Agreement on a Permanent Joint Council (PJC) was signed in May 1997, which is intended to strengthen the co-operation and partnership between the two sides. This agreement paved the way for NATO's formal enlargement decision.

After prolonged debates and internal reforms (a key element of which was the development of a European Security and Defence Identity), at the Madrid summit in July 1997 Poland, Hungary and the Czech Republic were invited to open accession negotiations while Romania and Slovenia were characterised as aspiring members.[7] NATO also decided to consolidate and expand the scope of NACC and PfP by bringing them together in a new Euro-Atlantic Partnership Council (EAPC) with the aim of providing the non-member states with a more permanent framework of consultation and co-operation. NATO has declared an 'open door' policy but the decision to offer membership to only three applicants (who joined the alliance in March 1999) caused scepticism among the other candidate countries. Still the Madrid summit carried a special significance, as the resolutions regarding the broadening of NATO changed the strategic perspectives in Europe, aiming not to allow the emergence of new partition lines. Indeed, NATO proceeded faster than the European Union in accepting new members from Central and Eastern Europe, but this was perhaps because joining NATO is less demanding than EU membership. Although NATO has laid down a number of political and military criteria – comprising mainly the acceptance of democratic principles, elimination of border disputes and maintaining good relations with neighbouring countries, civilian control over the military and the restructuring of the military itself – it is no fixed or rigid list of criteria. 'That explains why there was little public debate in the candidate countries about what the shared values and responsibilities of NATO membership entailed' (Rupnik, 2000: 122). Yet that was not the case in Bulgaria, as the debate over membership of NATO became the subject of argument between the UDF and the BSP and an issue that created a division in society.

THE DEBATE IN BULGARIA

The issue of joining NATO was raised during the transition process, when it was brought up by the opposition in the round-table negotiations.

> At that time, the meaning attributed to NATO was symbolic; the alliance was not even considering a possibility to expand to the East. NATO was regarded as an

> important element of the West, and the choice of NATO was a choice of a social model. The security issue, if at all discussed, was of secondary importance. In fact, the dialogue between Bulgaria and NATO at that time boiled down to icebreaking, with no specific plans involved. (Todorov, 1997: 30)

At the time, the political elite did not regard the issue as pressing but it was still the first time that the political parties had declared their positions. The BSP was reserved about NATO without firmly opposing the idea of accession but raising questions such as the financial cost of membership and supporting special relations with Russia, while the UDF was generally pro-NATO and deeply suspicious of Moscow. When the UDF assumed power and Zhelev, a consistent NATO supporter, became President, Bulgaria developed into an active promoter of closer association with NATO. In a lecture delivered in 1993 President Zhelev asserted that 'the NATO emblem is the compass by which Bulgaria orients itself in its striving to construct guarantees for its national security, to defend its national interests, to give meaning to and enrich its participation in international life' (Moser, 1994: 260). The political division was expressed in an ambiguous declaration adopted by the National Assembly in December 1993 stating that Bulgaria's membership of NATO was a matter for a future decision in the light of Bulgaria's national interests.[8] In accordance with this declaration, in February 1994 Zhelev signed the PfP structure on behalf of Bulgaria. It was particularly during the time of the BSP government that NATO membership became more significant as an issue of internal political debate rather than a matter of foreign policy orientation. The BSP government failed to clarify its position and adopted a rather ambiguous stand. The issue acquired an ideological character and became a choice between Russia and NATO, between East and West, between democrats and non-democrats. For example, 'whenever UDF political tactics required an acute differentiation from the BSP or an emphasis on its archaic character, the issue of NATO membership was brought up' (Todorov, 1997: 33).

Bulgaria managed to articulate its unequivocal intention to join NATO only after the dramatic events of 1996–97 and the resignation of the BSP government when in February 1997 Bulgaria submitted an official application for membership. Despite the initial optimism of the UDF government, at the NATO summit in Madrid Bulgaria was not recognised as a candidate even for the second wave of expansion. In Madrid it became clear that the accession of Bulgaria would not be on NATO's agenda at least until 2004–05. The outcome of the Madrid summit came as no real surprise, bearing in mind the late nomination of the candidature, the general condition of the country and the opportunities wasted in previous periods.[9]

In line with the political elite, public opinion in Bulgaria has been largely divided over the issue of NATO, showing one of the lowest rates of support for membership among the CEECs. In a survey in mid-1996 52 per cent of the respondents answered that Bulgaria ought to become a full member (Dainov, 1997: 54). Paradoxically, a positive attitude towards NATO seems to prevail among the majority of army officers, who are still largely Soviet-trained. 'An internal opinion poll conducted among serving army officers revealed that more than half the senior officers, and more than three-quarters of junior officers, are in favour of full NATO membership'[10] (Lyutskanov, 1997: 4). More recent surveys, however, indicate that public opinion was strongly influenced by NATO's reaction to the Kosovo crisis. Despite the fact that Serbia has traditionally been Bulgaria's arch-enemy, the majority of the Bulgarian people did not approve of NATO's air strikes and public opinion, which believed that neither side in the conflict was right, was divided. The government, with the approval of the National Assembly, supported the NATO operation and also granted NATO the use of Bulgarian air space (although the alliance took care not to carry out any operations through it).

> Before the war in Yugoslavia the idea that EU and NATO membership were two sides of the same coin – Euro-Atlantic affiliation – was commonly accepted and broadly communicated by the media. After the conflict turned into a real war, and especially after NATO became involved, this was no longer the case. Support for NATO membership is much lower than support for EU integration. Support for the former was 59 per cent in November 1998 and 48 per cent in April 1999. One-third of the respondents opposed NATO membership in April 1999, compared to only one-fifth in November 1998. (UNDP, 1999: 6)

Although there is still a majority in support of integration with NATO, the Kosovo crisis created an anti-NATO and anti-American outcry, rather short-lived and circumstantial in character. A momentous decision in the parliament in March 2000 demonstrated that at last there was a political consensus and that the political debate over NATO was over. Though its electorate has traditionally been against the alliance, the BSP, taking into account the international situation, agreed on full NATO membership. The BSP maintained its position that there should be a referendum but the political consensus on NATO membership certainly strengthens Bulgaria's application. Yet the question that more than anything else influenced the political debate over NATO as well as the debate in society during the 1990s and will continue to be a decisive factor in the future is the country's relations with Russia.

Bulgaria and Russia

For Bulgaria, unlike the other countries of the former Warsaw Pact that have reoriented their foreign policy to the West, relations with Russia remain a sensitive and complicated issue in an economic, political, military and even ethno-psychological respect. The reason is rooted in the fact that, apart from the years of close integration with the Soviet Union during the Communist era, over a period of more than 120 years Bulgaria developed traditionally close ties with Russia and a relationship of dependence. In fact Russia continues to be Bulgaria's sole resource supplier and one of the most important trade partners, which influences Bulgarian economic, political and social life.

Relations between Bulgaria and Russia made an encouraging beginning in the post-Communist period when in June 1991 President Zhelev sent a message of warm congratulation to Boris Yeltsin on the occasion of his election as President of the Russian Republic, referring to the 'deep historic, Orthodox and Slavonic feelings' which unite the two nations (Moser, 1994: 266). The links between Bulgaria and Russia further improved when Zhelev condemned the attempted *coup* of August 1991, immediately backed Yeltsin and expressed his full support, unlike Bulgaria's ex-Communists (BSP) who kept a 'neutral' stance, silently approving of the hard-liners. It was a move that initiated a personal relationship and rapport between Zhelev and Yeltsin. Bulgaria was also the first country (outside the former Soviet Union), months before the disintegration of the Soviet Union, to recognise, in 1991, the independence of Russia and establish full diplomatic relations. A year later, in August 1992, Yeltsin paid an official visit to Bulgaria and, after difficult negotiations, the two countries signed a new bilateral Treaty on Good Neighbourliness and Friendly Relations, replacing the one signed in 1967. The new friendship treaty provided the foundation for economic, cultural, military, scientific, technological and educational exchanges, covered minority rights issues and included guarantees that neither country would be actively or passively involved in activities against the other. Yeltsin's visit to Sofia, furthermore, was highly symbolic: 'It was his first trip to an East European capital as Russia's leader, and it was also the first time he had gone in person to Eastern Europe to sign a treaty … It was a clear sign that Russia was trying to reassert its traditional influence in the Balkans' (Haramiev-Drezov, 1993: 35, 38).

Despite these positive developments, the relations between the two countries made little further progress. The post-Soviet conditions led to a waning of Russia's influence in the Balkans while for a number of years Moscow's interest in the region decreased. Besides, the conceptual orientation of Bulgarian society and the shift in foreign policy towards the West certainly were not welcomed in Moscow. The situation was further complicated by the fact that between 1994 and 1996 Bulgaria was governed by the BSP, which, despite its pro-Russian attitude, was on poor terms with Yeltsin and his administration. As a result, relations with Moscow in this period were neglected while economic agreements between the two countries stalled. Paradoxically the party most strongly promoting closer relations with Russia failed to re-evaluate and upgrade them when it was in power..

Following the disappointment with the BSP government, Russia's initial response to the UDF electoral victory was favourable. Nevertheless, the situation abruptly changed and instead of warming up the cold climate of 1994–96 Bulgaria's entire relationship with Russia deteriorated when the UDF government announced its intention to seek NATO membership. Apparently Russia still considered Bulgaria part of its sphere of influence, and by officially applying to join NATO Bulgaria came into direct confrontation with the ex-Communist majority in the Duma as well as with Russian foreign policy strategy. The crisis between the two sides blew up when the government failed to reach agreement on prices and delivery terms with the Russian gas monopoly Gazprom, which exclusively supplies natural gas to Bulgaria. The issue was of grave importance for

Bulgaria, as any cuts in deliveries of Russian natural gas could bring industry and heating supplies to the point of collapse.[11] The purely commercial question of the agreement went beyond the bounds of economic argument and became a heavily political matter when Moscow hinted that it would apply pressure on Gazprom to adopt a more reasonable position if the Bulgarian government slowed down its NATO affiliation policy. Bulgarian–Russian relations became tense and great diplomatic friction followed. First, it was the exclusion of Russia from the October 1997 meeting in Sofia of the defence ministers of South-eastern Europe with the participation of the United States and Italy, and then came the refusal of the Russian foreign minister, Yevgenii Primakov, to meet his Bulgarian colleague, Nadezda Michailova, during the fifty-second session of the United Nations.

Bulgaria put its relations with Russia on a new footing when the National Assembly in December 1997 issued a declaration on Bulgarian–Russian relations articulating the principles on which relations must be based. 'The Republic of Bulgaria is minded to develop friendly equality in rights and mutually beneficial relations with Russia as one of its foreign policy priorities … The Republic of Bulgaria develops its relations with the Russian Federation on a long-term basis and in a spirit of friendship, mutual benefit and equal rights in accordance with its national interests' (*Insider*, 1997b: 13). The purpose of this vague declaration, which was based on the 1992 Treaty, was to express Bulgaria's commitment to the historical relationship with Russia but also to indicate that any such relationship should be based on equity and respect for the sovereignty and independence of the other. Soon after, following a meeting between President Stoyanov and Premier Chernomyrdin, the tension between Sofia and Moscow seemed to be overcome. After the principal political problems had been settled the gas issue was resolved early in 1998 in specific technical terms with a protocol signed by Bulgaria and Gazprom.

From this crisis between Sofia and Moscow it became clear enough that in spite of the NATO–Russia agreement the problems concerning NATO enlargement had not been resolved. Bulgaria is still of particular value to Russia as the only reliable partner in the Balkans and as the only former Communist Bloc country that is actually well disposed towards Russia. Although Russia will not object if Bulgaria joins the European Union, it vigorously opposes the idea of Bulgaria's potential NATO membership. Immediately after the application to join the alliance, Russia reminded Bulgaria of its dependence for natural gas and other energy supplies. Bulgarian foreign policy faces the challenge of seeking full participation in the integration process in Europe without disturbing its traditional friendship and good relations with Russia.

The Kosovo conflict has had a significant impact on the question of enlargement. First, it proved NATO's role as an important provider of stability in the Balkan region while raising expectations on the part of a number of countries, Bulgaria among them, which assisted NATO in one way or another. On the other hand, the Kosovo crisis tested NATO's relations with Russia, confirmed

Russian strategic interests in the Balkans and reminded everyone that Russia will be a continuing factor in any further decision on enlargement. It is evident that future developments depend on how the political situation in Russia evolves as well as whether the dialogue between NATO and Russia on the modalities of expansion progresses. Modern Bulgaria seems to stand once again in the shadow of European power politics.

Bulgaria's Balkan policy

Although the regional countries alone are not responsible for it, the Balkan peninsula has a long-standing reputation as a region of turmoil and instability. Communism and the Cold War polarisation imposed an artificial (and unusual) stability in the region but without eliminating or settling the differences among the regional ethnic groups and communities. The Communist system was not only guarantor of political unity and uniformity but also of national cohesion and the homogeneity of the Balkan countries. The fall of Communism and the end of the Cold War order created a political and security void and brought a resurgence of nationalism, ethnic conflict and enmity and economic depression, and the Balkans became a region of daunting problems. The paternalist nature of communal culture, the disintegration of state structures, shallow democratic traditions and the absence of strong political and democratic institutions capable of integrating citizens into political and economic life allowed authoritarian forces, nationalists and criminal groups to assume or retain power and led to violence that seems like echoes of the Balkan past.

In the course of the 1990s a maelstrom of events swept over the region and created a new reality in the Balkans: the disintegration of Yugoslavia and the creation of new states, the war in Bosnia-Herzegovina, the collapse of the pyramidal structures and the economic crisis in Albania, the conflict in Kosovo, outbursts of ethnic tension in the Former Yugoslav Republic of Macedonia (FYROM) and the permanent tension in Greek–Turkish relations. Despite the magnitude of events, Bulgarian Balkan policy since 1989 has been characterised by a moderate, balanced, consistent and constructive approach adhering to the aim of regional co-operation and commitment to international and democratic norms. Bulgarian Balkan policy is based on three fundamental principles accepted by all major political forces:

- Non-engagement in the region's problems and instead a permanent orientation to build structures aiming to restore security and co-operation at a regional level, promoting good neighborly relations.
- Good relations with all the Balkan countries, adopting a realistic, well balanced policy of equidistance, supporting multilateral co-operation procedures, refusing to join regional triangle configurations and avoiding a return to the pattern of forming an 'axis' in the area.

- Seeking solutions and the settlement of problems relating to the inviolability of existing states' boundaries and respect for the sovereignty and integrity of all Balkan countries.

Based on these principles Bulgaria succeeded in determining its regional foreign policy priorities, its permanent position and interests and managed to become a factor of stability in the Balkans.

Bilateral relations

The development of Bulgaria's bilateral relations is determined both by tradition and by reason, as dictated by the changing circumstances in the Balkans during the 1990s. In accordance with one of the basic criteria for obtaining NATO membership, Bulgaria has made considerable efforts to strengthen bilateral relations with neighbouring countries and to find solutions to historical problems as well as those arising from the years of transition.

TURKEY

Since Bulgaria achieved its autonomy from the Ottoman Empire (1878) relations with Turkey have been complicated, burdened with historical animosity and prejudice, and almost always cold, even hostile. During the Cold War relations between Bulgaria and Turkey – the first a member of the Warsaw Pact, the latter of NATO – were a reflection of the suspicions between the West and the East as a whole. But they became particularly strained in the mid-1980s when the two countries came close to military confrontation when the Communist regime in Sofia decided the enforced assimilation of Bulgaria's Turkish minority (the 'Revival Process'). For that reason immediately after the fall of Zhivkov's regime the first priority of the Bulgarian government was to re-establish bilateral contacts with Turkey.[12] With the quick ending and denunciation of the 'Revival Process', the restoration of full rights to ethnic Turks and the participation of the MRF in the political establishment, relations between Turkey and Bulgaria improved markedly. In 1991 President Zhelev met twice Turkish President Ozal (in Amsterdam and in New York) while discussions of bilateral military concerns got under way. The following year a number of bilateral agreements in all fields of co-operation were signed between the two countries, including the Treaty of Friendship, Good Neighbourliness, Co-operation and Security (1992), while Turkey, for its part, provided financial support and, as a goodwill gesture, withdrew significant forces from the common border. These developments proved sufficient to change the whole relationship between the two countries and in 1992 the Bulgarian Defence minister, Dimitar Ludzhev, acknowledged that 'Turkey is not an opponent country any longer' while the general climate of *rapprochement* was expressed by the Turkish foreign minister, Hikmet Cetin, when he asserted that 'Turkey and Bulgaria give the best example of a sincere, amicable, and friendly relationship' (Perry, 1992: 38, 39).

In the same period, attempting to strengthen its regional influence after the disintegration of the Soviet Union, and with no clear prospect of EU membership, Turkey promoted the idea of a Black Sea Economic Co-operation Zone (BSECZ), envisaging the establishment of a free-trade zone among member countries. Bulgaria, being among the most important Black Sea countries, joined in 1992 but rather hesitantly. As the Black Sea co-operation concept was under direct Turkish influence, and wishing to reorient its foreign trade to the West, Sofia preferred to co-operate on lower-level (such as ecological) rather than economic issues. Especially when Bulgaria became an EU associated partner, with the ensuing development of its relationship with the Union, the BSECZ became of secondary importance.

With the BSP electoral victory and the escalation of the Bosnia crisis progress in the bilateral relations between Bulgaria and Turkey somewhat stalled. The BSP first sought to correct the foreign policy balance by renewing contacts with Greece and, second, the BSP, traditionally pro-Slav in attitude, attempted to restore a Slavic orientation to foreign policy. (Because of the BSP's problems in dealing with Moscow, as discussed, this Slavic orientation found expression mainly in relation to Serbia.) The emergence of Turkey as a regional power awakened historical prejudices and fears, but the war in Bosnia turned the attention of the public away from Turkey. When the UDF came to power, at a time when Bulgaria needed support for its NATO candidacy, and for attracting foreign investment, new possibilities emerged to develop Bulgarian–Turkish relations further. President Stoyanov's visit to Ankara in July 1997, and the formal apology he offered for the oppression by the Communist regime of Bulgaria's Turkish minority, removed one more problem from relations between the two countries. The visit to Sofia by Turkish Prime Minister Mesut Yilmaz in December 1997 was the first official visit by a Turkish Premier for eighteen years and opened a new chapter in Bulgarian–Turkish relations. The half-century-long border dispute in the delta of the river Rezovska was resolved and during this visit Yilmaz pledged the support of his country for Bulgarian membership of NATO. The two countries signed a memorandum for liberalising trade and agreed to co-operate in law enforcement, customs and culture, and to work towards setting up a free-trade zone in order to boost bilateral trade and co-operation. As a result, the relationship has reached a significant level of interaction and Turkey tends to be Bulgaria's priority partner in the Balkans.

GREECE

Distrust and territorial disputes were the main characteristics of relations with Greece throughout their history. The two countries were enemies in the Second Balkan War (1913), in the First World War and in the Second World War. Bulgaria was also among the countries that supported the Communist insurgency in post-war Greece. Paradoxically, despite past animosity, and despite their membership of opposing military alliances, Bulgarian–Greek relations started to improve in the mid-1960s and were strengthened in the 1970s when a declaration on the principles of friendly relations was signed (1973). The Bulgarian-Greek *rapprochement*, which was based upon wariness of a common enemy (Turkey), culminated in 1986 with the Declaration of Friendship and Good Neighbourliness which among other things provided for the consultation between the two countries in the event of a threat to the national security of either, forming thus a Sofia–Athens 'axis'.[13]

During the initial transitional period the links between the two sides were maintained, and Bulgaria and Greece signed a new Friendship Treaty in 1991.[14] But then, with the coming to power of the UDF, relations became more complicated. The fact that the UDF government was dependent on the parliamentary support of the MRF, and especially Bulgaria's decision to recognise the independence of Macedonia in January 1992 (which Greece strongly opposed because of the use of the name 'Macedonia'), tarnished relations between the two countries. With the return to power of the BSP in 1994 Bulgaria's good relations with Greece were gradually restored. The fact that Videnov chose Greece for his first visit to a Balkan country in his capacity as Prime Minister was a sign of Bulgaria's foreign policy orientation. Favourable to this development was the fact that the government in Greece was that of the Socialists, trusted partners of the Bulgarian former Communists. It is also important to note the active involvement of Greek investors and the strong business interest Greek firms have shown in the Bulgarian economy and the expansion of bilateral trade. The problems in the Balkans forced Greece and Bulgaria to maintain frequent contact and their relationship of co-operation has been strengthened, especially since there are no open issues or differences. Greece has consistently pledged to support the Bulgarian case for EU and NATO membership (Greece is the only Balkan EU member) while, on the other hand, Bulgaria, taking advantage of its geographical position and the close relationship with both Turkey and Greece, is playing the role of bridge builder between the two and has promoted the idea of a trilateral 'non-aggression pact'.

THE FORMER YUGOSLAV REPUBLIC OF MACEDONIA

The area included under the term 'Macedonia', which is composed of various peoples and national groups (mainly Serbs, Albanians, Bulgarians, Greeks, Turks and Valaks), has been in the past the apple of discord in the Balkan region. The whole region of Macedonia was liberated from the Ottoman Empire at the conclusion of the Balkan Wars in 1913 and was partitioned among Bulgaria, Greece and Serbia. The section of geographical Macedonia that was later to become FYROM was annexed to the newly founded Kingdom of Serbs, Croats and Slovenes and was officially designated Southern Serbia. The Macedonian national identity was first recognised as separate from that of the other Balkan peoples in 1934 by the inter-war Communist movement and the Comintern and later during the Second World War by Josip Broz Tito. After the war, in an attempt to nurture the Macedonian national autonomy, Tito created the People's Yugoslav Federal Republic of Macedonia, a component of the Federal Yugoslavia, and also promoted the concept of a Macedonian Slav nationality with its own officially recognised language, which is close to Bulgarian. With the break-up of Yugoslavia, Macedonia in November 1991 declared its independence.

In the course of the twentieth century over a million people moved from Macedonia to Bulgaria, while the latter has occupied Macedonia three times and historically has regarded Macedonia as western Bulgaria, the Macedonians as Bulgarians and the spoken language as a regional Bulgarian dialect. The widespread perception in Bulgarian society is that Macedonians are in fact ethnic Bulgarians who are not part of Bulgaria only because the country was on the losing side in the Second Balkan War and in both World Wars. Bulgaria also regarded the Macedonian nation as artificially fabricated by Tito in order to undermine Bulgarian territorial integrity and assert future territorial claims.[15] Despite the feeling of historical deprivation, in January 1992 Bulgaria was the first country in the world to recognise FYROM as an independent sovereign state but was reluctant to recognise a Macedonian nation or a Macedonian language. Sofia feared that recognition of 'Macedonian' as a distinct language would allow FYROM to raise territorial claims in south-western Bulgaria (the Pirin region), where, according to Skopje, there is a Macedonian ethnic minority. Sofia was also concerned about Article 49 of Macedonia's constitution, which states that Skopje has a right to protect its ethnic minorities abroad. Nonetheless, 'the recognition of Macedonia was the first brave and categorical act of the post-Communist Bulgarian government in international affairs. It was done autonomously, without gaining the prior approval of any of the Great Powers or even consulting with friendly Greece'[16] (Nikova, 1998: 291).

The decision to recognise Macedonia promptly can be explained by the fact that, from a strategic point of view, the existence of an independent Macedonian state on its borders is far preferable for Bulgaria to a federal republic in the grip of Belgrade or a state partitioned between the neighbouring countries, which could revive the conflicts of the beginning of the twentieth century. After almost half a century of Communism nationalist feelings and the idea of a Greater Bulgaria had faded away and, given the county's problems in the post-Communist era, Bulgaria was in no position to pursue irredentist designs. On the contrary, policy towards FYROM has been based from the beginning on co-operation, support, respect for its internal affairs and the inviolability of its borders. In this respect Bulgarian President Zhelev managed to influence Russian President Yeltsin in deciding to recognise Macedonian sovereignty. Zhelev became the first head of state to visit Macedonia in February 1993, while Bulgaria offered its assistance and the Black Sea port of Burgas when Greece imposed a trade blockade on FYROM.

The two countries, however, did not manage to build on this good beginning and their relationship in the mid-1990s became stagnant. With the end of the Greek blockade, the gradual improvement of the Greek–Macedonian relations and the *rapprochement* between Belgrade and Skopje, Bulgaria's role in Macedonian affairs declined. To make matters worse, the language dispute dominated the Bulgarian–Macedonian relations as the two sides were caught up in a nationalist fever. Skopje insisted on the bilateral agreements being drafted 'in the Macedonian and Bulgarian languages' while Sofia called the demand unacceptable, since it would mean *de facto* recognition of the Macedonian language. As a result, nearly twenty vital accords on bilateral co-operation, already prepared by Bulgaria and Macedonia, were not finalised. The issue was protracted for years as the two sides approached the matter in an emotional way, unable to overcome the legacy of the past and to alienate the nationalist elements in both countries. A compromise was reached in February 1999 when Bulgaria agreed to sign the agreements in 'the official languages' of the two countries (thus implicitly recognising the Macedonian language) while Skopje agreed not to apply Article 49 to Bulgaria (accepting thus that there is no Macedonian minority in Bulgaria). A joint declaration, signed by Bulgarian Prime Minister Kostov and his Macedonian counterpart Ljubco Georgievski, stated that neither country had any territorial claims on the other and both pledged not to undertake, incite or support actions of a hostile nature (Synovitz, 1999). The settlement of the language dispute put an end to the artificial problem in bilateral relations and allowed the two sides to unblock the stalled agreements that opened up the way to trade and economic development, the free movement of goods, services and capital, relaxed customs and border formalities, promoted reciprocal investment, the construction of transport links and the development of culture of co-operation. With the joint declaration, therefore, Bulgaria and Macedonia resolved potential territorial disputes. (Sofia even went so far as to donate $3.5 million worth of decommissioned weaponry to Macedonia).

After the signing of the declaration relations between Bulgaria and Macedonia qualitatively improved. As long as the Kosovo problem and the spread of extremist views in Macedonia generate instability and uncertainty on Bulgaria's south-western border the only logical and realistic choice for the political elite in Sofia is to turn their back on the differences and controversies of the distant past and assist stability in Macedonia. The signs in the new decade are that this is exactly the orientation of the Bulgarian foreign policy.

THE FEDERAL REPUBLIC OF YUGOSLAVIA

Bulgarian relations with Serbia, considering the overall situation in the Balkans and the past animosity between the two countries, have been reasonably free of bilateral problems. From the outset of the Yugoslav conflict, Bulgaria made it clear that it had no intention of heightening tension further by making territorial or other demands upon Serbia, despite the existence of a small Bulgarian minority (about 30,000) in the borderland between the two countries (Bulgarian territory ceded to Yugoslavia under the Neuilly Peace Treaty of 1919). Bulgaria adopted a cautious approach and a policy of non-interference in the Yugoslav crisis, seeking to keep away from the conflict while contributing to the success of the international efforts to find a stable solution. Against its own economic interests Bulgaria supported and participated actively in imposing financial sanctions on the

Republic of Yugoslavia. Bulgaria completely closed its economic borders with Yugoslavia, though it suffered enormous losses as a result of the trade sanctions.

The relationship with the Milosevic regime was perhaps the only major difference between the UDF and the BSP in regional policy. The first UDF government (1991–92) and particularly President Zhelev kept a rather tough position on Belgrade by calling for more decisive NATO involvement, while during the BSP government the rift widened as the Videnov Cabinet re-established contact with Serbia and preserved close ties with the Serbian Socialist party, headed by Milosevic. At the time of the Kosovo conflict the UDF government demonstrated full solidarity with NATO policy but the BSP was openly against the NATO operation. At the end of the conflict, however, both parties hailed Milosevic's ousting and the election of President Kostunica as a landmark for the prospects of economic growth across the entire Balkan region. Bulgaria expects to benefit from democratic changes in Yugoslavia and bilateral relations are expected to acquire impetus, especially in the economic domain.

ROMANIA

Relations between Bulgaria and its northern neighbour have for decades been calm and friendly. At the moment Bulgaria and Romania are more like European partners, sharing mutual interests and having the same goals – EU and NATO accession. The good-neighbour relations between the two states were confirmed with a treaty of friendship signed in January 1992. In the post-Communist period the thorniest issues were environmental problems and the construction of a second bridge over the Danube. Bulgaria frequently complained in the past about pollution of the Danube and air pollution drifting in over the cities of Russe and Silistra. The issue is expected to be resolved eventually with the implementation of the EU legislation.

The issue of the Danube bridge, which is of extreme significance to all Balkan countries, has been more complicated and exemplifies Balkan behaviour. When the main transport route between South-east and Central and Western Europe was cut by international sanctions against Yugoslavia in the 1990s, Bulgaria and Romania were eager to create an alternative transport route bypassing Serbia. Because the only bridge over the Danube between Romania and Bulgaria was inadequate (that meant considerable delays) the two countries decided on the construction of a second but could not agree on the location, and this reflected on the whole spectrum of bilateral relations. Especially when all Serbia's Danube bridges were destroyed in NATO's air campaign in 1999 the construction of the bridge became more pressing while the issue of its location assumed geopolitical significance. After nine years of negotiations a mutually acceptable site was found, under pressure from the European Union, in March 2000.[17]

The regional setting

For more than ten years the Balkan region has been politically, economically, institutionally and socially unstable and characterised by enormous insecurity.

Despite the Dayton Peace Agreement in 1995, NATO's military intervention and the end of the Kosovo conflict, the various initiatives conceived by the international community in attempts to foster a spirit of co-operation, the emergence of more liberal and democratic governments in countries like Croatia, FYROM or Romania, and despite the fall of Slobodan Milosevic, the Balkans remain a volatile region. The initial approach of the international community in the beginning of the 1990s was that Balkan conflicts were generated by the undemocratic nature of the old political system and that political change and democratisation would reduce ethnic tension and ensure stability and security in the region. 'This explanation has some validity but the lessons of the last decade demonstrate the limits of democratisation *per se* as a security provider. The dissolution of Yugoslavia demonstrated that when a society has to choose between democratisation and self-determination, the latter comes first' (Krastev, 2000: 14). The persistence of ethnic tensions even after the political change in Serbia stands as a reminder that the promotion of democracy alone cannot solve regional problems. The precedents of Bosnia and Albania, furthermore, demonstrate that simply providing assistance through underdeveloped state institutions that cannot guarantee law and order creates aid dependence and increases the scope for corruption while those who profit from the situation tend to defend the *status quo*. Bosnia, therefore, despite massive international financial assistance, lost the chance to make a lasting economic recovery; thanks to the old Communist mentality, the intrusive and ineffective bureaucracy, the endemic corruption, the illegal economy and the existing interethnic friction, economic activity remains poor, the democratic institutional system remains fragile and the withdrawal of the international administration would bring chaos and a new stage of violence. The situation in Kosovo seems similar: the absence of coherent and efficient state structures, the failure of the international administration to administer the province effectively and the lack of clarity in the legal system offer criminal gangs great opportunities, to the extent that smuggling, extortion, drug and weapons trafficking are the major economic activities.[18] 'Weak states, that is, states that are unwilling or unable to create and enforce rules, are the basic source of insecurity in the Balkan region and if the international community is not ready to face this reality, all other policies will fail' (Krastev, 2000: 17). In this context it could be argued that after the Dayton Peace Agreement, stability in the Balkans is threatened not by conflicts between states but by the question of how to ensure and sustain peace and security within states. Besides, almost all Balkan countries decided to follow the path that leads to EU and NATO integration which includes regional co-operation, a commitment to find solutions to regional problems, the improvement of the good neighbourliness and the development of democracy.

Throughout the 1990s international engagement was based largely on crisis management and containment, short-term measures designed for post-conflict rehabilitation, and tended to treat issues in a piecemeal and country-oriented approach without provision for long-term, political and financial investment –

in the broader sense of the term. But rebuilding peace and security in the region requires more than an end of the conflict, emergency assistance and repairing destroyed infrastructure. The challenge for the international community is the articulation and implementation of a unified and concrete long-term regional strategy, a broader development and integration framework for the whole region involving military, economic, political and social instruments. Developments since the Kosovo crisis suggest that there is increased readiness, both within and outside the region, to foster genuine co-operation between countries. The aim must be to settle or eliminate differences, encourage collective work for the area's future and pave the way to sub-regional and, subsequently, continental integration. The Kosovo tragedy underlined the need to tackle the sources of the problems and placed the Balkan area at the top of the European agenda. Therefore, in the immediate aftermath of the cessation of hostilities in Kosovo a new approach was elaborated, with a new Balkan Stability Pact, under the auspices of the European Union, to aid the political and economic reconstruction of South-eastern Europe.[19]

The Stability Pact is the organisation charged with the co-ordination of the various assistance initiatives and national activities in the political, economic and security spheres. The aim of the pact, which was initially compared with the Marshall Plan and aroused great expectations and enthusiasm, is to drag the backward Balkans into the European mainstream at last by offering the region increased support in terms of trade, investment, economic development, infrastructure and security, as well as guidance in democratisation and institution building. The three major fields covered by the Stability Pact are democracy, economics and security/defence. Only parallel progress on all fronts, taking into account the interdependence between these three priority fields, can be effective. The Stability Pact also recognises the crucial role that NGOs can play and considers the building of a civil society that transcends state boundaries as an important prerequisite for promoting regional integration, which should be primarily a bottom-up process aiming to construct real communities of people. In this vein, the long-term task of the NGOs is to develop and co-ordinate an educational programme for the people of the region that can support and facilitate efforts towards *rapprochement* and reconciliation.

Moreover, after the fund-raising conference in March 2000, the Stability Pact is endowed with considerable resources ($2.3 billion committed to quick-start projects), which perhaps indicates that the international community is anxious not to repeat the mistakes of the past. Nonetheless, even though it had still not been fully unfolded by 2001, the pact has already been criticised for bad organisation, a bureaucratic approach and lack of co-ordination between international institutions, while the initial overoptimistic hopes seem to fade. The Stability Pact is not financially autonomous, either, as it is actually an umbrella organisation whose mission is to co-ordinate, not to fund, regional projects. There are even claims that the funds donated to it are funds that had already been allocated to the region under another label. There is also a real danger, mainly because of the regional institutional environment, that the funds will be misused. Indeed, the Stability Pact is not a magic formula that will solve the region's problems but certainly is a major challenge which is doomed to fail unless there is sincere and lasting determination among the countries to seize the opportunity and act in a new spirit of co-operation and neighbourly relations.

Bulgaria will not particularly benefit from the Stability Pact, having made considerable progress towards political and economic transformation and already initiated accession negotiations with the European Union. Yet the country has a key interest in strengthening stability throughout the region, having suffered enormous political and economic losses during the 1990s. In this respect Bulgaria co-ordinates all its activities in the area with the foreign and security policy of the European Union and with the terms and positions agreed upon in the context of NATO. Bulgaria is very active in promoting regional co-operation procedures, as it has initiated a series of multilateral meetings and participates in all regional initiatives that influence the process of transforming the Balkans into an integral part of the European democratic community. Examples of such initiatives are: the South-east European Co-operation Initiative (SECI), launched in 1996 by the United States with the aim of improving the transport infrastructure, private capital investment and the evolution of a regional common market; the Southern Balkans Development Initiative (SBDI), a US-sponsored initiative to improve the transport infrastructure linking Albania, FYROM and Bulgaria; the South-eastern European Defence Ministerial (SEDM), the meeting of the Defence Ministers of the South-east European countries aiming to harmonise national military policies and to bring together NATO member countries and applicants; the Multinational Peace Force in South-east Europe (stationed in Plovdiv), which has introduced a common military force to protect the security interests of countries in the region. This demonstration of regional thinking and approaches to the various political, social, economic and security issues certainly is not just Bulgaria's achievement but rather a common asset that needs to be further nurtured. Bulgaria's stance is also that Belgrade, after the political change, should play an important role in the process of stabilisation and development of the Balkan region.

Bulgaria (along with Romania and Slovenia) has a clear regional and European vision and tries through its regional policy to promote European patterns of behaviour among the countries of the area so as to accelerate the integration of the region into the European Union and NATO. That is because ultimately the strong incentive of incorporation into the uniform zone of European security and co-operation is the only way to avoid conflict and to attain a measure of state, democratic and economic consolidation. That said, in a region as unpredictable as the Balkans, where it is as easy to buy a modern machine gun as a bar of chocolate, only an amateur could claim to know what the future will be.

Notes

1. Unlike the three previous Association Agreements, the agreements signed with Bulgaria and Romania were made conditional on respect for human rights and democratic principles.
2. As the former Czech economics minister, Karel Dyba, put it, 'we were surprised by the speed of the collapse of our Eastern markets, and we were surprised by the speed of the common market's actions to close their markets' (Parker, 1994: 60).
3. Bulgaria's main exports to the European Union are textiles and base metals, its main import from the Union is machinery.
4. The findings of the 2000 opinion, though some progress since the 1999 opinion is recorded, are similar. As far as other candidate countries are concerned, the political criteria of accession appear to have been met by all countries except Slovakia, where, in the Commission's view, the rule of law and democracy is not sufficiently rooted in political life and there is insufficient protection of minorities. For that reason Slovakia was excluded from the first wave of enlargement. As regards the economic requirements, the five countries chosen for the first wave are considered to have viable market economies (while Slovakia is very close to this goal), having made progress in their ability to cope with competitive pressure and market forces within the Union.
5. There were frequent statements from political figures across the political spectrum about a 'new iron curtain', or the European Union considering Bulgarians 'third-rate Europeans', and there were demands for an unconditional and non-discriminatory visa-free regime for Bulgarian citizens.
6. The lack of knowledge in society about the actual meaning of EU membership indicates also a failure on the part of the European Union to provide adequate information on how its structures and institutions operate. It is indicative of this that there is still no EU information centre in Sofia.
7. As Avery and Cameron noted, 'it was the US that in the end carried the day, with President Clinton basing his decision on a limited enlargement to three countries as much on internal considerations (Senate ratification) as for any strategic rationale. The US was thus against accession of the Baltic states (as advocated by Denmark) and against the accession of Romania and Slovenia (as advocated by France and Italy)' (Avery and Cameron, 1998: 169).
8. The National Assembly declared that 'Bulgaria will continue the efforts for utilising the co-operation opportunities offered by NATO and the WEU. In case of their future expansion, Bulgaria will join them at the condition of full respect for its national interests' (Todorov, 1997: 31).
9. Furthermore, with the aim of bringing the army up to NATO standards, the government developed a plan for the reform of the army and the restructuring of the arms industry. The reform focuses on downsizing the total standing and enhancing the defence capacity of the armed forces. According to the plan, within five years Bulgaria will have to cut its army from 85,000 to 50,000 troops but will have to improve its funding, training and equipment. The army reform, however, is progressing slowly because of the financial burden.
10. An interesting fact is that the military elite usually identify NATO with the United States. This can be attributed to a natural reflex, left over from the past, when army officers identified the Warsaw Pact as an alliance with the Soviet Union. 'In the political and especially in the economic sphere there was a genuine sense of a socialist community, but that was not the case in the military sphere. The army officers perceived the Warsaw Treaty as a military alliance between Bulgaria and the Soviet Union rather than as a multinational alliance. The main reason for this situation was the exclusive dependence on Soviet military and other equipment, the word-for-word translations of the Soviet

guidelines, the presence of Soviet military advisers ... All other allied relations were so far-fetched that they had no real chance of producing allied thinking among army officers' (Ratchev, 1997: 47).

11 At the root of this dispute was a struggle for control of pipelines carrying Russian natural gas across Bulgaria and on to Macedonia, Turkey, Serbia and Greece. Gazprom is the largest and perhaps the most politically influential company in Russia. Allegations that Gazprom has a powerful say in Moscow's political decisions arise from the fact that Viktor Chernomyrdin headed the firm from its creation in the late 1980s until he became Prime Minister in 1992. It is estimated that about 11 per cent of the Bulgarian economy depends on the gas supplied by Gazprom. The story behind Russian supplies of natural gas is extremely difficult to trace, since it is a mixture of unlawful deals, mafia groupings, crime and corruption.

12 The first meeting between the two sides took place just days after the regime change, on 30 November 1989, when Bulgaria's deputy Prime Minister, Georgi Yordanov, met Turkey's foreign minister, Mesut Yilmaz, in Ankara. Several high-level meetings between Bulgarian and Turkish officials followed.

13 The Bulgarian–Greek Treaty of 1986 came at a time when the socialist PASOK government of Greece was attempting to conduct a more independent foreign policy within the alliance, while the Zhivkov regime was resuming its campaign to assimilate the Turkish minority. Furthermore, an indication of the close relations between Greece and Bulgaria is the fact that from 1975 to mid-1989 the two countries exchanged a total of twenty-eight visits of heads of state, Prime Ministers and foreign ministers (Moser, 1994: 268).

14 An example of the equal distance that Bulgaria wants to keep between Greece and Turkey is the fact that the treaty of friendship Bulgaria signed with Greece in October 1991 was quite similar to the one signed with Turkey in May 1992. Even more, parliamentary ratification of the treaty with Greece was delayed until after the signing of the treaty with Turkey.

15 Only after the Second World War did Bulgaria, in the spirit of Communist collegiality, recognise the Macedonians as a separate nation, but soon reverted to the old notion.

16 Despite the emotional stress, Bulgarian society accepted the recognition of Macedonia (an act attributed mainly to President Zhelev) rather well, and although there were voices against, the reaction was not so intense as some expected.

17 'The bridge is a key link in the EU project known as Pan-European Transport Corridor Four. That project aims to create a major north–south transport route linking Greece and Western Europe through Bulgaria, Romania, and Hungary. Under the March agreement, the new bridge will cross the Danube about twenty kilometers east of Serbia at the Bulgarian town of Vidin and the Romanian river port of Calafat. For years, Bucharest had lobbied for a bridge to be built further to the east, a move that would have put the north–south transport corridor closer to Bucharest as well as would have increase the amount of transit fees received by Romania' (Synovitz, 2000).

18 International experts estimate that Kosovo drug smugglers 'are handling up to five tons of heroin a month, more than twice the quantity they were trafficking before the war' (Arbova, 2000: 19).

19 The previous Stability Pact of 1994–95 was mainly aimed at getting EU accession candidates to resolve by co-operation outstanding border disputes and minority issues. These co-operation initiatives have been transferred to the OSCE.

7

Conclusion

The process which started with the extraordinary turn of events in 1989 will not be complete until the countries of Central and Eastern Europe reach the stage of democratic consolidation which involves the development of a vigorous civil society and the broad and widespread participation of citizens in public affairs not just in terms of voting but in terms of interest group and association activity. Nor will the process which started in 1989 be complete until the dividing lines that still cross Central and Eastern Europe, including the divisions between NATO members and non-members and between likely early EU members and other candidate countries, are replaced by an integrated Europe. In this context, this book has attempted to discuss the direction of the democratisation process in Bulgaria and the prospects of meeting the challenge of moving for the first time in its history from Europe's periphery and becoming a member of core European institutions.

The initiation of the democratisation process was due to three primary reasons: the failure of Communist policies, especially in the economic field, and the hostile treatment of the Turkish minority; the drastic change in Soviet foreign policy; and the decision of the Communist leadership to retain a central role in the new post-Communist reality by launching political and economic reforms. Despite the fact that even before November 1989 civic organisations had been formed openly criticising the regime on a number of ecological, cultural, economic and political issues, civil society was not among the factors that brought Communism down. The passive population only followed the course of events while the ruling elite negotiated and manipulated the transition period. Besides, one of the main features of the Communist era was the lack of a dissident movement, which is explained by the paternalist Balkan mentality, the absence of a democratic political culture and by the enormous economic successes brought by Communism until the 1970s. Though the successful post-war economic development, social modernisation and elevation of the literacy level created a large group with a middle-class lifestyle with changed political values and orientations, it remained largely submissive and became visible only after the introduction of reformist policies by Gorbachev. Therefore the fall of Communism was arguably an elite-centred transition, the outcome of a negotiated change between elements of the previous regime and a weak dissident group, not the result of the awakening of civil society. The new post-Communist elite, with the participation of the former Communists, faced the grim task of creating new political and economic foundations. The political leadership soon after the events of 1989, based on the round-table agreements and on a broad procedural consensus, managed quite successfully to create the necessary political institutions and political framework. As a result, since the downfall of the old regime Bulgaria presents all the minimum procedural characteristics of a modern democracy: representative government, a competitive plural party system, regular and fairly conducted elections, non-violent alternations of power, conflict resolution according to institutionalised democratic principles, an independent legal system and civil rights. Yet, despite the fact that Bulgaria has established all democratic institutions, they have not yet formed a smoothly operating system.

Although the early days of the transition were characterised by constructive debate and compromises, after the 1990 elections this pattern gradually altered radically. Tolerance was gave way to extreme polarisation of the two major political forces which, along with the lack of strategic thinking, short-termist policies, factionalism, frequent accusations of collaboration with the Communist authorities or of economic scandals, inexperience, arrogance and lack of political skills, contributed to the creation of social prostration, fatigue of the futile reformist strains and all-embracing disappointment. Under these conditions the political parties that came to the fore with the round-table talks failed to create the necessary conditions for democratic consolidation. The dismal performance of the bipolar political system is best reflected in the economic sphere, where successive governments proved incapable of handling the pressing economic problems of creating the foundations of a functioning market economy. The economic transformation proved to be very slow and did not yield the results the population had hoped for. The economic crisis deepened and produced a catastrophic collapse in living standards, unprecedented reductions in real wages and unique figures for unemployment, accompanied by an inadequate welfare and health-care system. Economic transition created an alienated underclass, impoverished the middle class and enriched the already wealthy. The last decade is hence perceived by most Bulgarians as a time of wrecked optimism, betrayed expectations and meaningless sacrifices that brought about negativism and social resignation amid unexpected hardship. It is estimated that more than 300,000 citizens left their homeland as a result of the economic and social situation. Since those who emigrate are particularly the most promising part of society, the younger and more educated, as long as Bulgaria continues to record negative population growth rates the demographic issue is another potentially explosive problem for the country.[1]

Arguably, economic success and the creation of greater wealth would have strengthened the prospect of democracy, while a more positive assessment of the political process would have provided a valuable time frame for the accommodation of the pain of economic restructuring. Still, the failure of economic reform had an effect neither on the legitimacy of market economics nor on democracy as a political system. Despite the fact that a large section of society saw its living standards fall rapidly in comparison with the Communist years, the negative effects of economic reform have not been associated with democracy and democratic principles and did not generate a widespread reaction. The economic crash and the collapse of the social notions moulded at the beginning of the transition, however, undeniably undermined the legitimacy of the new political establishment and political elite. It is no coincidence that the most popular man in Bulgaria at the end of the 1990s was President Stoyanov – by all means one of the more enlightened politicians – who lacks executive power.

Certainly that is not to imply that because successive governments were inefficient, corrupt, shortsighted, irresponsible, dominated by special interests and incapable of adopting policies demanded by the public good Bulgaria is not a democratic country. These qualities may make such governments undesirable and unpopular but they do not make them undemocratic. Yet as the existing party system failed to live up to expectations, to clarify and express the interests of society, to show morality and frankness, the bipolar political model of the 1990s seems exhausted. The BSP remains discredited as, along with the Communist past, it has to overcome the legacy of the gloomy and extremely negative period of the Videnov government. On the other hand, the popularity of the UDF government has waned owing to falling living standards, painful market reforms and a series of public scandals involving top officials. As a result the public is desperate for an alternative. This has apparently created fertile ground for a third force and, in this context, the emergence on the political arena in 2001 of the former King Simeon, who has lived in exile since 1946, may produce significant shifts and shatter the bipolar political system. Although society is not faced with the monarchy–republic issue, Simeon became the first monarch in post-Communist Europe to enter politics. In any case, as long as a large segment of society lives in real poverty the danger of succumbing to the appeal of demagogy has not yet been eliminated. Thus only real economic growth and prosperity, reducing poverty and increasing the competitiveness of the economy will ensure the legitimacy of the democratic system.

The prospects of democracy are also connected with the rapidly eroding capacity of the state, which has caused public disappointment and weakened public trust. Post-communist transformation lacked a regulatory framework as the state failed to help or guide the transition and did not fulfil its role as a regulator. The general feeling of mistrust towards the state is the reason for the lack of commitment to the public welfare generally, and this explains why private interest tends to prevail over the public interest. High levels of crime and corruption have been among the main elements of the first decade of post-communism, affecting even the most basic societal structures and leading to the domination of economic activity by predatory business and criminal groups. The creation of a market economy presupposed the existence of capital but since there was no capital in the Communist system a new class of capitalists emerged that acquired wealth by illegal means, by expropriating public property or by transforming political power under Communism into economic power. Democratic institutions, which tolerated these mafia structures, have largely lost the confidence of the public and thus have yet to gain genuine legitimacy, while Bulgaria is not yet functioning as a genuine market economy because 'instead of being marketised, the economy is being mobsterized' (Bulgarian Academy of Science, 1994: 10). The strengthening of institutions will reduce corruption and in so doing will assist poverty reduction and thus bring about improvements in the quality of life. Undoubtedly, steps were taken in this direction at the end of the 1990s but still the issue of corruption remains perhaps the biggest challenge for the political elite because, to quote President Stoyanov, 'if reforms are accompanied by corruption, democracy itself will be threatened' (*Economist*, 2000: 38). And the fact that corruption is acknowledged as a compelling issue is of itself an improvement.

The post-Communist political situation has not facilitated or encouraged political participation, whereas the state of the economy has led ordinary citizens to concentrate on their day-to-day financial problems, restricting citizen participation in the political process even more. The economic context within which a new civil society has attempted to develop has been far from perfect, as economic problems generated an all-pervading pessimistic realism and created a deficit of self-confidence since Bulgaria became the object of humanitarian concern to Western countries. Negativism and the absence of any worthy perspective are always a good excuse for civic passivity. The development of civil society is also obstructed by the political culture and the Balkan mentality that represents a paternalist type of communal culture. Only in the Balkans did former Communists retain a grip on political power in the period immediately after 1989 and they remain major players in national politics, even if many choose to redefine themselves as nationalists. The corruption of administrative bodies has enabled crime and smuggling to flourish, allowing the region to be dominated by international criminal structures and interest groups which are gaining political influence. In the still parochially based societies of the Balkans, tolerance and pluralism remain in short supply. Nonetheless, given the nationalistic and belligerent atmosphere, it is a substantial enough achievement for Bulgaria and its people not to be influenced by the surrounding environment. Bulgarians have consistently rejected nationalist agendas and ideologies, just as the situation of the Turkish minority has been considerably improved.[2]

In this political, economic and regional setting it became even more difficult to rebuild and regenerate civil society after forty-five years of absence. At the same time the active participation of civil society in national and local policy making as well as the enhancement of participatory democratic practices has become a prerequisite for the consolidation of democracy. Civil society has not significantly developed ten years after the democratic transition and still is in its formative stage. That much was revealed in our examination of the NGO sector. Certainly the third sector has expanded, has created channels for the articulation and representation of interests and has provided excluded groups (such as the Roma) with access to the decision-making process. It continues to suffer, however, from poor co-ordination, and its major weaknesses continue to be the difficulty of achieving sustainability and heavy dependence on international donor support. It is evident that the expansion of the third sector will progressively continue, though it may take several years before Bulgarian NGOs can match the performance and efficiency of those in consolidated democracies. But, as all the signs indicate at present, it is mainly a matter of time.

An acute danger for democratic politics, however, derives from the fact that once again an inferiority complex has started to reappear, stemming from modern Balkan culture. As the political scientist Ognyan Minchev points out,

> almost all Balkan countries are suffering from this inferiority complex, which basically boils down to the realisation that, for historical reasons, the Balkans remained apart from Europe in the most important ages of European development, the ages of the Renaissance, the Enlightenment and Modernisation. This is precisely why the process of emancipation and modern development in the Balkans was based above all on the prerequisite that we must 'catch up with Europe' and break away from the Balkan cultural legacy. (Minchev, 1997: 116)

In this context Bulgaria made a historic choice in 1989 which expressed itself mainly in foreign policy. Ever since 1878 modern Bulgaria has sought to associate itself with Europe. Despite the appeal of Russia, pre-communist Bulgaria relied mostly on European political and social models but, thanks to economic backwardness and consecutive wars, did not manage to get closer to mainstream Europe. Following the Second World War, the Soviet Union became the model of development and European affiliations were buried, coming back to life only in 1989 as the aspiration to membership of the European Union.

The post-Communist international and regional setting obliged Bulgaria to formulate a new national strategy and develop new concepts of national security. The changes have been reflected in foreign policy since 1989, which has corresponded to the demands of the modern world and in many respects has been commendable, on several occasions receiving the praise of the international community. The continuous ten-year period of political and economic instability in the Balkans and the resulting problems for both the international community and the countries of the region highlight the achievements of Bulgarian foreign policy. The country managed to associate itself with all the European structures and institutions, worked to build solid good relations with its Balkan neighbours, kept its distance from the Balkan conflicts, becoming an anchor of stability in the region; the handling of the Kosovo crisis boosted Bulgaria's international role and reasserted its place in the family of democratic values. The acknowledgement of the stability of its democratic institutions and the enhancement of its international image found expression precisely in the invitation by the European Union to enter into accession negotiations. This invitation promises the realisation of the longest-cherished dream in modern Bulgarian history, which will be fulfilled only when Bulgaria becomes a full and equal member of the European Union.

The issue of Bulgaria's membership of NATO is more complicated, as it not only confirms the country's pro-European orientation but also means, to a certain extent, a breaking with the traditional Russian affiliation. There are still many Bulgarians who see Russia as the country's traditional economic, political and cultural ally, while, on the other hand, Russia is not prepared to accept the expansion of NATO in its traditional sphere of influence and has activated economic leverage to assert its interests. It is obvious that Bulgaria's candidacy could fall victim to Moscow's interests in the Balkans and its desperate efforts to play a role on the world stage. Certainly, Bulgaria's successful integration into NATO will need hard work during the period before the alliance decides on the admission of new members, and it is certain that when that moment comes the primary concern of the current members will be effectiveness rather than enlargement. Hence most probably Bulgaria will not be included in the next wave of expansion but still the country must be given a clear perspective on its chances of accession. Besides, as long as regional problems remain unresolved the West must actively support the democratic factors in the Balkans. The spread of violence in Macedonia proves that sometimes the international community underestimates risks that may result in conflict. Though the Stability Pact is an updated strategy for solving problems in the region, no potent idea of how to surmount instability has yet been put forward. The settlement of the Kosovo problem is vital for the development of events in other parts of the Balkans and a final disintegration of Montenegro and Serbia may send disturbing impulses to other Balkan hotspots.

The prospect of accession to the European Union and NATO seems crucial to the future of Bulgaria, since it involves issues relating to the political, economic and social transformation of the country. It could even be argued that the aspiration to European integration has been instrumental in making the process of change more dynamic. Ten years of post-Communism, nonetheless, have been enough for Bulgarians to realise that the attitudes and behaviour of the Western countries are guided primarily by pragmatic calculations of self-interest and concern with their own well-being, peace and security, not by abstract humanist principles. The reluctance on the part of the European Union to admit free trade or the free movement of people across its borders has generated feelings of disappointment among the Bulgarian people. While the country has contributed to the goals of the international community in the Balkans and its efforts to achieve stability in the region, the belief is widespread that the Union and NATO have not done enough to help Bulgarian reform. This feeling is becoming even stronger, given the different treatment some other former Communist Bloc countries are enjoying.

> The magic word 'Central' (Europe), meaning the Czech Republic, Poland, Hungary and Slovakia, was promoted as a new division that sets apart the first pretendents for 'integration' from the rest, symbolically moving them closer to the West, while pushing the remaining former Socialist countries to a kind of new (inferior) East. (Daskalov, 1994: 31)

Still, in 2001, the EU Commission sees Bulgaria's prospects of EU membership as neither short-term nor medium-term. In the event of marginalisation or a lengthy pre-accession period, the political elite may encounter public opposition to the adjustment to EU standards and may cause discontent and a delegitimisation of the whole reform process.

> The legitimisation of the reform process is stemming from the fact that Bulgarians want to be a 'normal' people, having 'normal' lives, 'normal' homes, etc. But the 'normal' is equivalent to Western European standards of life. Thus if the West refuses to accept Bulgaria it will lead to a crisis as the people will lose orientation again. In that case, though they have never been strong in this country, nationalists will have a chance. (Dainov interview, 1998)

Western response and assistance have not been what Bulgarians were expecting in 1989, but they still feel that their political leadership is mostly to be blamed for the country's difficulties and hardships. If there is a change in this feeling while Western attitudes to Bulgaria remain unaltered, it might well provide fertile ground for nationalist political forces. To avoid any such risk, even if the economy is still unready to meet the strict criteria for EU membership, a political 'back door' should be opened to Bulgaria and the other candidates.

For years Bulgarian people used to share a rather vague and idealistic view of a perfect Europe that the real Europe cannot measure up to. Though the cost of integration into Europe is still unknown, the high expectations and the enthusiasm have started to abate as Bulgarians come to realise that Europe is not a panacea for the country's problems and that a segment of society will not be able to adapt swiftly and successfully to the new realities. In just a short period of time Bulgaria already has suffered many vicissitudes but still held to the right course. Some have witnessed their ideals collapse, others grew up with no ideals at all, and others have been living with the vision of today: transition to a democratic society based on a market economy and with the goal of becoming an integral part of Europe. Indeed, the 1990s were a very difficult period for Bulgarians. The false Communist illusions were replaced by the euphoria of the early years of post-Communism that evaporated quickly and a deep pessimism dominated society. With the new decade Bulgarians recognise that things are slowly starting to change and can discern a ray of hope on the horizon. Their expectations have acquired more realistic dimensions and they view the future with cautious optimism. According to an old Soviet saying, a pessimist is a well informed optimist. In the case of Bulgaria it may be reversed.

Notes

1 According to the early results of the 2001 census Bulgaria's population had fallen to 7,977,646 from 8,487,317 in 1992 and showed an overall drop of 970,000 from 1985 to 2001.

2 Over the course of the transition, opinion polls consistently confirmed the absence of nationalist sentiment. 'In 1996, polls revealed decidedly tolerant and peaceful attitudes toward the other Balkan countries: 77 per cent accepted the present borders of the country, 70 per cent declared that Bulgaria should have no territorial claims against its neighbours, 80 per cent wanted to see all the Balkan states join a unified Europe' (Nikova, 1998: 283).

References

Agh, Attila (1999), 'Processes of democratisation in the East Central European and Balkan states: sovereignty-related conflicts in the context of Europeanization', *Communist and Post-Communist Studies*, 32, 263–79.

Andreev, Alexander (1996), 'The political changes and political parties' in Iliana Zloch-Christy (ed.), *Bulgaria in a Time of Change. Economic and Political Dimensions*, Aldershot, Singapore and Sydney, Avebury.

Arbova, Antonina (2000), 'Balkan security system: one year after the Kosovo war' in *IRIS Quarterly Policy Report – Spring 2000*, Sofia, Institute of Regional and International Studies.

Avery, Graham, and Fraser Cameron (1998), *The Enlargement of the European Union*, Sheffield, Sheffield Academic Press.

Avramov, Roumen (1994), 'Macroeconomic stabilisation: three years later' in Roumen Avramov and Ventsislav Antonov (eds), *Economic Transition in Bulgaria*, Sofia, Agency for Economic Co-ordination and Development.

Batt, Judy (1993), 'The politics of economic transition' in Stephen White, Judy Batt and Paul G. Lewis (eds), *Developments in East European Politics*, London, Macmillan.

Bell, John D. (1977), *Peasants in Power*, Princeton NJ, Princeton University Press.

Bell, John D. (1990), 'Post-Communist Bulgaria', *Current History*, December, 417–29.

Bell, John D. (1998), 'Bulgaria's search for security' in John D. Bell (ed.), *Bulgaria in Transition. Politics, Economy, Society and Culture after Communism*, Boulder CO and Oxford, Westview Press.

Berend, Ivan T., and Gyorgy Ranki (1974), *Economic Development in East Central Europe in the Nineteenth and Twentieth centuries*, New York and London, Columbia University Press.

Black, Cyril E. (1976), 'The process of modernisation: the Bulgarian case' in Thomas Butler (ed.), *Bulgaria Past and Present*, Columbus OH, American Association for the Advancement of Slavic Studies.

Boyadjiev, Vladimir (1990), 'Socio-economic platform of the Bulgarian opposition', *Peace Research*, 22, 45–51.

Brown, J. F. (1970), *Bulgaria under Communist rule*, London, Pall Mall Press.

Brown, J. F. (1992), *Nationalism, Democracy and Security in the Balkans*, Aldershot and. Sydney, Dartmouth.

Bulgarian Academy of Science (1994), *Economic Outlook of Bulgaria 1995–97*, Sofia, Institute of Economics.

Bulgarian Parliament (1998), *National Strategy for the Preparation of the Republic of Bulgaria for Membership of the EU*, http://www.db.online.bg.

Centre for the Study of Democracy (1998), *Public Opinion on Non-governmental Organisations in Bulgaria (December 1996)*, http://www.online.bg/vr/ngo.

Centre for the Study of Democracy (2000), *Corruption and Trafficking. Monitoring and Prevention*, second edition, Sofia, Centre for the Study of Democracy.

Clark, John (1995), 'The state, popular participation, and the voluntary sector', *World Development*, 23: 4, 593–601.

Coppieters, Bruno, and Michael Waller (1994), 'Conclusions: social democracy in Eastern Europe' in Michael Waller, Bruno Coppieters and Kris Deschouwer (eds), *Social Democracy in a Post-Communist Europe*, London, Frank Cass.

Crampton, Richard J. (1987), *A Short History of Modern Bulgaria*, Cambridge, London and New York, Cambridge University Press.

Crawford, Keith (1996), *East Central European Politics Today*, Manchester and New York, Manchester University Press.

Creed, Gerald W. (1995), 'The politics of agriculture: identity and Socialist sentiment in Bulgaria', *Slavic Review*, 54: 4, 843–68.

Dainov, Evgenii (1997), 'Bulgaria's path to NATO in the mirror of public opinion and press in the mid-1990s' in Andrey Ivanov (ed.), *Bulgaria and NATO. The Debate at Five to Twelve*, Sofia, Centre for Strategic and Applied Studies/Atlantic Club of Bulgaria.

Daskalov, Roumen (1994), *Images of Europe. A Glance from the Periphery*, EUI Working Papers, Florence, European University Institute.

Daskalov, Roumen (1998), 'A democracy born in pain' in John D. Bell (ed.), *Bulgaria in Transition. Politics, Economy, Society and Culture after Communism*, Boulder CO and Oxford, Westview Press.

Davidova, Sofia, and Allan Buckwell (1994), 'Agricultural reform' in Andrew Schmitz, Kirby Moulton, Allan Buckwell and Sofia Davidova (eds), *Privatisation of Agriculture in New Market Economies. Lessons from Bulgaria*, Boston MA, London and Dordrecht, Kluwer.

Davidova, Sofia, and Allan Buckwell (1997), 'Political Design of Land Reform in Central and Eastern Europe. Was it backward-looking?' paper presented at the Agricultural Economic Society annual conference, University of Edinburgh, 21–4 March.

Deltcheva, Roumiana (1996), 'New tendencies in post-totalitarian Bulgaria: mass culture and the media', *Europe–Asia Studies*, 48: 2, 305–15.

Diamond, Larry (1994), 'Rethinking civil society: towards democratic consolidation', *Journal of Democracy*, 5: 3, 4–17.

Ditchev, Ivaylo (1997), 'Balkan vicious circles' in Ivaylo Ditchev (ed.), *Balkan Transition. Proceedings of the International Conference, December 1996, Sofia, Bulgaria*, Sofia, Access/BCN.

Dobrin, Bogoslav (1973), *Bulgarian Economic Development since World War II*, New York, Washington DC and London, Praeger.

East, Roger (1992), *Revolutions in Eastern Europe*, London and New York, Pinter.

Eatwell, John, Michael Ellman, Mats Karlsson, D. Mario Nuti and Judith Shapiro (1997), *Not 'Just another Accession'. The Political Economy of EU Enlargement to the East*, Amsterdam, London and Stockholm, European Forum for Democracy and Solidarity.

Economic Policy Institute (Sofia), Centre for the Study of Democracy (2000), 'Bulgaria and Romania' in Helena Tang (ed.), *Winners and Losers of EU Integration*, Washington DC, World Bank.

Economist (2000), 'Petar Stoyanov, Bulgaria's gladiatorial President', *Economist*, 355: 8175, 17 June, 38.

Edwards, Michael, and David Hulme (1996), 'Too close for comfort? The impact of official aid on non-governmental organisations', *World Development*, 24: 6, 961–73.

Elster, Jon, Claus Offe and Ulrich K. Preuss (1998), *Institutional Design in Post-Communist Societies*, Cambridge, Cambridge University Press.

Engelbrekt, Kjell (1994), 'Bulgaria's political stalemate', *RFE/RL Research Report*, 3: 25, 24 June, 20–5.

Engelbrekt, Kjell, and Duncan M. Perry (1992), 'The conviction of Bulgaria's former leader', *RFE/RL Research Report*, 1: 42, 23 October, 6–11.

European Commission (1995), *Agricultural Situation and Prospects in the Central and Eastern European Countries: Bulgaria*, Directorate General of Agriculture, Working Document VI/1119/95, Vol. 1.

European Commission (1996), *Central and Eastern Euro-barometer*, No. 6, Brussels.

European Commission (1998), *Regular Report 1998 on Bulgaria's Progress towards Accession*, Supplement 12/98 to the *Bulletin* of the European Union, Luxembourg, European Commission.

European Commission (1999a), *Bulgaria: 1999 Accession Partnership*, European Commission, http://www.evropa.bg.

European Commission (1999b), *Regular Report 1999 on Bulgaria's Progress towards Accession*, European Commission, http://www.europa.eu.

European Commission (2000), *Regular Report 2000 on Bulgaria's Progress towards Accession*, European Commission, http://www.europa.eu.

Eurostat (1991), *Country Profile. Bulgaria 1991*, Brussels, Statistisches Bundesamt.

Feiwel, George R. (1977), *Growth and Reforms in Centrally Planned Economies. The Lessons of the Bulgarian Experience*, New York, Washington and London, Praeger.

Financial Times (1997), Bulgaria. Survey, *Financial Times*, 21 October.

Friedberg, James, and Branimir Zaimov (1998), 'Politics, environment and the rule of law in Bulgaria' in Krassimira Paskaleva, Philip Shapira, John Pickles and Boian Koulov (eds), *Bulgaria in Transition. Environmental Consequences of Political and Economic Transformation*, Aldershot, Brookfield, Singapore and. Sydney, Ashgate.

Ganev, Venelin I. (1997), 'Bulgaria's symphony of hope', *Journal of Democracy*, 8: 4, 125–39.

Geremek, Bronislaw (1992), 'Civil society then and now', *Journal of Democracy*, 3: 2, 3–12.

Hadenius, Axel, and Fredrik Uggla (1996), 'Making civil society work, promoting democratic development: what can states and donors do?' *World Development*, 24: 10, 1621–39.

Haramiev-Drezov, Kyril (1993), 'Bulgarian–Russian relations on a new footing', *RFE/RL Research Report*, 2: 15, 9 April, 33–8.

Havel, Vaclav (1999), *Cold War*, BBC documentary.

Huntington, Samuel P. (1991), *The Third Wave. Democratisation in the late Twentieth Century*, Norman OK and London, University of Oklahoma Press.

IMF (1995), *Republic of Bulgaria. Recent Economic Developments*, Washington DC, International Monetary Fund.

Insider (1997a), 'Socialist economy: last act of the drama', *Insider – Business and Current Affairs*, 7: 1–2, 6–9.

Insider (1997b), 'Declaration for developing equality in rights and mutually beneficial relations with the Russian Federation', *Insider – Business and Current Affairs*, 7: 12, 13.

Jelavich, Barbara (1983), *History of the Balkans. Twentieth Century* II, Cambridge, London and New York, Cambridge University Press.

Jelavich, Charles, and Jelavich Barbara (1977), *The Establishment of the Balkan National States 1804–1920*, Seattle WA and London, University of Washington Press.

Karasimeonov, Georgi (1996), 'Bulgaria's new party system' in Geoffrey Pridham and Paul G. Lewis (eds), *Stabilising Fragile Democracies. Comparing new Party Systems in Southern and Eastern Europe*, London and New York, Routledge.

Kitschelt, Herbert, Dimitar Dimitrov and Assen Kanev (1995), 'The structuring of the vote in post-Communist party systems: the Bulgarian example', *European Journal of Political Research*, 27, 143–60.

Kolarova, Rumyana (1996), 'Bulgaria: could we regain what we have already lost?' *Social Research*, 63: 2, 543–58.

Koulov, Boian (1998), 'Political change and environmental policy' in John D. Bell (ed.), *Bulgaria in Transition. Politics, Economy, Society and Culture after Communism*, Boulder CO and Oxford, Westview Press.

Krastev, Ivan (2000), 'Debalkanising the Balkans: what priorities?' *International Spectator*, 35: 3, 7–17.

Lampe, John R. (1976), 'Special barriers to Bulgarian industrialisation before 1914' in Thomas Butler (ed.), *Bulgaria Past and Present*, Columbus OH, American Association for the Advancement of Slavic Studies.

Lampe, John R. (1986), *The Bulgarian Economy in the Twentieth Century*, London and. Sydney, Croom Helm.

Lewis, Paul (1997), 'Political participation in post-Communist democracies' in David Poter, David Goldblatt, Margaret Kiloh and Paul Lewis (eds), *Democratisation*, Cambridge, Polity Press and Open University.

Linz, Juan J., and Alfred Stepan (1996), *Problems of Democratic Transition and. Consolidation*, Baltimore MD and London, Johns Hopkins University Press.

Lovenduski, Joni, and Jean Woodall (1987), *Politics and Society in Eastern Europe*, London, Macmillan.

Lyutskanov, Vasil (1997), 'Officers go for NATO', *Insider – Business and Current Affairs*, 7: 4, 4.

McDonald, Frank, and Stephen Dearden (1994), *European Economic Integration*, second edition, London and New York, Longman.

McIntyre, Robert J. (1988), *Bulgaria. Politics, Economics and Society*, London and New York, Pinter.

Meininger, Thomas A., and Detelina Radoeva (1996), 'Civil society: the current situation and problems' in Iliana Zloch-Christy (ed.), *Bulgaria in a Time of Change. Economic and Political Dimensions*, Aldershot, Singapore and Sydney, Avebury.

Melone, Albert P. (1994), 'Bulgaria's national round-table talks and the politics of accommodation', *International Political Science Review*, 15: 3, 257–73.

Melone, Albert P. (1998), *Creating Parliamentary Government. The Transition to Democracy in Bulgaria*, Columbus OH, Ohio State University Press.

Minassian, Garabed (1994), 'The Bulgarian economy in transition: is there anything wrong with macroeconomic policy?' *Europe–Asia Studies*, 46: 2, 337–51.

Minassian, Garabed (1998) 'The road to economic disaster in Bulgaria', *Europe–Asia Studies*, 50: 2, 331–49.

Minchev, Ognyan (1997) 'The Balkans: an optimistic view' in Ivaylo Ditchev (ed.), *Balkan Transition. Proceedings of the International Conference, December 1996, Sofia, Bulgaria*, Sofia, Access/BCN.

Mindjov, Kliment (1995), 'Bulgaria' in Regional Environmental Centre for Central and Eastern Europe, *Status of National Environmental Action Programmes in Central and Eastern Europe*, Budapest, Regional Environmental Centre.

Mishew, D. (1971), *The Bulgarians in the Past*, New York, Arno Press.

Morris, L. P. (1984), *Eastern Europe since 1945*, London and Exeter, Heinemann.

Moser, Charles A. (1994), *Theory and History of the Bulgarian Transition*, Sofia, Free Initiative Foundation.

Mouzelis, Nicos (1986), *Politics in the Semi-periphery*, London, Macmillan; New York, St Martin's Press.

Nikolov, Stephan E. (1998), 'Bulgaria: a quasi-elite' in John Higley, Jan Pakulski and Wlodzimierz Wesolowski (eds), *Post-Communist Elites and Democracy in Eastern Europe*, Basingstoke and London, Macmillan Press.

Nikova, Ekaterina (1998), 'Bulgaria in the Balkans' in John D. Bell (ed.), *Bulgaria in Transition. Politics, Economy, Society and Culture after Communism*, Boulder CO and Oxford, Westview Press.

OECD (1997), *Economic Surveys – Bulgaria 1997*, OECD/Centre for Co-operation with the Economies in Transition.

OECD (1999), *OECD Economic Surveys 1998–99. Bulgaria*, Paris, OECD Centre for Co-operation with Non-members.

Oren, Nissan (1973), *Revolution Administered. Agrarianism and Communism in Bulgaria*, Baltimore MD and London, Johns Hopkins University Press.

Palairet, Michael (1995), '"Lenin" and "Brezhnev": steel making and the Bulgarian economy 1956–90', *Europe–Asia Studies*, 47: 3, 493–505.

Pantev, Andrei (1996), 'The historic road of the third Bulgarian state' in Iliana Zloch-Christy (ed.), *Bulgaria in a Time of Change. Economic and Political Dimensions*, Aldershot, Singapore and Sydney, Avebury.

Parker, Richard (1994), 'Clintonomics for the east', *Foreign Policy*, 94, 53–68.

Pateman, Carole (1970), *Participation and Democratic Theory*, Cambridge, New York, Sydney and Melbourne, Cambridge University Press.

Perry, Duncan M. (1992), 'New directions for Bulgarian–Turkish relations', *RFE/RL Research Report*, 1: 41, 16 October, 33–9.

Pirgova, Maria (1991), 'Political forces' motivation and conduct in 1990', *Bulgarian Quarterly*, 1: 1, 32–43.

Pundeff, Marin (1992), 'Bulgaria' in Joseph Held (ed.), *The Columbia History of Eastern Europe in the Twentieth Century*, New York, Columbia University Press.

Ratchev, Valeri (1997), 'Bulgaria's policy on NATO expansion: a challenge to military professionalism' in Andrey Ivanov (ed.), *Bulgaria and NATO. The Debate at Five to Twelve*, Sofia, Centre for Strategic and Applied Studies/Atlantic Club of Bulgaria.

Rau, Zbigniew, ed. (1991), *The Re-emergence of Civil Society in Eastern Europe and the Soviet Union*, Boulder CO, San Francisco and Oxford, Westview Press.

Rosenov, Rossen (1996), 'Removing barriers to growth in the current economic situation', *Institute of Market Economics Newsletter*, 3: 10, 11–15.

Rothschild, Joseph (1974), *East Central Europe between the two Wars*, Seattle WA and London, University of Washington Press.

Rupnik, Jacques (2000), 'Eastern Europe: the international context', *Journal of Democracy*, 11: 2, 115–29.

Schmitter, Philippe C. (1983), 'Democratic theory and neo-corporatist practice', *Social Research*, 50: 4, 885–98.

Schöpflin, George (1993), *Politics in Eastern Europe 1945–1992*, Oxford and Cambridge, Blackwell.

Smith, Karen E. (1999), *The Making of EU Foreign Policy. The Case of Eastern Europe*, London, Macmillan.

Stoychev, Kancho (1997), 'Videnov wielded immense power for no good', *Insider – Business and Current Affairs*, 7: 1–2, 18–19.

Strong, Ann Louise, Thomas A. Reiner and Janusz Szyrmer (1996), *Transitions in Land and*

Housing. Bulgaria, the Czech Republic and Poland, London, Macmillan.

Synovitz, Ron (1999), 'Bulgaria, Macedonia resolve language dispute', *RFE/RL Newsline*, 15 February, http:www.rferl.org.

Synovitz, Ron (2000), 'Agreement advances transport corridor around Serbia', *RFE/RL Newsline*, 29 March, http:www.rferl.org.

Szablowski, George J., and Hans-Ulrich Derlien (1993), 'East European transitions: elites, bureaucracies, and the European Community', *Governance*, 6: 3, 304–24.

Szajkowski, Bogdan, ed. (1991), *New Political Parties of Eastern Europe and the Soviet Union*, London, Longman.

Tanchev, Evgeni (1998), 'The constitution and the rule of law' in John D. Bell (ed.), *Bulgaria in Transition. Politics, Economy, Society and Culture after Communism*, Boulder CO and Oxford, Westview Press.

Task Force Report: Vassil Garnizov, Valery Roussanov, Evgenii Dainov, Krassen Stanchev, Mariana Miloseva, Deyan Kiuranov and Ivan Krastev (1997), *Initiative for Civil Society Building in Bulgaria*, Sofia, ACCESS.

Todorov, Nikolai (1977), *A Short History of Bulgaria*, Sofia, Sofia Press.

Todorov, Antony (1997), 'The Bulgarian political parties and NATO' in Andrey Ivanov (ed.), *Bulgaria and NATO. The Debate at Five to Twelve*, Sofia, Centre for Strategic and Applied Studies/Atlantic Club of Bulgaria.

Todorov, Antony (1999), *The Role of Political Parties in Bulgaria's Accession to the EU*, Sofia, Centre for the Study of Democracy.

Tomaszewski, Jerzy (1989), *The Socialist Regimes of East Central Europe*, London and New York, Routledge.

UNDP (1995), *Bulgaria. Human Development Report 1995*, Sofia, National and Global Development.

UNDP (1997), *Human Development Report. Bulgaria 1997*, Sofia, UN Development Programme.

UNDP (1998), *National Human Development Report. Bulgaria 1998. The State of Transition and Transition of the State*, Sofia, UN Development Programme.

UNDP (1999), *National Human Development Report. Bulgaria 1999. Bulgarian People's Aspirations* II, Sofia, UN Development Programme.

UNDP (2000a), *The Bulgarian Chitalishte. Past, Present and Future*, Sofia, UN Development Programme.

UNDP (2000b), *Development Co-operation. Bulgaria 1999 Report*, Sofia, UN Development Programme.

Videnov, Zhan (1998), 'The Gorbachev generation destroyed the Socialist party', interview by Stanimir Vuglenov, *Insider – Business and Current Affairs*, 8: 5, 8–9.

Vitosha Research (1999), *Evaluations of the Qualities of those in Power*, http://www.online.bg/vr/surveyeng.

Wyzan, Michael L. (1992), 'Bulgaria: shock therapy followed by a steep recession', *RFE/RL Research Report*, 1: 45, 13 November, 46–53.

Wyzan, Michael L. (1996), 'Stabilisation and anti-inflationary policy' in Iliana Zloch-Christy (ed.), *Bulgaria in a Time of Change. Economic and Political Dimensions*, Aldershot, Singapore and Sydney, Avebury.

Wyzan, Michael L. (1998), 'Bulgarian economic policy and performance 1991–97' in John D. Bell (ed.), *Bulgaria in Transition. Politics, Economy, Society and Culture after Communism*, Boulder CO and Oxford, Westview Press.

Zhelev, Zhelyu (1997), *Fascism*, Sofia, Zlatorog.

Zhelyaskova, Antonina (1998), 'Bulgaria's Muslim minorities' in John D. Bell (ed.), *Bulgaria in Transition. Politics, Economy, Society and Culture after Communism*, Boulder CO and Oxford, Westview Press.

Zhivkov, Todor (1997), 'The people love me, politicians hate me', interview by Valeria Veleva, *Insider*, 7: 11, 16–17.

Interviews

Dainov, Evgenii, President, Open Society Foundation, Sofia; Co-chairman, Centre for Social Practices; former Executive Director, Union of Bulgarian Foundations and Associations, Sofia, 29 May 1997 and 1 April 1998.

Kanev, Krassimir, Chairman, Bulgarian Helsinki Committee, Sofia, 9 April 1998.

Katsanis, Manolis, President, Bulgarian International Business Association (BIBA), Sofia, 29 May 1997.

Kiuranov, Deyan, Programme Director, Centre for Liberal Strategies, Sofia, 6 November 2000.

Koteva, Maya, delegation of the European Commission to Bulgaria, economic adviser, Europe Agreement, macroeconomic and trade issues, Sofia, 7 November 2000.

Marincheshka, Tanya, Programme Director, Bulgarian Helsinki Committee, Sofia, 3 April 1998.

Milosheva, Mariana, founder, Creating Effective Grass-roots Alternatives, Sofia, 1 April 1998.

Mindjov, Kliment, Director, Borrowed Nature, Sofia, 9 April 1998.

Mitev, Valentin, Executive Director, Civil Society Development Foundation, Sofia, 24 March 1998.

Ouzounov, Dimo, Member of Parliament (BSP), Sofia, 28 May 1997.

Petrova, Tanya, Executive Director, Bulgarian Charities Aid Foundation, Sofia, 27 March 1998.

Prodanova, Donka, Programme Director, and Ognyan Lipovski, Executive Director, Union of Bulgarian Foundations and Associations, Sofia, 24 March 1998 and 31 October 2000.

Stanchev, Krassen, President, Institute of Market Economics, Sofia, 20 May 1997.

Stoyanov, Alexander, Research Director, Centre for the Study of Democracy, Sofia, 26 March 1998.

Todorov, Boyko, Project Co-ordinator, Centre for the Study of Democracy, Sofia, 16 May 1997 and 1 November 2000.

Zhelev, Zhelyu, former President of the Bulgarian Republic, Sofia, 8 April 1998.

Select bibliography

Armijo, Leslie Elliott, Thomas J. Biersteker, and Abraham F. Lowenthal (1994), 'The problems of simultaneous transitions', *Journal of Democracy*, 5: 4, 161–75.

Baldwin, Richard, Pertti Haaparanta, and Jaako Kiander, eds (1995), *Expanding Membership of the European Union*, Cambridge, Cambridge University Press.

Berger, Peter L. (1992), 'The uncertain triumph of democratic capitalism', *Journal of Democracy*, 3: 2, 1–10.

Berglund, Sten, and Jan Ake Dellenbrant, eds (1991), *The New Democracies in Eastern. Europe. Party Systems and Political Cleavages*, Aldershot, Elgar.

Boyd, Michael L. (1990), 'Organisational reform and agricultural performance: the case of Bulgarian agriculture 1960–85', *Journal of Comparative Economics*, 14, 70–87.

Brogan, Patrick (1990), *Eastern Europe 1939–89*, London, Bloomsbury.

Brown, J. F. (1994), *Hopes and Shadows. Eastern Europe after Communism*, Harlow, Longman.

Creed, Gerald W. (1995), 'Agriculture and the domestication of industry in rural Bulgaria', *American Ethnologist*, 22: 3, 528–48.

Dahrendorf, Ralf (1990), *Reflections on the Revolution in Europe*, New York, Random House.

Daskalov, Roumen (1999), 'The emerging order: Bulgarian experiences with democracy' in Richard Sakwa (ed.), *The Experience of Democratisation in Eastern Europe*, London, Macmillan.

Dawisha, Karen, and Bruce Parrott, eds (1997), *Democratisation and Authoritarianism in Post-Communist Societies* II, *Politics, Power, and the Struggle for Democracy in South-east Europe*, Cambridge, Cambridge University Press.

Diamond, Larry, and Marc F. Plattner, eds (1993), *The Global Resurgence of Democracy*, Baltimore MD and London, Johns Hopkins University Press.

Glenny, Misha (1990), *The Rebirth of History. Eastern Europe in the Age of Democracy*, London, Penguin Books.

Grabbe, Heather, and Kirsty Hughes (1998), *Enlarging the EU Eastwards*, London, Royal Institute of International Affairs.

Henderson, Karen, ed. (1999), *Back to Europe. Central and Eastern Europe and the European Union*, London, UCL Press.

Holmes, Leslie (1997), *Post-Communism*, Cambridge, Polity Press.

Hristov, Hristo (1988), 'Foundation and activity of the Bulgarian learned society, 1869–1911', *East European Quarterly*, 22: 3, 333–9.

Hyde-Price, A. (1996), *The International Politics of East Central Europe*, Manchester and New York, Manchester University Press.

Kolodko, Grzegorz W. (1993), 'From recession to growth in post-Communist economies: expectations versus reality', *Communist and Post-Communist Studies*, 26: 2, 123–43.

Lewis, Paul G., ed. (1992), *Democracy and Civil Society in Eastern Europe*, New York, St Martin's Press, London, Macmillan.

Mason, David S. (1995), 'Attitudes toward the market and political participation in the post-Communist states', *Slavic Review*, 54: 2, 385–406.

Mason, David S. (1996), *Revolution and Transition in East Central Europe*, second edition, Oxford, Westview Press.

McSweeney, Dean, and Clive Tempest (1993), 'The political science of democratic transition in Eastern Europe', *Political Studies*, 41, 408–19.

Meiklejohn, Sarah Terry (1993), 'Thinking about post-Communist transitions: how different are they?' *Slavic Review*, 52: 2, 333–7.

Minassian, Garabed (1992), 'Bulgarian industrial growth and structure 1970–89', *Soviet Studies*, 44: 4, 699–711.

Mishler, William, and Richard Rose (1997), 'Trust, distrust and scepticism: popular evaluations of civil and political institutions in post-Communist societies', *Journal of Politics*, 59: 2, 418–51.

Nelson, Joan M., ed. (1994), *A Precarious Balance. Democracy and Economic Reforms in Eastern Europe*, San Francisco, ICS Press.

O'Donnel, Guillermo, and Philippe C. Schmitter (1986), *Transitions from Authoritarian Rule. Tentative Conclusions about Uncertain Democracies*, Baltimore MD and London, Johns Hopkins University Press.

Pridham, Geoffrey, and Tatu Vanhanen (1994), *Democratisation in Eastern Europe*, London, Routledge.

Ramet, Petra Sabrina (1995), *Social Currents in Eastern Europe. The Sources and Consequences of the Great Transformation*, second edition, Durham NC and London, Duke University Press.

Sjoberg, Orjan, and Michael L. Wyzan, eds (1991), *Economic Change in the Balkan States. Albania, Bulgaria, Romania and Yugoslavia*, London, Pinter.

Stark, David, and Laszlo Bruszt (1998), *Postsocialist Pathways. Transforming Politics and Property in East Central Europe*, Cambridge, Cambridge University Press.

Szoboszlai, Gyorgy, ed. (1991), *Democracy and Political Transformation. Theories and East Central European Realities*, Budapest, Hungarian Political Science Association.

Tong, Yanqi (1995), 'Mass alienation under state socialism and after', *Communist and Post-Communist Studies*, 28: 2, 215–37.

Vassilev, Rossen (1999), 'Modernisation theory revisited: the case of Bulgaria', *East European Politics and Societies*, 13: 3, 566–99.

Wadekin, Karl-Eugen (1982), *Agrarian Policies in Communist Europe*, The Hague, Nijhoff.

Welsh, Helga A. (1994), 'Political transition processes in Central and Eastern Europe', *Comparative Politics*, July, 379–94.

Wightman, Gordon, ed. (1995), *Party Formation in East Central Europe. Post-Communist Politics in Czechoslovakia, Hungary, Poland and Bulgaria*, Aldershot, Elgar.

INDEX

acquis communautaire, 135–8, 140
Agenda 2000, 137
agrarianism, 16, 52
agriculture, 14–17, 26, 83–4, 97–9
  collectivisation of, 28–31
  machinery for, 36
agro-industrial complexes, 30–1
Albania, 148, 155
Aldcroft, Derek, 35
Andreev, Alexander, 52
arms shipments, 65
authoritarian rule, 23, 61–2, 68
Avramov, Roumen, 102

Balkan states
  Bulgarian policy towards, 148–9
  culture of, 164
  instability of, 155, 164
  Stability Pact, 156–7, 165
banking system, 100
Batt, Judy, 24, 38, 81
Bell, John D., 13–14
Berend, Ivan T., 15
Beron, Petar, 62
Berov, Lyuben, 68, 87–9
bilateral relations between states, 149–54
Black Sea Economic Co-operation Zone, 150
Blagoev, Dimitar, 18
Boris, Tsar, 16–17
Bosnia, 148, 150, 155
Bozhkov, Alexander, 71
Brezhnev doctrine, 44
Brown, J. F., 19, 29, 67
Buckwell, Allen, 98
'Bulgaria 2001' programme, 70, 93
Bulgarian Academy of Sciences, 115
Bulgarian Agrarian National Union (BANU), 15
Bulgarian Communist Party (BCP), 16, 20, 45, 47–51, 54
Bulgarian Social Democratic Party, 18, 52
Bulgarian Socialist Party (BSP), 53–6, 59–60, 66–70, 87, 89, 92, 102, 125, 134, 143–6, 150–1, 154, 162
Bulgarian state, origins of, 10–12
Bulgarian Workers' Party, 18

central planning, 24–7, 36–8, 84
Centre for Mass Privatisation, 88
Cetin, Hikmet, 149
charitable organisations, 114
Chernomyrdin, Viktor, 147
Chervenkov, Vulko, 23
Chilingirov, Stilian, 115
chitalishte, 115
Christianity, 10–11
citizenship, 5–6, 111, 128
civic tradition, 114–16
civil society, 21–2, 36, 39, 50–1, 56, 63, 74, 106, 112, 116–17, 120, 124–31, 156, 160–4
  definition of, 5–6
Clark, John, 111–12, 130
clientelism, 55–6, 65, 71, 130
Coalition 2000, 124
Cold War, 149
  ending of, 133, 148
collectivisation, 25, 28–31
  dismantling of, 86
Communism, 2, 6, 18
  in the Balkans, 34–5
  legacy of, 74
  see also former Communists
Confederation of Independent Trade Unions, 73
Constitutional Court, 59, 89
constitutional provisions, 12, 51, 58
Copenhagen criteria, 135–6, 139–40
Coppieters, Bruno, 61
corruption, 38, 49, 55, 64–8, 71–3, 89, 124, 129, 140, 155, 162–3
Council of Mutual Economic Assistance (CMEA), 24, 31–3, 35, 80, 133
Crampton, Richard J., 11, 19, 27
Crawford, Keith, 20–1
Creed, Gerald, 28, 30
crime, 55–6, 61–5, 69, 71, 73, 119, 155, 162–3
  economic, 103
currency board, 92, 94, 106
Czech Republic, 86, 94

Dainov, Evgenii, 68, 89, 100, 166
Daskalov, Roumen, 60, 64, 166
Davidova, Sofia, 98
Dearden, Stephen, 80
decentralisation, 26–7, 38
Deltcheva, Roumiana, 74, 111, 127
demagogy, 60
democratic consolidation, 4–7, 51, 60, 63, 72, 128, 130, 160–3
  as distinct from democratic transition, 3
democratic culture, 72–4, 160
democratisation, 1–8, 13, 16, 44, 47–51, 155, 160
demographic change, 37, 161
demoralisation of society, 64–5
dependence, structures of, 122, 155
deregulation, economic, 7
developing countries, 34
Diamond, Larry, 5
Dimitrov, Georgi, 18, 20, 23
Dimitrov, Philip, 57, 67, 70
dissident movements, 46–9, 57, 62, 70, 160–1
Ditchev, Ivaylo, 35
Dobrin, Bogoslav, 11, 17, 33
Dogan, Ahmed, 58–9

Eatwell, John, 82
Eco-*glasnost*, 46, 57, 73, 117
economic consolidation, 6
economic reform programme, 84–5
  appraisal of, 99–100
  and civil society, 116
  failure of, 104–5, 162
  pressure for, 70–2
education, 115
egalitarianism, 74, 103, 116–17
election results, 53, 59, 67–70, 89
electoral system, 51
elites, political and economic, 3–4, 13, 49–55, 60–2, 69–70, 160–1
Elster, Jon, 55–6
energy shortages, 28, 36, 146–7
Engelbrekt, Kjell, 89
environmentalism and environmental policy, 37, 46–7, 117–19, 129
ethnic tensions, 155
Euro-Atlantic Partnership Council, 143
Eurobarometer, 62
Europe Agreements *see* European Union, Association Agreement with
European Commission, 72, 98, 137–40, 166
European Union, 56, 58, 71, 134–42, 150–1, 154–7, 160, 164–5
  Accession Partnership, 137–8, 140
  Association Agreement with, 88, 135–7
exchange rates, 91–2

factionalism, 56, 61, 70
Fatherland Front, 19–20
foreign debt, 36–7
foreign direct investment, 89–90, 96–7
foreign donors (to NGOs), 121–5, 130
Foreign Investment Act, 87
foreign policy, 133, 146, 149, 153, 164; *see also* bilateral relations; regional policy
foreign trade, 31–4
former Communists, 3, 69, 161, 163
Friedberg, James, 37

Gazprom, 146–7
Georgievski, Ljubco, 153
Germany, 17
glasnost, 44–5, 47
Gorbachev, Mikhail, 38, 46, 49, 161
gradualism in transition, 81, 100
Greece, 11, 150–1
Green parties, 57, 59, 118
growth, economic, 26–7, 37, 85–8, 91–2

Hadenius, Axel, 112
Haramiev-Drezov, Kyril, 146
Havel, Vaclav, 38–9
human rights, 46, 140
Huntington, Samuel, 4, 60

ideology, 102
institutional reform, 81–2, 90, 138
intellectuals, role of, 73
International Monetary Fund (IMF), 81, 84, 87–8, 102

Jelavich, Barbara, 15, 29
Jelavich, Charles, 15
judicial system, 63, 65, 71, 140
'July concept', 38, 45

Karasimeonov, Georgi, 36, 54
Katsanis, Manolis, 96
Khrushchev, Nikita, 133
Kitschelt, Herbert, 4, 45, 49
Kiuranov, Deyan, 48
Kosovo, 145–8, 153–6, 164–5
Kostov, Ivan, 57–8, 153
Kostunica, Vojislav, 154
Koulov, Boian, 47
Kozloduy power plant, 140–1
Krastev, Ivan, 155

land reform, 97–9
law enforcement, 63–5, 71

Law on Commerce, 87
Law on Competition Protection, 87
Law on the Ownership and Use of Agricultural Land (LOUAL), 86, 89, 98
Law on the Transformation and Privatisation of State-owned and Municipal Enterprises, 85
liberalisation, economic, 71–2, 136
Linz, Juan J., 3
liquidation councils, 86, 88
living standards, 15, 25, 31, 35, 37, 62, 93, 99, 104–5, 126, 134, 161–2
London Club, 88
loss-making enterprises, 90
Lovenduski, Joni, 22
Ludzhev, Dimitar, 149
Lukanov, Andrei, 55, 66, 84
'Lukanov scheme', 55

McDonald, Frank, 80
Macedonia, 148, 151–3, 165
McIntyre, Robert J., 10, 28–9, 37
media, the, 74, 118
  and civic organisations, 126–8
Meininger, Thomas A., 62–3, 119
Melone, Albert P., 3
Michailova, Nadezda, 147
Milosevic, Slobodan, 154
Minassian, Garabed, 94, 101
Minchev, Ognyan, 164
Mindjov, Clement, 118
Mishew, D., 115
Mladenov, Petar, 48, 66
modernisation programmes, 14, 35–6, 61
Mouzelis, Nicos, 16
Movement for Rights and Freedoms (MRF), 58–9, 67–8, 87, 149, 151
Multinational Peace Force in South-east Europe, 157

nationalisation, 24–5, 50
nationalism and national consciousness, 11–12, 166
New Economic Mechanism, 27, 31, 38
New Economic System, 26
Nikova, E., 62, 152
nomenclature, the, 3, 21–2, 45, 50, 52, 55, 57
non-governmental organisations (NGOs), 111–19, 156
  definition of, 111
  financing of, 119–25, 130
  and the media, 126–8
  number of, 112–13
  prospects for, 128–31
  and the state, 125–6, 129–30

North Atlantic Co-operation Council, 142–3
North Atlantic Treaty Organisation (NATO), 56, 58, 134, 142–60 *passim*, 165
nuclear power plants, 140–1

Oren, Nissan, 20, 30
Organisation for Economic Cooperation and Development (OECD), 90, 94
Ottoman rule, 11, 13–14, 48, 149
Ozal, Turgut, 149

Pantev, Andrei, 14
participation, political and civic, 5, 13, 16, 21–2, 62–3, 74, 111–12, 116–17, 128, 131, 160, 163
Partnership for Peace (PfP), 143–4
Parvanov, Georgi, 56
Pateman, Carole, 5
peasants, Marxist view of, 28
perestroika, 38, 44–6, 49
Permanent Joint Council (NATO–Russia), 143
Petkov, Nikola, 20, 57
Phare programme, 135, 138–9
pluralism, political, 50–1
Podkrepa (trade union), 46, 57, 73
polarisation of society, 67, 73, 103
political parties, 6, 12–13, 52, 65, 72–3, 130, 161–2; *see also* Bulgarian Communist Party; Bulgarian Socialist Party; Movement for Rights and Freedoms
politicians, attitudes to, 60, 68
pollution, 37, 46, 117–18, 154
Presidential powers, 51
press reporting, 74
Prices Act, 89
Primakov, Yevgenii, 147
privatisation, 60–1, 67, 69, 71, 81–95 *passim*
  'mass' and 'cash' types, 88, 95
Privatisation Agency, 85–6, 95
protest demonstrations, 69, 128
public administration, 63, 71

quality of life, 163

Radoeva, Detelina, 62–3, 119
Ranki, Gyorgy, 15
Rau, Z., 22
Red Army, 34
'reform fatigue', 103
regional policy, 154–7
restitution of land and property, 86, 88, 95, 98–9, 102
'return to Europe', 134
Roma population, 74–5, 104, 140, 164

Romania, 154
Rothschild, Joseph, 17
'round table' talks, 50, 57, 143, 161
rule of law, 56, 140
Russe, 46, 117, 154
Russia, 2, 12, 18, 51, 134, 143–8, 165

Schengen Agreement, 140–1
Schmitter, Philippe C., 4–5
Schöpflin, George, 19, 21
Second World War, 17–19
Serbia, 145, 150, 153–4, 165
shock therapy, 58, 81–2, 84, 100
Silistra, 154
Simeon, King, 162
Skopje, 152–3
Slavic culture, 10–11
Slavic orientation of foreign policy, 150
Smith, Karen E., 136
social exclusion, 74–5
social market economy, 56, 101
social partnership, 125
Socialist International, 54
Sofia University, 46–7
South Balkans Development Initiative, 157
South-east European Co-operation Initiative, 157
South-eastern Defence Ministerial (SEDM) meeting, 157
Soviet Union, 2, 32–6, 44–5, 133
Spain, 62
stabilisation, macroeconomic, 81, 83, 87, 90, 94, 102–5
Stalinism and Stalinisation, 20, 68
Stamboliski, Alexander, 16
Stambolov, Stefan, 12
state, the, role of, 111
state-owned enterprises (SOEs), 83, 88, 101
Stepan, Alfred, 3
Stoyanov, Petar, 69–70, 147, 150, 162–3
structural reform, 92–4, 103–5

Tanchev, Evgeni, 12
Task Force Report, 66, 113, 120, 125
Thatcher, Margaret, 1
third sector, 112–14, 119–24, 128–31, 164
Tito, Josip Broz, 151–2
Todorov, Antony, 13, 144
totalitarianism, 20–3, 45–6, 50–1
  dismantling of, 110
trade unions, 73; *see also* Podkrepa
transition to a market economy, 79–80
  from above and from below, 3
  failure of, 105, 161
  gradualism or shock therapy in, 81, 100
  objectives of, 80–1
trust, lack of, 63, 74, 124, 162
Turkey, 149–50
Turkish minority in Bulgaria, 47–50, 58–9, 74, 149–50, 160, 163
Turnovo Constitution, 12
'two turnover test', 4

Uggla, Fredrik, 112
uniformity, political, 23–4
Union of Bulgarian Foundations and Associations (UBFA), 124–5, 131
Union of Democratic Forces (UDF), 53, 56–60, 66–72, 84, 87, 93, 126, 134, 143–6, 150–1, 154, 162
United Nations Development Programme (UNDP), 64–5, 100–1, 104, 115, 118–19, 142, 145
urbanisation, 37

value-added tax, 88
Videnov, Zhan, 56, 69–70, 151, 154, 162
visa restrictions, 141
Vitosha Research Institute, 65
voluntarism, 30, 129
voucher privatisation, 88

Waller, Michael, 61
Warsaw Pact, 24, 133, 142
Woodall, Jean, 22
World Bank, 84, 102
Wyzan, Michael L., 84–5, 89–90

Yeltsin, Boris, 145–6, 152
Yilmaz, Mesut, 150
young people, activism of, 129
Yugoslavia, 51, 64, 80, 105, 134, 142, 148, 153–5

Zaimov, Branimir, 37
Zhelev, Z., 22–3, 45, 57, 66, 68, 144–6, 149, 152, 154
Zhelyazkova, A., 59
Zhivkov, Todor, 23, 38, 44–5, 47–50, 54–5, 69–70, 133